Reading, Analysing and Teaching Literature

Reading, Analysing and Teaching Literature

EDITED BY
Mick Short

LONGMAN

LONDON AND NEW YORK

Longman Group UK Limited,
Longman House, Burnt Mill, Harlow,
Essex CM20 2JE, England
and Associated Companies throughout the world.

*Published in the United States of America
by Longman Inc., New York*

© Longman Group UK Limited 1989

First published 1988

British Library Cataloguing in Publication Data
Reading, analysing and teaching literature.
  1. English literature – Study and teaching
  I. Short, Michael H.
  820'.7   PR35

ISBN 0-582-29157-7

Library of Congress Cataloging-in-Publication Data
Reading, analysing, and teaching literature/edited by Mick Short.
  p. cm.
  Bibliography: p.
  Includes index.
  ISBN 0-582-29157-7 (pbk.)
  1. Literature – Study and teaching. 2. Rhetoric. I. Short,
Michael H.
  PN59.R37 1988
  808'.042'07 – dc19

Set in 10/12 pt Linotron 202 Palatino

Produced by Longman Group (FE) Limited
Printed in Hong Kong

Contents

Acknowledgements

Thanks are due to all the contributors, for the patience with which they have witnessed the complicated path which this collection of papers has taken on its way to publication. Especial thanks to Ron Carter for his useful advice, and to Carole Bellard-Thomson for doing some of the typing. But thanks most of all to Hilary Short for her forbearance and bibliographical skills, without which we might never have made it!

Mick Short

We are grateful to the following for permission to reproduce copyright material:

Associated Book Publishers (U.K.) Ltd for the poem 'Death of a Son' by Jon Silkin from *Selected Poems*, Routledge & Kegan Paul Plc; Authors' Agents on behalf of the Estate of H. E. Bates for an extract from 'Tiger Moth' in *Song of the Wren* by H. E. Bates, Michael Joseph Ltd; Carcanet Press Ltd for the poem 'Off Course' by Edwin Morgan from *Poems of Thirty Years*; Faber & Faber Ltd/Farrar Straus & Giroux Inc. for the poem 'Vers de Société' by Philip Larkin from *High Windows*, copyright © 1974 by Philip Larkin; Faber & Faber Ltd/New Directions Publishing Co. Inc. for the poems 'In a Station of the Metro' & 'Alba' by Ezra Pound from *Collected Shorter Poems & personae* (source: New Directions), copyright © 1926 by Ezra Pound; Grafton Books/Harcourt Brace Jovanovich Inc. for the poem 'maggie & millie & molly & may' by e. e. cummings from *Complete Poems 1913–1962*, copyright 1956 by e. e. cummings; Martin J. Machat/McLelland & Stewart Ltd (Toronto) for the poem 'Adolph Eichmann' by L. Cohen from *Flowers for Hitler*; The Marvell Press for the poem 'Going' by Philip Larkin from *The Less Deceived*; Authors' Agents on behalf of Ted Hughes/Harper & Row Inc. for the poem 'Ariel' by Sylvia Plath from *Collected Poems*, Faber & Faber Ltd, © Ted Hughes 1965 & 1981.

The Contributors

Sylvia Adamson is a lecturer in the Faculty of English at the University of Cambridge, where she teaches stylistics and the history of the English language. She has recently moved back to Cambridge after a period at the University of Strathclyde, where she helped to found the Programme in Literary Linguistics.

Charles Alderson is senior teaching fellow in the Institute for English Language Education at the University of Lancaster. His main interests and publications are in the fields of language testing and reading in a second or foreign language. He has edited *Issues in Language Testing* (1981) with Arthur Hughes and *Reading in a Foreign Language* (1984) with Sandy Urquhart.

Christopher Candlin is Professor of Linguistics in the School of English and Linguistics at Macquarie University, Australia, a post which he has recently taken up after being at the University of Lancaster for many years. He is best known for his work in sociolinguistics and linguistics in relation to language teaching. He has published extensively in these areas, and has edited *The Communicative Teaching of English* (1981) and (with Geoffrey Leech) *Computers in English Language Teaching and Research* (1986). He is general editor of two series of books for Longman (*Applied Linguistics and Language Study* and *Language in Social Life*) and one for Prentice Hall (*Language Teaching Methodology Series*).

Ronald Carter is a lecturer in the Department of English Studies at the University of Nottingham, where he teaches English and linguistics. He is well-known for his work in the fields of stylistics and language teaching. His best-known publications to date are *Language and Literature* (1982), and *Literature and Language Teaching* (1986) which he edited jointly with Chris Brumfit.

Tom Hutchinson is a teaching fellow in the Institute for English Language Education at the University of Lancaster. His main interests are in the teaching of English as a foreign language. He has twice been awarded prizes by the English Speaking Union for his publications in this area. One of these prizes was for *Project English* (1985). Jointly with Alan Waters, he has written *Interface* (1984) and *English for Specific Purposes* (1987).

Mick Short is senior lecturer in the Department of Linguistics and Modern English Language at the University of Lancaster. His main interests are in stylistics and textlinguistics, and he is best known for *Style in Fiction* (1981) which he wrote jointly with Professor Geoffrey Leech. He and Geoffrey Leech also co-edit two series of linguistics books for Longman: *Learning About Language* and *Studies in Language and Linguistics*.

Graham Trengove is a lecturer at the University of Aberdeen, where he teaches English and is particularly involved with the teaching of English literature overseas. He has run a well-respected series of British Council seminars in this field at Aberdeen for some years.

Willie Van Peer is a lecturer in the Department of Language and Literature in the University of Brabant, Holland. His main interests are in stylistics, textlinguistics and literature pedagogy. He has published extensively in Dutch as well as English, and is the author of *Stylistics and Psychology* (1986).

Peter Verdonk is a senior lecturer in the Department of English at the University of Amsterdam, Holland. His major field of interest is in stylistics and its use in foreign language teaching, areas in which he is well-respected for the numerous articles which he has published.

ONE

Introduction
Mick Short

Although the common focus of this collection of papers is the stylistic analysis of literary texts, the relevant interests of the contributors are wide-ranging: stylistics and linguistic approaches to literary texts, literary theory, textlinguistics, psycholinguistics, reading theory, language testing, and language and literature teaching, both to non-native and mother-tongue speakers. The fact that academics and educators with such a broad span of interests have been willing to contribute to this volume is symptomatic of an interesting stage in the development of stylistic analysis and its relations with connected areas of study.

1.1 STYLISTICS

In many ways, stylistic analysis has come of age. In spite of the fact that literary critics are still wary about its role in the study of literature, stylistics has proved to be increasingly popular with *students* of English, both in the UK and overseas. Undergraduates find it genuinely useful as a tool for analysing literary texts. It helps them to understand what they read, and explain explicitly to others their intuitive responses, responses which they had before been unable to characterize and explain except in the most general and impressionistic of terms. The mere fact that they are provided with a descriptive analytical vocabulary enables them to see and appreciate features of literary texts which they would otherwise have overlooked.

Exactly how this process works is by no means clear, but Peter Verdonk's report (Ch. 10) of the enthusiastic response of his students to the work which he did with them is characteristic of what I and other stylisticians have experienced. As Ron Carter suggests in 'Directions in the teaching and study of English stylistics' (Ch. 2), stylistics is becoming increasingly confident and mature. It has been forced by its students to make itself less daunting and more relevant to their immediate concerns; it makes less grandiose claims than it used to; and many of the issues that it has raised in literary studies (e.g. literariness, and the objectivity or subjectivity of literary response) have been seen to be of increasing importance by literary critics.

Another symptom of stylistics' development is the burgeoning amount of work being done in the field. This can be seen in Carter's overviews in this volume and elsewhere (Carter 1985, 1986b). Yet one of the things which literary critics complain of is that stylisticians tend to be long on theory but short on practice. Amongst other things, this volume helps to increase the amount of published stylistic practice. It has plenty to say about theoretical matters, as we shall see below; and because stylisticians are in general more interested in *how* interpretations are arrived at than producing a new interpretation of some text, it will probably always be the case that stylistics articles will discuss theoretical matters alongside whatever practical analyses they provide; but in the eleven papers in this volume the reader will find nine fairly full descriptions of poetic and prose texts as well as a number of more limited, suggestive accounts of some others.

1.2 READING LITERATURE

In literary theory at present there is a large amount of interest in the notion of the reader and the reader's process of understanding (see, for example Iser 1978; Kintgen 1977, 1983). Often the literary critic wishes to focus on the reader in order to point to the essentially subjective nature of literary response. And it is true that each reader will to some extent interpret a text differently from others, merely as a consequence of the fact that we are all different from one another, have had different experiences, and so on. But it should be obvious that such a subjectivist view of literary understanding runs counter to the presuppositions of stylistic analysis, whose proponents assume that our shared knowledge of the structure of our language and the processes for interpreting utterances in our community imply a relatively large degree of common understanding in spite of some differences in individual response. For the stylistician, the major fact to be explained is that, though we are all different, we agree to a remarkable extent over the interpretation of texts. Indeed, if this were not the case, it would be difficult to see how communication could ever take place. Critics argue with one another over the interpretation of particular literary works, but I would suggest that the range of interpretations which have been produced for even the most discussed of texts is remarkably small compared with the theoretically infinite set of 'possible' readings.

The most extreme versions of reader-response accounts of literary texts are to be found in deconstructionist criticism, where it is often claimed that it is reasonable for the reader to take along to the text a set of attitudes totally at odds with the presumptions of the author. Thus deconstructionist readings on well-known literary works often 'explode' the text from within, producing readings radically different from those which critics have traditionally provided. Not all critics want to take such a radical view of course. Leavisite criticism, for example, tended to assume a relatively narrow range of appropriate response, probably too narrow for the taste of most critics in the 1980s. And critics defending all points between these two extremes can be found.

It should be clear that not all of these views of reading and reading outcomes can be correct. It is thus rather surprising to find how few attempts there have been within literary studies to establish the true facts. Honourable exceptions to date are the two works by Kintgen (1977, 1983) referred to above and Van Peer (1986a). These two scholars arrive at very different findings, and it is clear that much careful work in this field remains to be done. The contributions by Short and Van Peer (Ch. 3) and Alderson and Short (Ch. 4) provide interesting information for this debate. Short and Van Peer compare two written protocols obtained from independent readings of a poem by Gerard Manley Hopkins. The two authors, working independently, were given the text one line at a time and wrote down their immediate reactions as they struggled to interpret the text. This comparison of written protocols in reaction to a poem is matched by a similar experiment by Alderson and Short, this time on the first page of a piece of fictional prose. In this case the protocols are transcriptions of tape recordings; the experimenters spoke their thoughts out loud as they read the text. There are of course limitations and difficulties with experimental techniques such as these, but the two papers provide initial support for the idea of a large degree of common understanding with a peripheral amount of differing interpretation. These results are, of course, encouraging for the stylistician. But much more work of a similar kind needs to be done before we can be sure of the facts.

The three readers involved in the experiments reported in this volume are all highly educated, for example, and the database is narrow. An essential next step is to widen that database, and to determine whether readers from different educational and social backgrounds respond in similar ways to the same texts. But at least empirical work is now being done, and if they achieve nothing else, experiments like those reported here will give us a surer foundation on which to continue investigation. The discussions in Chapters 3 and 4 also point to what is likely to become a stronger connection between stylistics and psychology, a trend already begun in Van Peer (1986a). And, as Alderson and Short point out through some of their references, there is an interesting connection to be explored with English as a foreign language, where a number of people have been working on the reading processes of second-language learners. Comparative work on the reading outcomes of native and non-native speakers, with their different linguistic knowledge and reading purposes will put theories of commonality of interpretation to their severest test. Moreover, cooperation between empirical literary studies and second-language reading research should provide a fascinating complement to the current critical interest in literature written in English by writers whose culture and first language are usually considered 'exotic' by those in Britain, North America and Australasia.

An interesting by-product of the experiment by Short and Van Peer is the fact that in their protocols they produced, unbidden, explicit evaluative comments on the poem they worked with. As a result, they propose a rough-and-ready account of evaluative as well as interpretative procedures. Hopefully, their observations will act as a stimulus for more work in this area, and help to cast some light on a topic which many mention, few discuss and none understand.

1.3 ANALYSING LITERATURE

This volume contains a large number of extensive analyses of literary texts. Short and Van Peer provide a full stylistic analysis of Hopkins' 'Inversnaid' to compare with their protocol analysis, and the Chapters (7–11) which concern themselves primarily with the *teaching* of English literature also contain a number of analyses of poems. Ronald Carter (Ch. 7) examines Edwin Morgan's 'Off Course', Short and Candlin (Ch. 8) discuss 'All There is to Know about Adolf Eichmann' by Leonard Cohen, and the description of Mr Bounderby in Dickens's *Hard Times*. Peter Verdonk (Ch. 10) examines three poems: 'Going' by Philip Larkin; Jon Silkin's 'Death of a Son'; and 'Ariel' by Sylvia Plath. The analyses by Carter, Short and Candlin and Verdonk, and the shorter discussions of a number of texts by Willie Van Peer (Ch. 11) are all linked to particular teaching proposals; but the Chapters by Hutchinson and Trengove concentrate exclusively on particular texts. Tom Hutchinson (Ch. 5) examines *The Tiger Moth* by H. E. Bates from the point of view of speech and thought presentation. He argues that the work which has gone into establishing criteria for the various categories of speech and thought presentation needs to be supplemented by a concentration on the functions which the various categories are used for. He demonstrates the uses to which Bates puts the presentation categories in his story.

Bates uses free indirect speech to *summarize* conversations of varying lengths and even a whole series of conversations. In *blending* he uses FIS to 'fade' from one scene, or aspect of a scene, to another. Under the heading of *contrast* Hutchinson examines the way in which Bates uses contrasting patterns of speech presentation in relation to character. The use of free indirect speech as opposed to direct speech for a particular character's speech is often used for *distancing*. These four functions are combined strategically in *The Tiger Moth* in order to manipulate the reader's view of the two main characters, so that we identify with the man, Williamson, but feel distanced from the woman, understanding her no more than Williamson himself.

Graham Trengove (Ch. 6) analyses Philip Larkin's 'Vers de Société'. He begins with the assumption that advanced foreign learners of English will need to be able to respond to linguistic variation in English. The text exhibits frequent shifts in style from one variety of English to another, and in order to make sense of the poem we have to ascribe an appropriate value to each style and style change. Larkin often makes use of style variation in his poetry, but nowhere so extensively as in 'Vers de Société'. Trengove shows that to understand the poem we need to establish a coherent character for its persona, and that this in turn depends crucially on our identifying the language varieties he uses and relating them together to form a consistent interpretative viewpoint.

1.4 TEACHING LITERATURE

Over the last few years there has been a resurgence of interest in the use of literature in language teaching, and a number of the contributions to this volume reflect this. Stylistic analysis has been of particular concern to the foreign-language learner as it has been seen as a device by which the understanding of relatively complex texts can be achieved. This, coupled with a general interest in English literature, has led to the stylistic approach becoming more and more popular in the EFL context.

Graham Trengove's approach to the use of literature in language teaching and understanding is relatively traditional in stylistic terms in that he uses linguistic and stylistic analysis as an analytical tool to help him to see textual pattern and its significance. In turn, these insights can be used to help others come to terms with the text and discuss it in detail. In that sense, his approach for foreign-language learners is not far removed from what one might see in an elementary stylistics class in a British university, and indeed, it falls within the description of stylistics in English departments in some British universities outlined in section 1.1. above. The same can be said of Peter Verdonk's contribution (Ch. 10). Working with his undergraduates at the University of Amsterdam, he explored different stylistic approaches and then encouraged them to try out the methodologies in detail on particular poems. Language understanding was achieved, as a by-product of this activity. Verdonk's chapter thus has three different kinds of interest: (i) the texts which he and his students analysed and the interpretations they arrived at; (ii) the relative merits of the different approaches which they explored (Leech on cohesion of foregrounding, Widdowson's notion of a literary text as a 'secondary language system' and Cluysenaar's lexical approach); and (iii) the efficacy of using the study of literature and stylistics as a strategy for communicative language learning.

Sylvia Adamson's contribution (Ch. 9), has obvious connections with Trengove's approach. She argues that English literature is of particular interest in English language teaching because of its special status with respect to one facet of language variation, lexical diglossia. She first discusses the traditional literary distinction between High and Low style in terms of the work on diglossia by Ferguson (1959), and others, and then goes on to show how Shakespeare, Wordsworth and Dickens use lexical diglossia in interesting ways in their works. She points out that examples can easily be found where a small text-portion contains synonyms or near-synonyms, one from the High and one from the Low style vocabulary set. The two words thus gloss one another, but at the same time have different connotative values and so can be used for expressing textual contrasts related to characterization, viewpoint, etc. This diglossic juxtaposition in literature constitutes a simplification of the language varieties that abound in English and that Trengove explores in his analysis of Larkin's poem. Adamson suggests that the study of texts with this simple form of style variation is of particular use to the language learner.

The chapters discussed so far under the heading 'teaching literature' have been general and/or traditionally stylistic in approach. The other 'teaching' contributions to this volume concern themselves more closely with pedagogy. Ronald Carter's second contribution (Ch. 7), 'What is stylistics and why can we teach it in different ways?' takes Edwin Morgan's poem 'Off Course' and suggests how it can be used for eight different kinds of teaching. The poem is unusual in that it consists of twenty-one lines, each of which contain two noun phrases consisting of a determiner, an adjective and a noun. Moreover, the lexis is restricted and repetitive. It is thus an interesting vehicle for, amongst other things, exploring the structure of the English noun phrase, looking at lexical relations and lexical patterns related to the text's interpretation, and studying the nature of 'literariness' through a discussion of whether or not 'Off Course' constitutes a 'proper' poem. Carter thus shows how we can view literary texts not just as aesthetic objects, but as vehicles for teaching all manner of things *about* English language and literature.

Short and Candlin's Chapter (8) describes a course for teachers at the University of Lancaster which explored ways of integrating language and literature teaching in the EFL context. The course covered a large number of areas, but the approach made central use of the stylistic approach to literature, and also of a suggestion in Widdowson (1975) that the comparison of similar text-types from literary and non-literary sources can be used to advantage. Like Widdowson (and indeed Trengove and Adamson in this volume), they make use of the fact that literary texts often contain a number of varieties of English. But unlike Widdowson, they do not see literature and the rest of language as being distinct from one another. Rather, they suggest that students can profit by comparing the linguistic similarities and differences between texts in terms of similarities and differences of communicative function. For example, the poem by Leonard Cohen which they examine displays interesting similarities with a passport description, similarities which are intrinsically connected with communicative purpose. But in turn, there are differences between the poem and the passport which help to highlight the special use that Cohen makes of the text-type that he borrows.

Perhaps the most radical chapter in this volume in terms of its pedagogical proposals is the last one (11), 'How to do things with texts: towards a pragmatic foundation for the teaching of texts', by Willie Van Peer. Van Peer first suggests that the definition of text with which we operate is inadequate in various respects, and in particular because not enough emphasis is laid on pragmatic function. This narrowness of definition has led teachers to see texts almost entirely as sources of *information* about which to ask questions. Van Peer outlines a more adequate, multi-faceted definition, from which he develops various strategies for teaching texts. So, for example, it is possible to adapt the cloze-test into an instrument for teaching students about textual cohesion and what Van Peer calls the 'openness' of texts. By presenting students with doctored versions, with words missing, the class can explore the various alternatives which students propose for particular slots and then compare them with the original choices made by the author. This and the other activities he suggests encourage the development of inferencing skills, which have increasingly been seen to be important in foreign language learning and textual understanding.

The approaches of Carter, Short and Candlin, and Van Peer might well cause the raising of some eyebrows in traditional literary circles in that literary texts are being used for purposes for which they were not intended, and, indeed, in Van Peer's chapter, the literary text itself is interfered with. But such pedagogical devices appear to be popular with the students who have been exposed to them, and help to promote literary understanding and general linguistic awareness. For teacher and pupil what counts is what works; and it is in this sense that reading, analysing and teaching literature go so interestingly together. After a period when English literature all but disappeared from the EFL curriculum in many countries, it now appears to be making something of a comeback. But this new use of literature for language teaching purposes involves an approach which is unlike traditional literary study, and is instead inextricably linked with the stylistic approach and empirical theories concerning how people read and understand. The use to which the literary texts are being put in these EFL classrooms is, in tenor, not unlike the deconstructionist approach which is being hotly debated within literary criticism itself.

TWO

Directions in the teaching and study of English stylistics

Ronald Carter

An essentially interdisciplinary activity, like many areas of applied linguistics, the most immediately contingent area to stylistics remains that of literary studies, although recent years have witnessed extension into other domains such as lexicography (see Hartmann 1981) and teaching English as a Foreign Language. This short survey is divided into five main sections but, given the interrelatedness of the areas, there will be inevitable overlaps as well as potential cases for sub-categorization. The sections are: (i) Linguistic stylistics; (ii) Literary stylistics; (iii) Style and discourse; (iv) Pedagogical stylistics; (v) Stylistics and the foreign language learner. The survey draws on a previous review (Carter 1985) but considerably expands material in sections (iv) and (v) in order to meet the overall aims of this volume more adequately.

2.1 LINGUISTIC STYLISTICS

In several respects, linguistic stylistics is the purest form of stylistics in that its practitioners attempt to derive from the study of style and language variation some refinement of models for the analysis of language and thus contribute to the development of linguistic theory. Work in linguistic stylistics is generally less accommodating to the aims of non-linguistic disciplines and is thus, when applied, most likely to provoke reservations about its relevance. Linguistic stylisticians believe that in the analysis of language there are dangers in compromising the rigour and systematicity of analysis of stylistic effects and that practitioners in related disciplines are unwilling to accept the kind of standards of principled language description necessary to a genuinely mutual integration of interests. In literary criticism such debate appears interminable (e.g. Knight 1982; Ferrar 1984) and still bears traces of the Fowler–Bateson controversy at the end of the 1960s (see Fowler 1971a). The most recent studies in linguistic stylistics have tended to focus on applications of studies in discourse analysis and narrative organization to literary text study. For example, Burton (1980, 1982) employs models for spoken discourse analysis based on Sinclair and Coulthard (1975) for the analysis of drama dialogue; Short (1981) uses analysis based on Gricean and speech act theories; Carter and Simpson (1982) use narrative models based on Labov (1972); Fowler (1981; 1982) exploits Hallidayan models from within systemic linguistics; Armstrong (1983) applies communications-modelling systems based on work by the Soviet semiotician Yuri Lotman, while Stubbs (1982) and Weber (1982) analyse narratives with systematic reference to semantic-propositional and speech act models respectively. A large part of this work owes much to pioneering work by Pratt in the late 1970s (Pratt 1977).

2.2 LITERARY STYLISTICS

A distinguishing feature here is the provision of a basis for fuller understanding, appreciation and interpretation of avowedly literary texts. Although the precision of analysis made available by stylistic methods offers a challenge to established methods of close reading or practical criticism of texts, the procedures of literary stylistics remain traditional in character in spite of developments in literary theory (e.g. post-structuralism) which challenge assumptions about the role of language in depicting literary realities. Major recent text books by Leech and Short (1981) and Cummings and Simmons (1983) are characterized by systematic attention to effects brought about at different levels of language and see 'style' itself as the simultaneous convergence of effects at a number of levels of language organization. The latter study operates within a strict framework of systemic linguistics while the former is more eclectic and reflects recent developments in linguistics in its innovating chapters on speech presentation and literary pragmatics. Banfield (1982) and Fowler (1982) also provide impetus to study of what are termed in traditional literary criticism 'stream of consciousness' and 'point of view' (see also

O'Neal 1983): the former is a major study of this topic with reference to a wide range of literary writers (though see a very critical review by McHale 1983), the latter develops ideas on perspective in fiction with analytical reference to modality, deixis and transitivity. The general trend in literary stylistics appears to be sociolinguistic, that is, in a direction pointed by Traugott and Pratt (1980), and towards a view of style as less text-immanent than as existing within a more dynamic domain of social discourse processes. Recent articles on politeness phenomena (Wadman 1983), on literary text as *process* (Lindemann 1983) and on the interactive and discoursal properties of texts by Raymond Chandler (Crombie 1983) reflect such a trend. A corresponding shift in analyses of genre means rather more attention to dialogue and interaction in narrative and drama. However, more traditionally based stylistic-syntactic analyses continue to be published in major journals (e.g. Toolan 1983; Carter (ed.) 1982, which is a textbook with such a focus). See also Attridge (1982), Byers (1983), for the linguistic study of metrics and rhythm in poetry.

Most studies in literary stylistics aim to provide analytical procedures which are, at least, replicable; and stylisticians are now much less assertive in their claims for more objective analysis. The ideological character of their work has still to be adequately defended from charges made by Fish (1980), and re-opened by Thurley (1983: Ch. 3). The contents and methodological character of volumes such as those edited by Birch (1985) or journals such as *Poetica* and *Poetics Today* demonstrate that there is no easy division between literary and linguistic stylistics.

2.3 STYLE AND DISCOURSE

Work in stylistics within this category acknowledges that style is not an exclusively literary phenomenon and addresses itself to description and characterization of stylistic effects in a wide range of discourse types. Fowler's term for this (Fowler 1986) is 'linguistic criticism'. Neatly opposed as it is to literary criticism this reflects a claim that there is no distinction between literary and non-literary language and embodies an appeal to stylisticians to recognize the social character of all discourse and to direct analyses at the unmasking of the socio-political ideologies which underlie the construction of meaning in all literary and non-literary texts. In one sense, Fowler is arguing for a view of style as rhetoric, in the pre-1800 sense of the term (see also Carpenter 1982).

Work in this tradition has raised central questions and challenged presuppositions about the character of stylistics as a discipline. For example: (a) is there such a thing as a literary language? (see contributions to Herman (ed.) 1983; Short and Candlin 1986; Short 1986); (b) how politically 'neutral' is the stylistician-analyst? (Burton 1982); (c) what is the nature and function of established literary tropes such as irony and metaphor and are they exclusively literary phenomena? (e.g. Amante 1980; Pulman 1982; and pioneering work by Lakoff and Johnson 1980); (d) what exactly *is* the role of ambiguity, allusion, puns, metaphor in literature? (Ching, Haley and Lunsford 1980); (e) is there an identifiable discourse structure to literary narrative text? (Carter and Simpson 1982); (f) what is the linguistic basis of literary competence? (Reeves 1983). Two full-length studies of the stylistic-'rhetorical' character of texts with particular attention to compositional processes and the interactive role of the reader are Nash (1980) and Dillon (1981) (though see also Mailloux 1982: appendix). An empirical semic study which focuses on the psychological processing by readers of foregrounding in poetry is Van Peer (1986a).

The potential for growth in this area is considerable and it has to be noted that no single study has emerged in the 1970s or 1980s which builds systematically on work on non-literary style and language variation by Crystal and Davy (1969). The issues raised by such investigations compel fuller consideration of the theoretical and ideological status of literary and linguistic stylistics.

2.4 PEDAGOGICAL STYLISTICS

There has been much discussion in recent years about the applications of stylistics to the teaching of language and literature to native-speaking students of English. Textbooks have been written with more of an orientation towards the needs of the learner, and studies in both literary and linguistic stylistics, as well as the work in 'modern rhetoric' cited above, regularly contain accompanying exercises designed for further student investigation. The main examples of such textbooks are Traugott and Pratt (1980); Leech and Short (1981); Carter (ed.) (1982); Cummings and Simmons (1983) and Carter and Burton (eds) (1982) – the latter of which is more linguistic-stylistic in orientation and aimed at teachers interested in using literary texts for the purposes of language as well as literary study.

In the ten years following its publication, there was little discussion of the pedagogy of stylistics in the manner of Widdowson (1975), though this gap has, to some extent, been remedied by this volume, by Brumfit and Carter (eds) (1986) and by Brumfit (ed.) (1983) which is directed at the teaching of literature in non-British contexts overseas.

There are a number of issues which emerge in the context of debates concerning the pedagogical relevance of stylistics. Some are perennial issues deriving from deep-rooted divisions between linguistics and literary critics but which still require to be considered; others derive from recent advances in literary theory. It is impossible to do justice here to the intricate character of such debates and any highlighting of particular issues will be an inevitably subjective one. The following points, then, relate to areas which the present author considers to merit fuller consideration by all teachers of English as a mother tongue and as a foreign language at an advanced level. But the fact that some issues are probably unresolvable without fundamental changes in assumptions concerning the nature of literature should not be taken to mean that these issues are best buried.

One of the main issues is the fundamentally *descriptive* nature of stylistics as a discipline. Some stylistic analyses stop at this level and naturally invite criticism that interpretative and evaluative dimensions are being ignored. A further objection here, too, is that the greater the literary work the less amenable it will be to systematic description and that only those works or 'texts' (as stylisticians are held – disparagingly – to refer to them) which are not 'worth' much will be reducible to the descriptive procedures of stylistics. A related objection is that a teaching of stylistics which treats all texts as discourses and juxtaposes them in terms of description of styles of language organization further serves to dislocate the 'literary', reducing it to the common denominator of a descriptive framework, relegating to the periphery the essentially non-linguistic but distinctive characteristics of literature such as symbolism, allusion and intertextuality. This results in teaching which singularly fails to promote discrimination of the relative value of the materials and which therefore denies the place of the individual, imaginative response to the text. For a classic and less crudely summarized statement of this position readers are referred to Knight (1982).

It is, of course, untrue that stylisticians do not interpret. Many do, though few would see their primary role as an evaluative one of ranking texts in divisions of excellence. Interpretation is the subject of much literary-theoretical analyses and here, too, stylisticians need to answer the kind of charges made against the general nature of literary interpretation, particularly when, as with stylistics, the model tends to be that of New or Practical Criticism. In particular questions concerning the 'objective' nature of all description, the ideology of the interpreter, the isolation of the text as a language artefact from broader historical, sociocultural and political determinants, the inevitably arbitrary and invariably subjective nature of the 'iconic' fit between linguistic forms and literary meanings (see Fish 1980; Thurley 1983), *all* feed into the nature of the interpretative procedures taught and the kind of literary competence which is acquired, particularly in the case of the more advanced students. For fuller discussion of such issues with particular reference to pedagogical considerations, see Eagleton (1983) and Taylor and Toolan (1984), and for discussion of the nature of 'interpretation' in stylistics, Carter (1986b). And for a clear account of some issues of literary linguistic interpretation in relation to historical study and to Foucaudian discourses, see MacCabe (1981).

A general result of such debate has been to engender less grandiose claims for the explanatory potential of stylistics in the teaching and study of literature. There is now a greater eclecticism linguistically (reflecting advances across all linguistic levels, especially discourse and pragmatics) and a more modest awareness that any approach to literary texts presupposes a theory of literature. Accompanying this has been fuller investigation of literariness in language use with much detailed exemplification of the presence of literary language uses in all discourses. The position defended by stylisticians is still one of arguing strongly that, if the medium of literature is held to be worth describing, then it should be done precisely, systematically and retrievably. And, if features of literary language or language organization in literature are to be properly investigated, then this should be done in a scientific manner, involving bold hypotheses, a process of providing examples and counter-examples, leading to refinement of the hypotheses and the setting up of provisional analytical models of sufficient predictive power to provide for a process of continually refined and theoretically self-aware analysis. Interpretations of texts will thus be more provisional, relative to the analytical model or level of language analysis which predominates and will not assume any automatic, one-for-one correlations between linguistic structure and literary effect. Within this framework students will be brought to a fuller understanding of the workings of language and thus to a firm and clearly principled basis for interpretation as well as to an awareness that language, though only one component in a literary semiotic, is a central feature which it is important to respond to *without* impressionism or *adhocery*. The development of 'A' level courses in Language Studies devoted to enhancement of analytical skills will do much to serve the cause of stylistic studies in higher education in England (Freeborn 1982). But see also Brumfit (1980, 1981) for some measured and cautious discussion of the nature of language study in relation to both courses in linguistics and literature, as well as Trengove (1983) and Pickett (ed.) (1982).

2.5 STYLISTICS AND THE FOREIGN LANGUAGE LEARNER

Perhaps because questions of language and learning are more widely addressed in the domain of foreign language learning than in the no less important area of mother-tongue language development, issues of pedagogy in relation to stylistics, literature and language study can be more easily surveyed. Discussion of the relationship is at a relatively embryonic stage so any survey must necessarily reflect, again selectively, problems and procedures which in some cases are being explored, have yet to be adequately tested in learning contexts or which the present writer feels have yet to be put squarely on an agenda. What is clear, however, is that there is growing recognition that integration of language and literature can be of mutual benefit in the context of foreign or second-language education and that a situation of literary education, conducted by exposure to a canon of texts in English literature mainly through a method of lecture, may be in need of modification on a number of counts. In terms of assessment, too, perennial questions such as: 'In "Daffodils" Wordsworth gives a very limited account of nature. Discuss'; or 'Write an essay on Jane Austen's innovations in plot structure' require re-examination in the light of students' inevitable reliance on criticism and second-hand sources. The tentative and exploratory nature of such relations and developments is best served by a list of points and issues for discussion (though for a more extensive recent survey see Muyskens, 1983).

(i) Debate here concerns the extent to which literary texts may be used in the classroom (a) to teach language (b) to teach about language. The case of the former has been advanced (Holst 1980 and to a certain extent Walker 1983) but has few adherents. This is connected with a fairly widespread recognition that there would be little justification for teaching the conditional in English by means of Kipling's 'If-' or the present tense in conjunction with Bradbury's *The History Man*. There is a real danger that the text as a text could emerge totally emasculated and a further problem would be that, in linguistic terms, a literary text will only very rarely provide the structured repetition, graded variation or range of forms and functions needed to enforce the discrete grammatical points. In the case of (b), however, literary texts can be used to pose seminal questions about the nature of language, the differentiability of 'literary' from 'non-literary' English and to explore the organization of literature as a communicative discourse (see Widdowson 1975: Ch. 6). It is likely however that the answers to questions would be relatively abstract and theory-laden and that such activity may be best confined to more advanced students.

(ii) One of the boldest claims for the uses of literature in foreign language teaching has been made by Widdowson in an interview in *ELT Journal* (Widdowson 1983). There Widdowson develops ideas first put forward in Widdowson (1979b) to the effect that reading literary discourses can assist students in the development of sense-making procedures of the kind required for the interpretation of or sensitization to language use in any discoursal context. Here is an extract from the interview:

> WIDDOWSON:. . . If you're a sensible teacher you use every resource that comes to hand. But the difference between conventional discourse and literature is that in conventional discourse you can anticipate, you can take short cuts; when reading a passage, let's say, you often know something about the topic the passage deals with, and you can use that knowledge while reading naturally in order to find out what's going on in the passage. This is a natural reading procedure: we all do it. The amount of information we normally take out of something we read is minimal, actually, because we simply take from the passage what fits the frame of reference we have already established before reading. Now, you can't do that with literature . . . because you've got to find the evidence, as it were, which is representative of some new reality. So, with literary discourse the actual *procedures for making sense* are much more in evidence. You've got to employ interpretative procedures in a way which isn't required of you in the normal reading process. If you want to develop these procedural abilities to make sense of discourse, then literature has a place.

Thus, according to Widdowson, 'meanings' in literature are contained in the language but are not to be located by appeal to conventional formulae; rather they are to be inferred by procedural activity. Such training in deciphering the communication, working out the precise nature of its communicative acts, by projecting yourself backwards and forwards, in and outside and across the discourse can be a key element in the acquisition of discoursal skills in the target language, whether they be in the service of native- or foreign-language development.

Widdowson's general position has received support from others, notably Short and Candlin (this volume) who place more stress than Widdowson on the need for students to study literature along a continuum of discourses thus appreciating the degree to which literary styles are coterminous with language styles across a curriculum or across a language as a whole. Apart from generating the more abstract discoursal questions raised above, the juxtaposition of literary and non-literary discourses in the classroom emerges as a strong teaching recommendation (see also Littlewood 1976). For a statement of opposition to such teaching based on the kind of assumptions outlined in section 2.4 (and thus containing arguments which may be more relevant to mother-tongue teaching contexts) see Gower (1984) and Barry (1983), responding to papers by Sopher (1981) and Deyes (1982).

(iii) The issues here are not as generally well-developed as in the preceding two sub-sections. The basic point at issue is whether the kind of stylistic analysis developed for language and literature studies in the mother-tongue can be transferred without modification or impairment to a foreign- or second-language learning context. Some writers and textbook authors introduce established language-teaching strategies such as cloze procedure, comprehension questions, pair-based oral interaction, prediction, structured re-writing as prior to more detailed and explicit stylistic analysis (see Carter 1986a; Long 1985; Boardman and McRae 1984). Much depends, of course, on the levels of language competence involved but the principle of pre-analysis language work is worthy of further attention. It also leads directly into questions of response to language, grading of text and appropriate 'simplification'.

(iv) However, a student's capacity to respond to language is not exclusively dependent on language. Language is the medium and can be taught as such but response is a matter of personal, cultural *and* linguistic experience. Indeed, the primacy of any one feature is very difficult to isolate. This leads directly into the taxing question of *selection* of texts for students whose backgrounds will be inevitably diverse. How do we therefore grade texts? Is there such a thing as an introductory or advanced literary course and by what criteria can such a course be defined?

Writers such as Hemingway who use mostly simple language structures (e.g. *The Old Man and the Sea*) can be complicated for students as a result of inconclusive plots or complex symbolism or difficult ideas. A poet such as Philip Larkin whose syntax is straightforward employs vocabulary which demands special socio-cultural knowledge of Britain. His poem, 'Mr. Bleaney', for example, contains references to English football pools, landladies and 'digs', English seaside souvenirs, etc., and requires an ability to recognize the associations created by reference to the town of Stoke and to summer holidays in Frinton. Similarly, John Osborne's *Look Back in Anger* is accessible on a number of levels but assumes knowledge of the English class system. Short and Candlin (this volume) report the kinds of difficulties encountered with an ostensibly simple sentence, *It was necessarily a Registry-Office Wedding*, the socio-cultural connotations of which were important for their students' understanding of the text. Linguistically simple texts are not always 'simple'; and, by turns, it will be clear what kind of effects are lost when literary texts are turned into simplified readers.

It is also interesting to observe that *modern* literature is generally not always the most accessible, especially for non-European students. Many modern texts present experience obliquely or deal with alienation from an impersonal, industrialized world where spiritual values are absent. Also, although modern and 'relevant' English is used, it is often linguistically experimental and can be perplexing even for British undergraduate students. In such cases, the 'distance' of, for example, eighteenth-century writers such as Goldsmith or Crabbe who deal with the break-up of rural communities can produce more personal responses and more direct involvement.

(v) It could be argued that the teaching of background in terms of socio-historical, cultural and political contexts is an essentially non-linguistic matter. As we have seen, however, language is continually impregnated with culture and no easy divisions or separations are possible. Although this is not the place to debate the role of literature in the introduction of students to the target culture, the construction of a syllabus in language and literature study presupposes theories of literature which are in their turn reflections of socio-political ideologies. The whole area is one not widely discussed in stylistics where the assumption of a value-free, 'neutral' analysis (see Burton 1982) is still widespread; but among the questions in need of debate are the extent to which English literature is or should be seen as consisting of institutionally canonized British authors or whether the definition of 'literature' should be extended to cover not only 'popular' literature in English (see Van Peer 1984), but writing in English within cultures where English is a recognized or institutionalized language or where it is the medium of education (e.g. Nigeria, India, Singapore, Hong Kong, Kenya). This raises questions to do with the bilingual's creativity (see Kachru 1983) and with the fact that the *values* involved are political and social as well as aesthetic ones.

2.6 CONCLUSIONS

Most of the areas covered in this short survey have involved some kind of demarcation between what is properly literary and what is properly linguistic. Interdisciplinary work of any kind brings with it these kinds of problems of definition of appropriate practice, particularly when pedagogical considerations are involved. And a continual refinement of theory, however important, will not necessarily provide illumination where attitudinal factors are involved. More positively, however, the place of stylistics in literature studies and in the teaching of literature is now being articulated with sharper theoretical awareness, increasingly numerous and explicit examples of analytical practice and rapidly growing illustrations of classroom stylistics in operation in different teaching contexts (see the recent edition of *Forum* (1985) vol. XXIII, No 1). The openness to problems on the part of stylisticians is a signal of a confidence that may in the past have paradoxically masked a defensiveness about their discipline; but the open, clear and explicit means by which their positions are articulated serves the end of explicit internal and external criticism without which progress and development are only obstructed.

THREE

Accident! Stylisticians evaluate: Aims and methods of stylistic analysis

Mick Short and Willie Van Peer

3.1 INTRODUCTION

Accidents do happen. Sometimes they are even beneficial. This chapter is a description of an experiment which produced, in part, very different results from those expected. Although we would not claim that our work is revolutionary in nature, we do think that it throws up a number of important insights into the processes of interpretation and evaluation, and that it suggests areas for future research by stylisticians and others interested in the interpretation and evaluation of texts.

The predominant mode of work in stylistic analysis has been geared towards text-description. We felt that not enough attention had been paid to the reading process and so we designed a simple experiment in which we wrote down independently our line-by-line reactions to a poem we had not studied before. By comparing these protocols we hoped to discover some essential insights into the act of literary interpretation. We also hoped that a comparison of the protocols with a thorough stylistic analysis of the poem would show the explanatory limits of linguistic criticism and thereby indicate areas for future study. Our most striking findings were that:

(a) Our interpretations and strategies for arriving at those interpretations were very similar;
(b) we had made very explicit and very similar evaluative remarks on the text;
(c) these evaluative statements centred on practically identical text locations.

What follows is:

(i) a description and discussion of the methodology used in arriving at the protocols (section 3.2);

 (ii)   the poem used as the basis for the experiment (section 3.3);
 (iii) the protocols (section 3.4);
 (iv)   a discussion of the similarities and disagreements between
        the two protocols (section 3.5);
 (v)   a discussion of the reading strategies employed by the two
        readers (section 3.6);
 (vi)   a stylistic analysis of the poem (section 3.7);
 (vii) a comparison of the results of the protocols and the stylistic
        analysis (section 3.8);
 (viii) a discussion of the evaluative remarks found in the proto-
        cols and the suggestion that readers use a set of evaluative
        as well as interpretative strategies when they read poetry
        (section 3.9);
 (ix)   concluding remarks (section 3.10).

3.2 THE EXPERIMENT

3.2.1 *General design*

Unlike literary critics, stylisticians often assume that their work
is independent of value judgements (although, like critics, they
tend only to discuss texts deemed to be of literary merit). The
experiment described here was also based on this assumption.
The general aim was to put the two experimenters in the kind of
position that new readers of a poem would be in. To this end,
a third party was invited to choose a poem (randomly, out of a
set of poetry volumes) and tell us its title in order to check that
we were not familiar with it. The poem selected was 'Inversnaid'
by Gerard Manley Hopkins.

In their discussions of poems both literary critics and stylisticians 'pretend' that they are reading the text line by line and for
the first time (see, for example, Fish 1970; Empson 1961 *passim*).
This 'pretence' is a convention which idealizes the reading
process and controls illicit variability in reader response in order
that rational discussion may take place. In fact a critic always
reads the poem in question a number of times before he puts pen
to paper; and readers almost always glance down the page as
they read, picking up information which occurs later in the text
in order to help them interpret the earlier parts. However,
different readers will pick out different pieces of 'advance' infor-

mation and different critics will not have read a poem the same number of times before they write about it.

In order to cut down the number of variables affecting reader reactions, we arranged for the poem to be given to us one line at a time so that we could write down our detailed reactions to each line in turn as the poem unfolded. (For a description of this method, see McHoul 1978.) The form of the reading process thus replicated the critics' conventional ideal. The experimenters worked completely independently and at their own pace and only compared notes when they had both finished the poem. The intention then was that the two accounts arrived at would be discussed in general terms. This was to be followed by a detailed comparison of the reactions to each line, in order to observe the ways in which the experimenters had built up their interpretations.

To make the situation as 'real' as possible we were allowed to know in advance the name of the poet and the poem's general shape (i.e. that it had four 4-line stanzas). Readers normally have this kind of information in advance, and it may affect the kind of interpretation they are likely to form, just as knowledge about the people we converse with allows us to understand more easily and more fully what they mean. Access to dictionaries and general reference works was also allowed, as this would normally be available to readers.

3.2.2 Methodological remarks

Two aspects of the method used in the experiment are to be considered here: firstly, the use of introspective techniques in *general* as an attempt to understand what goes on when a (poetic) text is read, and secondly, the use of the *particular* introspective technique chosen on this occasion.

Introspection in general

The main advantage of 'on-line' introspection is that it does allow at least some insight into the *reading process*. It is in principle impossible to gain direct access to what goes on inside people's heads when they read, and attempts to get readers to say or write down what thoughts come to them as they read is probably the nearest one can get to the observational ideal. It has an advantage over more leisurely critical methods in that: (a) it helps to prevent forgetfulness and *post-hoc* rationalization; and (b) it captures as well as we can the sequence of thoughts that the readers produced. The main disadvantages of introspection are that it probably distorts the act of reading to make it a conscious activity, and it is likely that quite a lot of what is involved in reading, particularly at the subconscious level, passes by unnoticed. Moreover, the resulting protocols are relatively inelegant, imprecise and 'messy' compared with more traditional critical and stylistic accounts. It is also difficult to *quantify* introspective data for comparison. Do slightly different linguistic formulations count as the same thing? If they do, how different do the formulations have to be before they are no longer two different ways of saying the same thing? The *relevance* of the data is similarly difficult to decide on. In particular, it is difficult to tell from the set of remarks about a particular text-portion which parts are the most salient. Once it is also realized that the two informants in this case were not trained introspecters, it can be seen that the technique is not without its problems. However, it appears to be the best we have until more sophisticated techniques are developed. And it at least gets nearer the actuality of reading than the traditional critical or stylistic discussions. For a somewhat different introspective technique on literary data see Alderson and Short (this volume); for an alternative approach to introspection see Harri-Augstein and Thomas (1984).

Written introspections

As in so many other areas of human enquiry, the text/reading analyst has to make a decision, conscious or otherwise, as to how far he is going to idealize his data. At one extreme we have the general approach of textual criticism, which contains a considerable amount of idealization. Allusions to the process of reading are often made, to describe, for example, effects of surprise, which must make reference to the sequence of reading, or irony, which often involves comparing the statement one reads with the real or fictional world, noticing that there is a mismatch which is unlikely to be explained by mere error, and then coming up with a sense different from the literal interpretation contained in the original statement. That the reading process is considerably idealized in this situation is evidenced by the mass of theoretical critical talk about ideal and average readers, e.g. Leavis (1952: 211–22); Riffaterre (1972); Iser (1978). These concepts assume a commonality for readers of a particular text and to a great extent ignore individual differences between readers. Traditional critical discussion also avoids the performance errors considered to be irrelevant (e.g. if one misreads a word through lack of attention and thus misinterprets, or if one skips a portion of text because one is tired). It thus idealizes in order to cut away those aspects of reading felt not to be relevant to 'good' textual understanding.

At the other, impossible, extreme would be a situation where an analyst sits inside the reader's head observing the conscious and subconscious mental operations as they take place. The nearest one can get to this is probably tape-recorded introspection (see Alderson & Short, this volume). But even here idealization will occur as a result of selection and the necessary fact that: (a) what is spoken must be coded in surface linguistic form; and (b) whatever subconscious thoughts are recorded are made conscious, and thus probably distorted to some extent.

The method we chose was intermediate between the two extremes. It may thus have missed points which tape-recorded data might have thrown up; and as it takes longer to write things down than to say them, it may well involve a little more reflection. This seemed a good compromise to us as we were interested in the relations between stylistic analysis and the reading process, and it allowed us some kind of attachment to both worlds. Oddly enough, it may be the case that written introspections are in some ways closer to the actuality of the reading process than spoken ones. In Alderson and Short's tape-recorded protocols the introspections are realized in a 'full-grammatical' way. The written situation chosen here seemed to encourage the readers to produce language in a more 'telegram style' manner, which, it might be claimed, is closer to what happens in people's heads. It also allowed the possibility (taken up by the informants) of producing tables and diagrams instead of linear constructs. It is of course extremely difficult to know exactly what mental operations are performed when people read and so it is not really possible to say whether the written or spoken mode is closest to what occurs.

But the written format chosen here seemed to allow for more possibilities of presentation than the spoken form.

One extra problem created by the methodology was the conversion of the protocols into printed form for this article. It is not possible to reproduce them exactly, with arrows, circling, half-diagrams, etc. as they would have been impossible for an outsider to read. Thus there is some distortion in the presentation of the protocols in section 3.4.

3.3 THE POEM

(Reprinted from *Gerard Manley Hopkins: Poems and Prose*, selected and edited by W. H. Gardner, Penguin, 1953, pp. 50–1)

[0]   **Inversnaid**

[1]   This darksome burn, horseback brown,
[2]   His rollrock highroad roaring down,
[3]   In coop and in comb the fleece of his foam
[4]   Flutes and low to the lake falls home.

[5]   A windpuff-bonnet of fáwn-fróth
[6]   Turns and twindles over the broth
[7]   Of a pool so pitchblack, féll-frówning,
[8]   It rounds and rounds Despair to drowning.

[9]   Degged with dew, dappled with dew
[10]   Are the groins of the braes that the brook treads through.
[11]   Wiry heathpacks, flitches of fern,
[12]   And the beadbonny ash that sits over the burn.

[13]   What would the world be, once bereft
[14]   Of wet and of wilderness? Let them be left,
[15]   O let them be left, wildness and wet;
[16]   Long live the weeds and the wilderness yet.

3.4 THE PROTOCOLS

Below, each line of the poem is presented in turn, along with the remarks which the two authors wrote down as they read the poem. As has been pointed out, these are *not* an exact replica of the original protocols. However, every effort has been made to ensure that no significant details are omitted.

[0] *Inversnaid*
MHS Name of Scottish town (cf. Inverness)? Meaning of *inver*?
WVP Proper name (cf. Inverness)? Not in atlas. A real place?
     Inverse?

[1] *This darksome burn, horseback brown,*
MHS Inversnaid = *this*? Poet is next to it, possibly addressing
     reader. *Darksome* is a neologism – 'made up of dark'. *Horse-
     back brown* = a metaphor, 'Brown as a horse's back'. Why
     bring in the horse and its back? Brown and dark = death?
     The burn is certainly dark coloured. So far only the subject
     NP (Noun Phrase).
WVP Narrator is pointing to *this*. *Burn* is pre- and post-modified
     by *dark* and *brown*. *Burn* = Scots river. Possibly ambiguous:
     (a) something burnt; (b) a wound; (c) a stream. (c) is most
     likely, given the title of the poem. So the narrator points to
     a stream somewhere – Scotland (but does it exist?) and says
     it has a dark colour and compares it to a horse's back. Why
     is it compared to a horse? Is the water fast (cf. *horse*) or
     streaming gently (cf. smoothness of horse's back)? The
     comma at the end of the line = a strong caesura. More qual-
     ities of the stream to come. Suggestion of something heroic
     (cf. the horse and dark colours, possibly associated with the
     past).

[2] *His rollrock highroad roaring down,*
MHS i.e. roaring down his roll-rock highroad. *Roaring* = fast
     flowing (cf. high road = large road). Hence a big river? *His*
     – capital letter but at the beginning of a line – God (from my
     general knowledge that Hopkins is a religious poet)?
     Possibly refers anthropomorphically to the river – or the
     horse? *Rollrock* = neologism. A high-road down which rocks
     can be rolled. *High* + *rollrock* + *roaring* = river coming
     down the side of a mountain or steep hill. (Is the moun-
     tainside God's high-road?) A problem with reviewing the
     poem line by line is that we do not get it in sense units.
WVP Does *his* refer to the burn? The first verb is *roaring down*: the
     burn is roaring down from a great height. Could explain the
     horse comparison in the first line. 'Gentle' possibility
     cancelled. *Rollrock* = neologism – rolling down from the
     rocks? Rolling down and rocking (fierceness)? *Highroad*:

stream can't be running down a public road. So *road* = river's course, and *high* is opposed to *low*. The river comes straight down. Highwayman associations (cf. the horse)? The expectation about more information was confirmed. More to come? Rhythm is quite regular.

[3]   *In coop and in comb the fleece of his foam*

MHS   Still more of the clause to come. *His* must now mean the river's – no capital; *foam* is also found in rivers. *Coop* = place of confinement/basket – for catching/holding fish? *Comb* – for hair? cockerel? crest of a hill? wave? Is the foam caused by going over and in between the rocks? *Fleece* = white and woolly. Sheep as well as horses? *Fleece of his foam, coop* and *comb* are all metaphorical and all have possible animal connotations.

WVP   *Foam* seems to settle the ambiguity of *burn*. *Fleece* – animal (cf. horse!). *Coop* = ambiguous – chicken basket or fishing gear. Latter seems most likely in context. *Comb* = crest of a wave or comb of a bird. Former most likely. If the latter, *coop* might mean *chicken basket* after all. No verb – deleted or still to come? Is the river running down in the shape of a coop? Explains the foam and the roaring. Another description of energy – stream is running fast and gets trapped. Hence the waves, the crests (*comb*) of which form into a thick fleece. *His* = burn? Most likely (internal *comb/foam* rhyme strengthens this interpretation). Where is the river going next? What has the narrator to do with it? Will the description go on for ever? No rhyme with previous lines.

[4]   *Flutes and low to the lake falls home.*

MHS   The verb! Metaphorical – so it makes a musical (high pitched?) sound and then falls straight down into the lake (cf. the sound patterning and positioning of *low*). *Home* = end; but also anthropomorphic meaning (cf. *his*)?

WVP   A verb. Subject = *the fleece of his foam*? *Falls home* is deviant (but cf. *to plunge home*). Makes a musical sound? And grooves? Note vowel parallelism in *coop* – *comb/flutes* – *low*; also the rhyme (*home/foam*). Hence this stanza 'describes' a stream thundering down from a height and dropping into the lake. In this dive the water seems to come to a standstill: connotations of rest and peace – *home, flute, low.*

[5]   *A windpuff-bonnet of fáwn-fróth*

MHS   Subject of new sentence and stanza. *Fawn-froth*: alliteration and lexical connection with foam (and fleece). *Fawn* = possibly brown (cf. first line). Verb meaning for *fawn* looks unlikely (no suitable contextualization). More animal images? (cf. line 3). *Windpuff* = very light and probably blown by the wind. *Bonnet* = hat, and so high – a metaphor. *Froth* = light, and on top of the water. Hence a light piece of brown froth on top of/above the water. It must now be a description poem – same subject matter as first stanza. Note the light words so far: *windpuff, froth, foam, (fleece, bonnet?).* Brown colours: *foam, horse, brown, darksome.*

WVP   NP – a verb in the next line? *Bonnet* – Scotland. *Fawn* – (a) young deer, (b) pregnant with, (c) colour? (b) is highly unlikely. (a) and (c) give parallels with *horseback brown* in first line. *Froth* refers back to *foam.* Hence brown coloured foam shaped like a puffed bonnet. Rhythm staccato here as opposed to flowing rhythm of previous stanza.

[6]   *Turns and twindles over the broth*

MHS   *Broth* = river – a liquid, and the right colour – brown. It also has froth over it. *Twindles* = neologism – *twine* + *dwindle*? cf. also *twinkle.* *Twinkle* and *dwindle* both = small (cf. the phonaesthetic quality of the first vowel in both words). So it is turning and disappearing down the river? Presumably not at the lakeside – he is watching the froth go down the river.

WVP   The verbs! The broth = the lake – leaves and plants in the water. *Broth* contrasts with the noise and speed of the stream – homely and banal. The froth, one of the reminders of fierceness, is coming to an end? (cf. *dwindle*). *Twindles* = neologism – *dwindle* + *twinkle* – light movement. More information to come on the lake? So the heroic tumbling of the stream comes to a quiet homely (and uninteresting?) end.

[7]   *Of a pool so pitchblack, féll-frówning,*

MHS   I didn't expect the NPs to go on so long. I was wrong about the foam – it is falling down a waterfall. The pool is even darker than the river – *pitch* + *black* + *frown. Frown* can also connote disapproval/anger – *fell* (cf. *fall*). Is this the fall from grace? Possible light/dark contrast between the foam and the pool. The *so* means the second half of the comparative is still to come. This should help make the reason for the contrast clear – the content of stanza 3?

WVP Postmodification in the NP. *Pool* = lake, with rather banal connotations (cf. *broth*). The water is black and in contrast with the brown stream (cf. *pitch*). Associations with DEATH of the stream. *Fell* – noun or adjective? Adjective most likely. So, something is going to be predicated of the lake, which is pitch black and frowning in a cruel way. *Frowning* = first verb with human meaning. Is the lake human? Stream animal? Is the lake 'killing' the stream?

[8] *It rounds and rounds Despair to drowning.*

MHS *It* = foam, not pool. *It rounds and rounds* – cf. parallel in form and idea with *turns and twindles*. So the foam goes round and round Despair and then drowns. *To* – in order to, or before? Is *drowning* a noun here? Despair ties up lexically with *drowning* and *frowning*. Note the capital letter. We now seem to have two sets of colours, brown and black, and also a set of despair words which can be linked with blackness. *Rounds* = intransitive here. This and the repetition gives aimless quality (hence despair?). Although *despair* is possibly anthropomorphic too, it doesn't seem that the earlier possible anthropomorphic or animal references have any pattern relevant to interpretation. *Brown – frown – drown*: hence brown connected with falling, death and despair too? Yet before it seemed to be contrasted with the black. Is the point of the comparative the transformation of the light to the dark?

WVP What is *it*? (a) bonnet or (b) pool? Although searching for the closest previous NP would select (b), can the pool be rounding? Hardly, so the bonnet of froth rounds and rounds in (deleted) Despair to drown (in the lake). Death of the stream now explicitly alluded to for the first time. So, the stream of the first stanza is now less homely, associated with despair, threatening, death, cruelty, etc. The last part of the stream is swallowed up, though it has clung to its existence to the very end.

[9]   *Degged with dew, dappled with dew*

MHS *Degged* – association with *drenched, dredged*? More likely encrusted with jewels – cf. the parallelism of the two phrases. Also, *d-gg-* looks a bit like *dagger*, and they sometimes had jewels on the hilt (is this a purely personal association?). Presumably a subject NP to do with grass is to come. Certainly a different topic now – a two half poem? Alliteration on /d/ – tie up with despair? No obvious connection. *Dappled* – light and dark (cf. the horses and deer (fawn?)!!!). The lighter (God) side of things to come?

WVP *Dappled* brings in the image of the horse (first line). *Degged = decked*? No, *sprinkled* – but obscure in English. Something (the lake?) is covered with (patches of dew).

[10] *Are the groins of the braes that the brook treads through.*

MHS *Brae* = steep bank or hillside. *Groin* = edge? – either 'vault' meaning, or a variant of *groyne*? Why use *groin* and not *bank*? – to avoid echoes of the Loch Lomond song? – when was it written? Possibly to indicate steepness of the sides. Were groynes invented then? *Brook = burn*. *Tread* = anthropomorphism. Also slow, steady, heavy associations. Rather inappropriate? It often has unpleasant associations if the dictionary entries are anything to go by. [*Webster's Third International*]

WVP *Groin* – (a) belly? (b) support of a vault? (c) breakwater on a beach? Not enough sea context for (c). (b) opposite image of vault given through the hills. If (a) lower part of belly = lower part of braes – therefore valley. So *the groins of the braes* are the valleys that the stream treads through, and these are covered with water. Now a wider (more panoramic?) view: stream – lake – braes. Syntactic unit with previous line.

[11] *Wiry heathpacks, flitches of fern,*

MHS The subject of a new clause. *Wiry heathpacks* = lumps of heath; hence strong and firm. *Flitches of fern* = larger lumps. *Flitch* = side (of bacon normally!). *Heath* possibly brown – though possible contrast with the burn? *Burn* to come as a rhyme?

WVP Further surroundings: fern, heath. *Packs* and *flitches* have animal associations.

[12] *And the beadbonny ash that sits over the burn.*

MHS So, [11] was not a subject NP for a new clause. [11] +
[12] = a series of NPs enumerating items near the brook –
a series of impressions. I was right about the rhyme –
unfortunate (cf. repetition from line [1]). *Beadbonny
ash* = ash that is beautiful (plus Scots associations), because
of beads (red berries) on it. Rowan tree? *Sits* – stative.
Anthropomorphic? N.B. dynamic terms all to do with the
brook. It now looks as if the land surrounding the burn is
meant to contrast with the river.

WVP Further enumeration – NPs still referring to the burn's
surroundings. *Ash* can only mean tree here. *Bonny* – Scots
associations. But why *beadbonny*? *Beads* = drips of water
splashed on the tree? N.B. mountain ash = rowan (hence the
beads). There is no verb. Has it been deleted or is the
sentence to run on into the next stanza? Strange rhythm for
the end of a stanza.

[13] *What would the world be, once bereft*

MHS The first question; and a change of topic to the world.
Internal deviation. *Once bereft* = 'once it did not have' – i.e.
hypothetical, not historical meaning most likely because of
the question. *The world* – definite article – hence our world.

WVP Change of focus. Burn – lake – surroundings – world (foregrounding). An everyday sentence after the previous poetical stanzas. Strong expectation – once bereft: 'of this
stream'.

[14] *Of wet and of wilderness? Let them be left,*

MHS *Wet* = burn; wilderness = heath, etc. (by lexical association). A rhetorical question – implies world would not be
up to much. Then a command – Hopkins' or God's?

WVP Oh boy!

[15] *O let them be left, wildness and wet;*

MHS Another command. Almost exact repetition of previous line.
Is this intended to indicate strength of feeling about the
matter? cf. the *O*. Isn't this all a bit too loose for Hopkins?
Alliteration again. Is it just wildness and wet, or nice and
nasty he is talking about? Wilderness (heath) can also be
wet. Relevant or not? Good or not?

WVP A moral story. What was the point of the poetical effects in the previous stanzas? To illustrate the moral? Quite likely, but the wording of the moral is in sharp contrast to the description.

[16] *Long live the weeds and the wilderness yet.*

MHS An exhortation! What kind of a speech act is this? *Wilderness* is repeated, but with *weeds*, not *wet*. This should indicate weeds = river??? But it doesn't. *Weeds* can mean mourning clothes (cf. *despair, drowning*). But this is not systematic and there is too much repetition – cf. also the alliteration. Water weeds? Very unlikely. Odd use of *yet* at the end – merely for rhyme? The problem is that even if the weeds equal death, the possible symbolic values don't seem to work out. So why set up all the stuff about despair? And why should they both carry on if they have no real value in the poem? – no real contrast articulated.

WVP Ends like a traditional song. Last stanza – anticlimax. The dynamic interaction of the elements of nature is replaced by a static human moral outlook. Also a large jump from the elaborate description of the particular to the general.

3.5 SIMILARITIES AND DISAGREEMENTS BETWEEN THE PROTOCOLS

In order to compare the extent of agreement and disagreement between the two readers we first of all composed lists of such comments. In order not to bias the evidence in favour of agreements we restricted ourselves to relatively noncontroversial items in the similarities. In the disagreements list we included the more marginal disagreement cases. This was an attempt to ensure that we did not bias the data towards what we were predisposed to find. The list of similarities and disagreements is presented below.

3.5.1 Similarities between the protocols

Line [0]

Both MHS and WVP take the title to refer to a Scottish geographical location. From their remarks it is obvious that the presence of the prefix 'inver-' leads them to this conclusion. Both wonder (WVP in his comments on [1]) whether Inversnaid really exists.

Line [1]
Both remark on the use of the deictic *this*. Both remark on the colour terms *dark* and *brown* and wonder why the stream is compared to a horse. Both note that the information about the stream is syntactically incomplete.

Line [2]
Both MHS and WVP remark on the introduction of the human pronoun *his* and worry about what it refers to. Both suggest among other things that it refers to the river. Both (a) note that *rollrock* is a neologism and attempt to interpret it, and (b) comment on *high* and *roaring*, and combine what they know about these terms and *rollrock* to infer that the stream is falling straight down a steep slope.

Line [3]
Both now decide that *his* must refer to the river and use the presence of the word *foam* to arrive at the conclusion. Both (a) see *coop* as ambiguous but see its most likely interpretation as a fishing basket, (b) note that the word *fleece* brings in another animal reference and wonder about the connection with horses, (c) supply possible alternative meanings for *comb* and (d) set up similar situational descriptions to relate *coop*, *comb* and *fleece* together. WVP explicitly mentions that the water is fast-flowing, and this is presupposed in MHS's description.

Line [4]
Both note the occurrence of the verb, thus indicating something that has only been explicitly present in WVP's protocol up to now, namely the fact that the clause has been arrested over a number of lines. (For a discussion of the concept of *arrest* see Sinclair 1972.) Both note the musical associations, and perhaps partly because of this, both notice phonological correspondences within the line. Both also remark on the use of the word *home*, noting that the stream has come to an end. WVP notes that the line is deviant and MHS that it is metaphorical.

Line [5]
In spite of its occurrence as a modifier, both MHS and WVP note the

possible animal associations of *fawn*. Both see the line referring to froth on top of the water which is light and blown by the wind and notice parallels between this line and line [1].

Line [6]
Both MHS and WVP note that *twindle* is a neologism. They both see it as a lexical blend involving *dwindle* and probably *twinkle*. They also come up with similar interpretations for the word.

Line [7]
In the previous line MHS interpreted *broth* as referring to the river. Now he changes his mind, thus agreeing with WVP's belief that it refers to the lake into which the river is falling. Both note that the pool is black in contrast to the brownness of the stream. Both comment on *fell-frowning* and both see the pool as threatening in some way.

Line [8]
Both comment on *it* and decide that it refers to the froth, which is drowning in the pool. Both notice the grim overtones of *Despair*.

Line [9]
Both remark on *dappled* and relate it to the earlier horse references. The two readers also come up with similar meanings for *degged* even though they get there by different routes (MHS treats it as a neologism, WVP looks it up in the dictionary and finds a relevant meaning for it).

Line [10]
Both readers have difficulty with the head noun (*groins*) of the noun phrase which constitutes the majority of the line. Possibly as a result of this, there is no real agreement on the meaning of the line, although some of the tentative hypotheses put forward are similar.

Line [11]
Neither reader says much about this line. Both note the animal associations of *flitches*. WVP also sees such possible associations for *packs*.

Line [12]
Both MHS and WVP see the *beadbonny ash* as a rowan tree, with red berries. They also note the Scots associations of *bonny*. Both note that the structure is one of further enumeration.

Line [13]
Both MHS and WVP note the sudden change at this point. MHS calls it a change of topic and WVP a change of focus. They also both notice 'structural' changes. MHS remarks on the change to a question and the hypothetical structure; WVP notes the everyday lexis as opposed to the previous poeticalities.

Line [14]
No correspondence here as WVP loses patience with the poem.

Line [15]
At this point MHS also makes comments of a negative evaluative nature, suggesting that the writing is too loose. This backs up earlier comments he has made (cf. comments on lines [11] and [13]) and ties up with WVP's *Oh boy!* on line [14]. WVP also indicates at this point that the relation between what he calls the story and the moral is not close enough.

Line [16]
Most of the comments on this line are evaluative and derogatory. The particular points which the readers choose to comment on are, however, different.

3.5.2 *Disagreements between the protocols*

There is something of a difficulty in deciding what to put into this category. There is the possibility of not being able to decide whether two somewhat different comments count as a disagreement. It might be deemed better to list *differences* rather than *disagreements*. We have chosen to restrict ourselves to disagreements as there is an obvious (statistical) sense in which one would expect different people to notice different things just because, by definition, they are different. For this reason we feel that for theories of reading, stylistic analysis and literary criticism, agreements and positive disagreements are of more interest. Hence we do not list examples like the comments on line [1], where WVP notes that *burn* has both pre- and post-modification but MHS makes no such comment. First, it is not possible to say that MHS did not *notice* such a structural fact subconsciously; indeed there is a sense in which he *must* have done so in order to be able to process the line at all. In any case, this example is one which concerns grammatical structure rather than meaning.

The list below thus restricts itself to statements about meaning or interpretation which show some disagreement between the readers in their understanding of words, lines, etc., and where only one reader notes a particular aspect of meaning. We have tried, however, bearing the above criteria in mind, to be as *inclusive* as possible. This means that, if anything, any bias in the evidence should favour disagreement rather than agreement. We have not included in this list examples where the two readers agree on meaning but make their statements at different points in their protocols (for example, WVP notes the fast-flowing quality of the river in his comments on line [1]; MHS does this in his line [2] comments).

General

It should be noted that WVP makes comments on the rhythm of the poem throughout, whereas MHS does not. This may be due to differences in their backgrounds or different perceptions of the task they set themselves. The initial impetus for the production of the protocols was an investigation into *interpretation*. It could be that one of the respondents sees metrical structure as important in the interpretative process and the other does not.

Lines [1] and [6]
WVP sees a heroic quality in the stream in line [1], which he refers to again in line [6]. MHS makes no such mention.

Line [2]
WVP notes possible highwayman associations for *highroad*, given the mention of a horse as well. This notion is not referred to again in his protocol, however.

Lines [2], [8] and [12]
MHS notes the possibility of anthropomorphic references or interpretations (although in his comments on line [8] he states that these and the various possible animal references do not appear to be patterned in a way which allows them to be interpreted in a systematic fashion). WVP often notes possible animal references (as does MHS; see agreements), but he does not pick out possible anthropomorphic meanings.

Line [4]

WVP notices possible connotations of peace and rest for the word *home*. MHS does not. As these connotations seem more inherent to the meaning of the word than the highwayman associations for *highroad* (see line [3]) it is difficult to tell whether MHS also noticed these connotations and failed to mention them, or whether he did not notice them at all. Another difficulty here is that MHS does mention a possible 'anthropomorphic' meaning for *home*, and it *may* be that he is referring to qualities similar to those which WVP notices.

Lines [7] and [8]

WVP concentrates on the notion of *death* with respect to these two lines. MHS, on the other hand, talks of *despair*. It is difficult to assess how much of a difference this is as the two notions are often linked in English in any case, and the two readers say things which at least presuppose their awareness of the concept that the other concentrates on.

Line [9]

The two readers differ somewhat on the meaning they assign to the word *degged*. MHS treats it as a neologism and infers its meaning *via* his knowledge of the phonetic patterns and meanings of English words. WVP resorts to the dictionary and finds an archaic entry for the word. They thus arrive at different meanings; 'encrusted' and 'sprinkled'. Even so, the meanings they assign are not far apart.

Line [14]

MHS sees the command as possibly being God's. There is obviously some attempt in his mind to give the poem a religious interpretation because of his general knowledge about Hopkins. In line [2] he also wondered whether *His* might refer to God. However, he rejects this possible interpretation in his comments on line [3] on syntactic grounds, noting that the capital letter can be seen as a necessary consequence of the word's initial position in line [2]. His attempt at a possible religious interpretation for line [14] may be influenced by his earlier attempt. It is interesting, however, that he makes no further reference to this notion, and therefore presumably discards it. WVP makes no such reference.

Lines [15] and [16]

WVP sees the poem as ending with a moral, although he does not say what that moral is. MHS makes no such comment (though see his comments on line [14] for a possible parallel). Both readers make evaluative comments suggesting that they do not think very much of the poem, but the *grounds* for saying so appear to differ somewhat.

3.5.3 Comments on the similarities and disagreements between the protocols

It is difficult to make a straight numerical comparison between the similarities and disagreements for the following reasons:

(i) Some instances are more important to overall textual understanding than others, and because it is not really possible to rank the comments on a scale of importance, a merely numerical account cannot be taken at face value.

(ii) The list of similarities includes remarks about structure (e.g. the internal deviation in line [13], the occurrence of the delayed verb in line [4]) as well as meaning. There are no disagreements of a structural kind, however, and it seems intuitively unlikely that there would be many. It is thus difficult to know whether to include them in comparative figures or not.

(iii) One or two items, particularly the comments on *degged* appear to have a right to representation in both lists.

(iv) In any case, as the reader will discover if he attempts the task, it is not that easy to supply an adequate count. Should MHS's anthropomorphic attempt at interpretation (lines [2], [8] and [12]) be counted as one or three instances, for example? Should the fact that MHS and WVP note the change in *topic* in line [13] be included as an agreement over meaning or not? And so on.

Given these difficulties, there is still some point in attempting a numerical comparison, however, as it is otherwise difficult to assess at all whether the set of agreements is larger than the set of disagreements or *vice versa*. In any case, if the two sets of figures are widely dissimilar, they should be significant even given the difficulties over computation. This is indeed the case. The list of disagreements number ten or under. The list of agreements, when only aspects of *meaning* are taken into account are over twenty, and if the more 'structural' agreements are included the figure is in excess of thirty (the figures are approximate precisely because of the difficulties mentioned above; however, they do represent an attempt to be fair to the data).

Given a null hypothesis predicting that two different readers should show very little agreement and a lot of disagreement because of their different backgrounds, these, albeit crude, figures suggest a non-random degree of agreement both on what to comment on and what interpretation to give to those items.

To the ordinary working stylistician this may all seem so unremarkable as to appear trivial. But it is worth remembering that many literary critics, psychologists and deconstructionists working in the theory of reading tend to argue that individual, non-agreeable interpretations are much more widespread than stylisticians would believe (cf. Kintgen 1977: 7; Crane 1970: 6; Harri-Augstein and Thomas 1984; Johnson 1981: 241–2; De Man 1979: 69). Two other possible objections might be made to the above numerical comparison:

(a) The two readers are both stylisticians and know one another. So they are likely to come up with similar accounts. To some extent this may be true. For example, it may explain their mention of the internal deviation in line [13]. Their familiarity with stylistic theory may well predispose them both to notice such things. But it is not at all obvious that any two stylisticians would automatically agree, and in any case there are substantial differences between the two readers to set against their similarities. One is a native speaker and the other is a non-native speaker. They also grew up in different countries (England and Belgium) and therefore experienced different educational systems. All this suggests that *prima facie* they ought to be fairly unlikely to agree (and indeed they do employ somewhat different reading strategies (see section 3.6).

(b)   The poem is an easy one and therefore is unlikely to provoke disagreements. In a sense this matter was out of the readers' hands as a third party chose the text, except for the fact that a short poem was asked for, which probably (although not necessarily) implies lack of overall structural complexity. But even so, the poem abounds with the neologisms, difficult and archaic words, metaphors and truncated syntax associated with Hopkins. So, although it is only a descriptive poem, it is quite complex linguistically, making the extent of the agreements more striking.

The kinds of agreements which the readers display are interesting:

(i)   reference of words;
(ii)   reference of pronouns;
(iii) the meaning of neologisms and unusual or difficult words;
(iv)   the meaning of metaphors;
(v)   the 'meaning' of structures, e.g. enumeration, topic change;
(vi)   the associations for words;
(vii) commenting on the incompleteness of structures at line ends.

Numbers (iii)–(vi) in the above list are of particular significance because they represent aspects of *meaning* which ought to be among the most difficult for readers to agree upon. Given the different backgrounds of the two readers, it seems reasonable to conclude that the agreements are a result of the interaction between textual clues of various kinds and shared assumptions concerning linguistic structure and the procedures governing interpretation.

The disagreements between readers are over:

(i)   associations and connotations of words;
(ii)   emphasis;
(iii) meaning supplied *via* the application of background knowledge;
(iv)   more 'general' aspects of meaning e.g. the 'heroic' quality of the stream as observed by WVP;
(v)   the grounds for evaluation.

It is likely that (iii) influences the other categories. There is, of course, no inconsistency in the fact that particular word associations turn up in both the similarities and the disagreements sections. The informants agreed over the associations for some words but not for others. Agreement is in itself of interest here as associative meaning is the area of language where one might expect least agreement *prima facie*.

The overall impression that the two respondents had when first comparing their understanding of the poem was that their interpretations were very similar. This appears to be borne out by a more careful and systematic analysis of the protocols. We are aware, of course, that it is difficult to make completely objective comparisons on data of this kind and that the investigative technique used might possibly bias the results. However, we have tried to guard against favouring agreement in our analysis of the protocols, and, given the fairly substantial differences between the backgrounds of the two readers, this experiment throws up substantial evidence against the more subjectivist literary theories. It also suggests that linguistically based textual criticism will be among the more fruitful analytical approaches to literary texts, and in section 3.7 we present a stylistic analysis of the poem in order to compare the results it throws up with those from the protocols. Before this, however, we turn our attention to a comparison of the reading strategies employed by both readers.

3.6. A COMPARISON OF READING STRATEGIES

In section 3.5 above we have examined agreements and disagreements in the protocols over meaning and what is commented on; it is also possible to examine the protocols in order to compare the reading strategies of the two informants:

(i) Both readers make predictions about the *syntactic structure* of lines which they have not yet seen, particularly where essential parts of clause structure have not yet appeared (cf. the comments on lines [4] and [5]). They also both comment when the predicted structural item finally occurs.

This is partly a result of the task which has been set (the poem can only be read a line at a time), but although the normal reading process allows the reader the possibility of skipping from line to line in order to make sense of the syntax, the frequent reference to enjambement, end-stopping, etc. in critical debate indicates that the relation between syntax and line-end is a particularly salient one for readers of poetry.

(ii)   Both readers make predictions about *aspects of meaning* to come, e.g. lines [1], [2] and MHS line [9]. This appears to be based sometimes on syntactic knowledge (e.g. the fact that at the end of line [7] the second part of the comparative structure is still to come), and sometimes on expectations about textual/semantic relations. In particular, both readers look for patterns of similarity and contrast between parts of the text.

(iii)   Both suggest *alternative possible meanings or associations* for words, lines and structures, which must then presumably be disambiguated (e.g. lines [3], [8] and WVP lines [1], [2]). They also set up single hypotheses for later confirmation (e.g. MHS line [1]). Sometimes, *but not always*, the readers explicitly state at a later stage that a hypothesis has been confirmed (e.g. WVP line [3]) or that one of the alternative readings is now more certain (e.g. MHS line [3] and WVP lines [2], [3]).

(iv)   They both ask questions about the *references* for words or the meanings of words (e.g. line [0]). Although the questions are answerable at a later stage (e.g. by line [1], the question about the reference of *Inversnaid* is pretty certain) the readers do not always state explicitly that the problem is 'solved'.

(v)   Both deduce aspects of *the situational context* in which they conceive the discourse of the poem taking place. In particular this involves deductions based upon the meaning of deictic items, e.g. *this*, line [1] and *the*, line [4].

(vi)   Both go through similar interpretative processes in order to understand the *meanings of metaphors* (e.g. *rollrock*, line

[2]) and *neologisms* (e.g. *twindles*, line [6], *beadbonny*, line [12]). In these cases, the process involves separating out the elements of meaning from the word or construction involved and then finding connections between the meaning of the parts in order to arrive at a meaningful whole. This appears to involve not just lexical and syntactic, but also phonetic processing. MHS, moreover, explicitly notes the phonaesthetic quality of the close front vowel in *twindle*, line [6], and WVP is almost certainly reacting to phonetic structure in part when he talks of 'light movement' as part of the meaning of *twindle* (comment on line [6]).

(vii)   Both readers make *recourse to dictionaries* in order to understand difficult words e.g. lines [10], [11]. There is some difference in that MHS, the native speaker, does not look up *degged*, line [9], but treats it as a neologism. WVP does look it up. By using cues from the surrounding linguistic context and from similar associations for this lexical item, as evidenced in the protocols, they arrive at very similar (inferred) meanings.

(viii) Both note aspects of *textual pattern*, particularly the animal references. Once a pattern is observable they both try to fit items into the pattern which in other contexts would be considered to be marginal or not to have the relevant aspect of meaning at all. *Fawn* in line [5] is a good example of this. It is highly unlikely that the adjective in e.g. 'fawn sweater' has any animal associations for native speakers of English, in spite of its derivational history. But in the context of other animal references, both readers consider the possibility of that kind of association in this text (cf. also the stylistic analysis in section 3.7.1). The fact that a pattern occurs also prompts both readers to look for a *reason* for it. Their failure to find one which satisfies them helps to prompt their negative evaluative comments on the poem (see section 3.9).

(ix)   Both note the occurrence of *stylistic notions* like parallelism and deviation, as well as linguistic structure, presumably as a result of their academic training.

(x)   Both remark on the *rhymes* in the poem, although not consistently, (e.g. MHS line [11], WVP lines [3] and [4]). Both readers appear to want to use the rhyme as a form of parallelism to help structure the meaning of the poem (although this is difficult to do in this text – see sections 3.7–3.9 *passim*).

(xi) Both make *value judgements*, even though the task they set themselves did not call for them. They also produce them at roughly the same point (cf. the comments on lines [14] and [15]).

(xii) They both set up hypotheses about the *general interpretation* of the poem which later turn out to be unfounded (MHS tries hard to find religious significance in the poem, and WVP wants to assign a heroic quality to the writing. Both of these attempts are based on background knowledge that the two readers have). The text does not *positively* disconfirm either hypothesis. Rather, no positive evidence comes forward to support either view. Here, as with (ii), (iii) and (iv) above, there are two later possibilities: either the reader will forget about the hypothesis or explicitly notice at some later point that the hypothesis is unfounded. WVP does the former and MHS the latter. The possible explanations for this differential behaviour are various. It may be that one reader perceived the point in the text where the hypothesis occurred to him as being more foregrounded than the other reader did, that is, the hypothesis was more *textually salient* for one reader than the other (for a detailed discussion of foregrounding see Van Peer 1986b). Alternatively, it could be the case that religion is more important to MHS than heroic qualities are for WVP (i.e. religion as a theme in the poem is *personally salient* for MHS, but heroic qualities are not for WVP). Another possibility is that the size of the readers' short-term memory varies.

(xiii) WVP makes continual remarks on the *rhythm* of the poem, but MHS does not. Instead, he appears to search for *sound-symbolic* structures. This difference may just be one of personal preference, particularly when one remembers that phonetic structure is the linguistic level which is least directly relatable to interpretation, and therefore probably permits a wider range of individual perceptual preference than other linguistic levels.

(xiv) MHS comments on his *own reading process* (line [7]) and on the task which they as readers have set themselves (line [2]). WVP's comments on line [8], although not so explicit, also indicate an awareness of his reading process.

There are obviously some differences in reading strategy between the two readers, and they do not always exhibit the same strategies at the same point. This demonstrates the well-known fact that readers differ. But the list above contains (as does the list of meaning agreements and the evaluative remarks) a quite considerable number of correspondences both in general reading strategies and the points at which those strategies are applied. In that sense, the results found here and in Alderson and Short (this volume) counteract the emphasis on variability of reading strategies and reading outcomes of Kintgen (1983).

3.7 A STYLISTIC ANALYSIS OF THE POEM

3.7.1 *Semantics*

Each of the four stanzas of this poem is concerned with a different, albeit related, topic: the burn (I), the bonnet of fawn-froth (II), the groins of the braes (III), and the world (IV). The first two stanzas deal with the stream in front of the 'observer' in the poem and the third stanza takes in the surroundings of the stream. The fourth stanza widens the focus much more dramatically and considers the world in general. In the first three stanzas, a more or less neutral observer describes the scenery, while in the final stanza he is heard commenting on the state of affairs of nature and its hypothetical future state.

The poem begins with the demonstrative *This*. Since there is no context from which the reader may deduce the meaning of this pronoun, he has to conjecture that someone (the writer, the addresser, the persona, . . .) is addressing him and pointing to the stream. Hence *This* is to be taken as a deictic, which refers to the presence of the stream in the neighbourhood of the speaker. This aspect of reference is mirrored in the use of the definite article, which is used with exophoric reference throughout the text. Hence *the lake* (line [4]) should be interpreted roughly as 'the lake near to the point on the stream at which the observer is standing'. Again the speaker/addresser is interpreted as 'pointing' to the object in reality. Note that the switch from *description* in the first three stanzas (where the definite article also carries specific meaning) to the generalized *question* in the last stanza is accompanied by a switch to the generic and homophoric use of the article: *the world, the weeds, the wilderness*.

What is predicated of each of the four topics may be summarized roughly as follows:

(a) the burn: *falls* into the lake;
(b) the bonnet of fawn-froth: *dies* in the lake;
(c) the groins of the braes: *are covered with*: dew, heath, fern, rowan-tree;
(d) the world: *is less valuable* without (a), (b) and (c).

The verbs in these predicates also show a decrease in activity, from the very active *roaring* and *falls* via *turns* and *twindles* and *rounds* to the passive *degged* and *dappled*, and finally to the statives *sits, be, be left* and *live*. We have already hinted at the break that may be observed in the poem between stanzas I–III and the final stanza. In what follows we shall demonstrate that this last stanza is set off from the rest of the poem in a number of different ways. This will be illustrated through an analysis of the lexical make-up of the poem, summarized under the following six groups:

(i)   changes in subcategories of the lexis of the poem;
(ii)   Scots words;
(iii) obsolete words;
(iv) neologisms;
(v)   figurative meaning elements;
(vi) contrasting lexical sets.

The most noticeable change in lexical subcategories is provided by the verbs of the poem: a change is effected from intransitive verbs in the first three stanzas to transitive verbs in the final stanza, which have generic noun phrases referring to the nouns of the preceding stanzas as their objects: *them, the world, the weeds,* etc. The fact that there is a sharp increase in the number of verbs in the final stanza (twice as many as in the preceding one, and more than three times as many as in the first two stanzas) also sets off the last stanza from the rest. There is a similar change in the subcategories of nouns, with CONCRETE nouns in the first three stanzas being replaced by GENERIC nouns in the final stanza. Note also *Despair* in line [8] is the only truly ABSTRACT word in the whole poem, and therefore strongly internally deviant. We shall return to this point later. The adjective in the final stanza does not refer to colour, in contrast to those in the preceding stanzas (although *wiry* in line [11] must be discounted from this movement, and *beadbonny* (line [12]) only indirectly reflects colour, by way of its reference to the berries of the rowan-tree). The final stanza also contains the only pronouns in the plural and the only adverb referring to time.

If we now turn to the *Scots words* in the poem we may notice the following lexical items: *burn* (line [1]), *bonnet* (line [5]), *braes* (line [10]), *burn* (line [12]). They heighten the local atmosphere of the Scottish scenery, but note again that such words are completely absent from the final stanza.

Obsolete words are similarly restricted to the three initial stanzas: *darksome* (line [1]), *flutes* (line [4]), *fell* (line [7]), *degged* (line [9]), *flitches* (line [11]). These obscure words may find a vague echo in *bereft* (line [13]) and the syntactic function of *yet* (line [16]) of the final stanza, both of which have vaguely archaic overtones. Some of these obsolete terms, such as *degged* are so archaic that they may well be interpreted as *neologisms* by the reader. This is in fact what can be observed in one of the protocols. All neologisms likewise occur in the first three stanzas: *rollrock* (line [2]), *twindles* (line [6]), *heathpacks* (line [11]), *beadbonny* (line [12]). The compounds *fáwn-fróth* (line [5]) and *féll-frówning* (line [7]) may be considered as mild forms of neologism, interpretable as 'froth with the colour of fawns' and 'frowning inexorably' respectively. Note that the neologisms decrease in boldness as the poem progresses, so that the following relations may be construed as shown in Fig. 3.1.

Clearly *heathpacks* (line [11]) can be interpreted as 'packs of heath' and *beadbonny* (line [12]) as 'beautifully covered with beads'. The latter forces the reader to hypothesize that the tree referred to may be a rowan-tree, because of its brightly coloured fruits, and because of the meaning of mountain ash = rowan. In *twindles* one may find a Carrollian blending of 'twinkle' and

Fig. 3.1

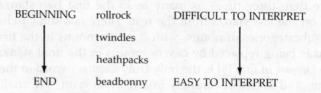

'dwindle'. Both the sense of 'rapid movement' and of 'disappearing' seem to be present in it. The meaning of *rollrock* (line [2]) is much harder to work out, even in the context of the surrounding lines. Gardner (1969) takes it to be of the 'verb-object' form; if this holds then the compound word would refer to something or somebody rolling down rocks. The parsing of the sentence or the breaking up of the compound seems to make little difference, however, as the constituent morphemes present in *rollrock* exert a powerful constraint on its total meaning. Hence the phrase could indicate the movement of rocks, or the movement of the river over the rocks, or that the movement of the stream is of a rolling and rocking kind. The context provides little evidence to resolve these ambiguities.

A number of lexical items clearly have *figurative* meanings: *horseback* (line [1]), *highroad* (line [2]), *fleece of foam* (line [3]), *bonnet* (line [5]), *broth* (line [6]), *frowning* (line [7]), *groins* (line [10]) and *beadbonny* (line [12]). Again no such cases can be found in the final stanza. Of these instances, *highroad* and *beadbonny* are quite mild cases of figurative language. Of the others, *horseback* and *fleece* have strong ANIMAL connotations, while all the others have HUMAN associations. Note, finally, that the overflow of ANIMAL and of HUMAN meaning potential on to the various descriptions of the stream and its surroundings has the effect of personifying the stream. This is also further corroborated by the use of the personal pronoun *his* in lines [2] and [3].

Until now the major finding of the semantic analysis has been that the final stanza is set off quite markedly from the rest of the poem. This is reflected in the generality of its theme, in the distinct subcategories of NOUN, VERB and to a lesser degree of PRONOUN, ADJECTIVE and ADVERB classes, and finally in the absence of any neologisms, obsolete or Scots words, and figurative language use. It will later be shown that a similar break can also be observed on the grammatical level. We now wish to concentrate on a crucial issue in the analysis of the poem's semantic material, i.e. the way in which lexical items may be grouped together as belonging to the same lexical 'set' or 'field'. (The readers' perception of these sets can easily be seen in the protocols.)

We have already alluded to one such lexical field: that of the words carrying figurative meaning, which were shown to possess ANIMATE characteristics, either of ANIMAL or of HUMAN quality. Another such set groups words that refer to dark colours: *darksome* (line [1]), *brown* (line [1]), *fawn* (line [5]), *broth* (line [6]), *pitch-black* (line [7]), *fell* (line [7]), and perhaps also *horseback* (line [1]). This lexical set is to be found in the first two stanzas. Notice, however, how the darkness of the colour becomes thematically linked to the notions of despair and death in line [8]. This link is brought about by the comparative construction 'so . . . that' (in which the relative pronoun has been deleted however: see section 3.7.2), through the grammatical construction, in which *Despair* is the object of the verb *rounds*, through the strong internal deviation created by *Despair* (which has its first letter capitalized and is the first ABSTRACT noun in the poem) and through the grammatical deviation of *Despair*, being the object of a verb demanding a CONCRETE NP as its object. The link with death is brought in by *drowning*, supported by the alliteration of the two words. Hence the darkness encountered in the first stanza takes a new direction in the second stanza, becoming associated with despair and death.

Schematically, one may represent this association as shown in Fig. 3.2: roman numbering refers to stanzas. The third stanza then brings in a new lexical set, consisting of words that can be associated with LIGHT: *dew, degged* and *dappled* in line [9], and *bead* (line [12]) which must refer to the red berries of the rowan tree. As such one may say that line [9] contrasts sharply in its associative potential with line [8]: the latter calls for a dark and death-

Fig. 3.2

I   DARK

II   DESPAIR/DEATH

like atmosphere, the former introduces the notion of light in a verse that also contrasts sharply with the preceding one in its phonological make up (see section 3.7.3). Note also that the lexical set associated with *Despair* should perhaps include morphemes such as *fell* (line [7]), *frown* (line [7]), *fall* (line [4]), *low* (line [4]), and of course *drown* (line [8]).

If one combines these associations with the gradual movement of the focus of the description the reader is witnessing, one may paraphrase the movement as one which sees the death of a (personifed) stream in the lake, after which, by moving still further to the general surroundings of the brook, an image of light is introduced in the third stanza. In the same way that an equivalence relationship was established between DARKNESS and DESPAIR/DEATH, one may now notice a contrast between the DARK-NESS of stanza I and the LIGHT of stanza III. Schematically, this may be represented in Fig. 3.3:

Fig. 3.3

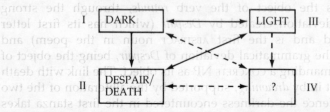

(Note: *single-headed* arrows denote a rough equivalence relation; a *double-headed* arrow denotes a contrast; *dotted* arrows indicate potential contrasts or equivalences to complete the set of relations.)

From this set of relations we suggest that at the end of the third stanza, a reader sensitive to the patterns set up so far would expect the last stanza to establish a topic roughly equivalent to HOPE/LIFE, an opposite to DESPAIR/DEATH, which would be represented symbolically in terms of the LIGHT symbolism intro-duced in stanza III. Close investigation of the poem does reveal a degree of realization of this expectancy. HOPE is expressed, though somewhat indirectly, as a wish for the preservation of nature in the raw, and the idea of LIFE is clearly found in the exclamation of the final line. However, these notions are somewhat indirectly related to the themes of the previous stanzas, and, more important, the pattern of light and dark previously set up is not exploited at all, and so no special symbolism emerges from the explicit statements of the last stanza. Instead, there is merely the expression of a vague hope for the wilds of nature, and the symbolism and patterning set up in the previous stanzas is wasted.

What is of essential interest here is that the evidence of the stylistic analysis so far provides good confirmation of the stated expectancies of the readers when dealing with the last stanza of the poem. The fact that their expectancies were not met also leads them to make negative statements about the worth of the poem. We will return to the subject of evaluation in section 3.9 of this Chapter.

3.7.2 Grammar

Firstly the poem exhibits a number of grammatical parallelisms, which increase as it progresses, with only one case in the first stanza, two in the second, two in the third, and three interconnected instances in the fourth stanza:

> *in coop and in comb* [3];
> *turns and twindles* [6];
> *it rounds and rounds* [8];
> *degged with dew, dappled with dew* [9];
> *wiry heathpacks, flitches of fern* [11]; *the beadbonny ash that sits over the*
> *burn* [12];
> *of wet and of wilderness* [14];
> *wildness and wet* [15];
> *the weeds and the wilderness* [16].

All of these examples of grammatical parallelism contain supplementary phonetic parallelism and are characterized by a pattern of straightforward equivalences rather than contrasts. Moreover, the equivalences become more obvious as the text progresses, so that in the last stanza they are reduced to a series of near-synonyms and repetitions. This is important as it ties up with the semantic observations about the final stanza. Contrary to normal expectations the text reduces in complexity and entropy as it unfolds. This tendency is confirmed by other aspects of the poem's grammar. Thus the final stanza is separated sharply from the others in terms of general grammatical structure. Before turning to these, however, it should be noted that most fore-grounded devices are spread out over the whole of the poem fairly evenly. The only places where some density of grammatical foregrounding may be located are lines [8]–[9], and to a lesser degree, lines [2]–[3]. The major devices employed there (and else-where in the text) are:

(i)   fronting;
(ii) arrest;
(iii) violations of selection restriction rules;
(iv) deletion.

We shall discuss each of these. We will examine the first two locations just pointed out for their extra density in foregrounding devices. Then the remaining cases will be examined.

Fronting of adverbial phrases occurs in line [2] (*His rollrock high-road*), [3] (*in coop and in comb*), and [4] (*low to the lake*), while the whole of line [9] is fronted as well. In each case the fronting has the effect of emphasizing characteristics of the stream, or of its movement or surroundings. Those in lines [3] and [9] are the most striking cases, as they occur in combination with *arrest* (cf. Sinclair 1972) which renders their syntactic status dubious until the following line appears. Further cases of arrest may be found at the end of lines [1], [3], [5], [7], [9] and [13]. *Extension* occurs at the end of line [6]. The effect will be slighter here than with the arrest cases (for the related concepts of *arrest*, *release* and *extension* see Sinclair 1966). In lines [1] and [5] the arrest operates at clause level, while in line [13] it occurs at phrase level. As enjambement effects become more noticeable as one goes down the grammatical hierarchy from sentence to morpheme, the effect of line [13] will be the strongest, especially since in lines [1], [3] and [5] the line-ends coincide with the boundary of the subject of the sentence, and in line [9] with the fronted complement.

The poem contains several cases of *selection restriction violation*. Four obvious examples may be reported:

lines	*His*	*burn*
[2]–[3]:	ANIMATE PRONOUN	INANIMATE REFERENCE

lines [3]–[4]:	*fleece* INANIMATE	*flutes* usually ANIMATE subject
line [8]:	*rounds* usually CONCRETE OBJECT	*Despair* ABSTRACT
line [12]:	*ash* INANIMATE	*sits* usually ANIMATE subject

All of these cases involve a violation of the ANIMATE – INANIMATE opposition; the result is that elements of natural scenery acquire animate associations. Notice how three out of the four cases mentioned occur in the lines singled out for their density of fore-grounding devices, while the one that does not is only a mild case of a selection restriction violation, and one that may perhaps be encountered frequently in everyday language use. The deviation in line [8] is more striking than the others because of the higher feature of meaning that is departed from. (CONCRETE – ABSTRACT features are superordinate in lexical meaning to ANIMATE – INANIMATE contrasts, since the latter can only apply to CONCRETE referents.) Morever, the deviation occurs in a line that seems almost impossible to parse in any elegant and straightforward way.

In our discussion of the poem's semantic organization we pointed out the fact that the final stanza was marked off from the rest. The poem's grammatical structure reinforces this argument. While the first three stanzas are declarative in form, the last stanza opens with a rhetorical question. The mood of the verb also changes here, from indicative to conditional (*would be*, line [13]) and subjunctive (*Long live*, line [16]). Thus the descriptive aspect of the three initial stanzas is mirrored in their syntax, and so is the pleading speech act of the final stanza. Moreover, the latter contains the only imperatives (*let*, lines [14] & [15]) and the only auxiliaries (*would*, line [13], *let*, lines [14] & [15], and *be*, lines [13], [14] & [15]). The fact that there are five such auxiliaries in this stanza, against none in the preceding twelve lines, further supports the contrast. We also encounter the first subordinate clause in this stanza and the only interjection (*O*, line [15]), together with the first arrest at phrase level (lines [13] & [14]). We have already mentioned in the semantic analysis that this stanza contains the only plural pronouns in the poem, and the only adverb that refers to time.

3.7.3 Phonology

Various observations about the phonological make-up of the poem can be made. After Leech (1969) these will be categorized into devices of:

   (i)   syllable structure;
  (ii) rhyme and alliteration;
 (iii) chiming;
 (iv) assonance;
  (v) onomatopoeia;
 (vi) statistical deviations;
(vii) metre and rhythm.

Most syllables in the poem are of the CVC (consonant – vowel – consonant) type. The number of initial consonant clusters (never more than two) gradually increases as the poem progresses (5 in the first stanza, 6 in the second, and 8 in the third) with a culmination point in line [10] where there are 5 syllable-initial clusters of 2 consonants. In the final stanza, however, not a single word-initial consonant cluster appears. A similar tendency may be noted at the ends of syllables: the first two lines of the poem contain no end clusters, lines [3]–[5] contain 6 clusters of 2 consonants, while lines [6]–[9] contain the highest number of 3- and 4-consonant clusters (a 4-consonant cluster in line [6] and two 3-consonant clusters in line [8] with another 3-consonant one in line [9]). This part of the poem was pointed out for its density of grammatical foregrounding devices too, thereby adding support to the present observations. There is also, as with initial clusters, a drop in lines [11]–[12], while the final stanza contains, in contrast to its lack of initial clusters, the highest number of end clusters in the whole poem: 10 clusters of 2 consonants appear in it. Thus we again notice, apart from a density of devices in lines [6]–[9], that the final stanza is separated from the rest of the poem, this time in its syllabic make-up. However, it is difficult to interpret the finding, since the two observations go in opposite directions: initial consonant clusters are totally absent, while final clusters have their highest frequency in the final stanza.

The rhyme scheme of the poem is that of the couplet: AA, BB, CC, etc. This yields the following rhyme pairs in the poem:

(a)	lines [1]/[2]	brown – down
(b)	lines [3]/[4]	foam – home
(c)	lines [5]/[6]	froth – broth
(d)	lines [7]/[8]	frowning – drowning
(e)	lines [9]/[10]	dew – through
(f)	lines [11]/[12]	fern – burn
(g)	lines [13]/[14]	bereft – left
(h)	lines [15]/[16]	wet – yet

Of these, pairs (a), (e) and (h) contain words from different lexical classes, and any semantic relationship between them is difficult to perceive. The rhyme between *fern* and *burn* is highly predictable (cf. MHS's protocol), and therefore will contribute little to the special effects that could be gained by exploitation of rhyme as a poetic device. In rhyme pair (g) the relationship is clearly one of contrast: the world without the elements of wild nature just described contrasts with the addresser's wish to have them preserved. This contrast is perhaps the only one that can be observed between rhyme words in the poem. Rhyme pair (c) clearly constitutes one of equivalence: *froth* and *broth* may be associated with each other. Similarly in (d), *frowning* may be associated with *drowning*, evoking a gloomy note in the poem. Line [3] may present the reader with the strongest rhyme effect because of the extra internal rhyme: *comb – foam – home*. The first pair may be interpreted as coming from similar lexical fields: it is the *comb* that causes the *foam*, or it is the foam's top, etc. while perhaps the second pair (*foam/home*) is the easiest to interpret in terms of contrast: the foam on top of the wave finds its end in the lake. On the whole, then, the rhymes in this poem do not offer the reader much interesting material. We are therefore tempted to interpret them as mainly decorative devices. In any case, their description on the phonological level offers little connection with the other levels of linguistic organization.

Moving on to alliteration, we should first of all point to the impressive number of instances to be observed in the text: forty-five words (approximately 38 per cent) are in clear alliterative pairs:

(i)	*b*urn	*b*rown		
(ii)	*r*ollrock	*r*oaring		
(iii)	*d*arksome	*d*own		
(iv)	*c*oop	*c*omb		
(v)	*f*leece	*f*oam	*f*lutes	*f*alls
(vi)	*l*ow	*l*ake		
(vii)	*f*awn	*f*roth		
(viii)	*t*urns	*t*windles		
(ix)	*p*ool	*p*itchblack		
(x)	*f*ell	*f*rowning		
(xi)	*D*espair	*d*rowning		
(xii)	*d*egged	*d*ew	*d*appled	
(xiii)	*b*raes	*b*rook	(*g*roins	*t*reads *t*hrough)
(xiv)	*f*litches	*f*ern		
(xv)	*b*eadbonny	*b*urn		
(xvi)	*w*hat	*w*ould	*w*orld	once
(xvii)	*w*et	*w*ilderness	*w*eeds	*w*ildness
(xviii)	*l*ong	*l*ive		
(xix)	*l*et	*l*eft		

All of these connections *via* alliteration are interpretable in terms of an equivalence relationship, so that in the first pair, for instance, the burn is interpreted as having a brown colour, the pool is pitchblack, etc. No instances of clear contrast between alliterative words can be pointed to. This strengthens our earlier observations on the associations between lexical items. Thus by virtue of appearing among a long list of equivalence-evoking alliterations, the reader feels prompted to interpret *Despair* as being linked to *drowning*.

Out of the list of alliterations, some may be isolated for their high frequencies such as (v), with four words alliterating on the /f/ sound, (xi–xii) for the five words alliterating on /d/, and (xvi–xix), where eight words alliterate on /w/ and four on /l/. Notice that those in (v) and (xi–xii) coincide with locations pointed out for density of grammatical foregrounding devices.

Out of the above list, the only cases which can be considered as candidates for the device of chiming are those in (v), (vii), (x), and (xi). *Fleece* and *foam* may now be interpreted as equivalent, while *flutes* and *falls* form some kind of contrast. Therefore, this case may be the most striking amongst the chiming effects, since it is the only one 'between words which are grammatically paired but which contrast in reference and associations' (Leech 1969: 96). The other chiming cases clearly evoke relations of equivalence, and the associations between the two terms are so obvious that they carry little aesthetic reward.

Four cases of assonance may be easily perceived by the reader because they are tied to (or lead up to) rhymes;

lines[2]–[4]:	/əʊ/:	rollrock	highroad low
line [5]:	/ɒ/:	bonnet	froth
lines [13]–[16]:	/e/:	wet	let

Other cases of assonance may be observed in:

lines[9], [11], [12]:	/æ/:	dappled	heathpacks	ash
lines[11]–[12]:	/i:/:	heathpacks	beadbonny	
lines[13]–[16]:	/ɪ/:	bereft	wilderness (x2) be (x2)	
		wildness	live	

Onomatopoeic devices may be found in lines [2]–[3], where the /r/-sound and the high-low vowel alternation may be interpreted as symbolizing the noise of the stream thundering down, in lines [5] and [7] (where the /f/s can be seen as representing the sound of the current against the stones in the stream), while the /d/ and /b/ phonemes in line [12] onwards are a strong contrast to the many fricatives in the preceding lines. In the final stanza, the /w/ and /l/ phonemes are extremely frequent, and this is in contrast to the rest of the poem. Both belong to the softest group of consonants in English, and may therefore be mimetic for the addresser's feelings of warmth and respect for the wildness of nature and its beauty.

Apart from the observations made in the previous paragraphs, a study of the sound inventory of the poem shows several cases of statistical deviations in the text. The /əʊ/ and /aʊ/ sounds are statistically deviant in stanzas I and II respectively. The first stanza contains four times as many /əʊ/ sounds as could be expected on the basis of Fry's tables of average frequency (see Gimson 1970: 148), while /aʊ/ in stanza II is present six times more than could be expected on the basis of chance. Two more factors contribute to the fact that these instances of statistical deviation must be prominent in the perception of the text. The first is the length of the sounds: they are amongst the longest diphthongs in the English sound system; secondly these sounds are not very frequent by themselves, according to Fry's tables. Hence the fact that they appear much more frequently in the text must be all the more striking.

Stanza III shows a mild statistical deviation of /æ/ and /u:/, the latter due to the exact repetition of *dew*. The final stanza shows higher frequencies than average for /ə/ and /e/ sounds. But these are probably not very prominent perceptually. /ə/ only occurs in unstressed positions, and the density of /e/ is partly a consequence of straight lexical repetition in lines [14]–[15] (*let, left, wet*).

If we look at classes of vowels, we can note that as the text unfolds:

(a)   there is a gradual increase in closed vowels and a corresponding decrease in the openness of vowels as the text unfolds;

(b)   there is a gradual increase in front vowels and a corresponding gradual decrease in back vowels as the poem progresses.

When we compare this tendency with the distribution of subclasses of consonants, we observe a similar trend:

(c)   soft consonants increase, while hard consonants decrease;

(d)   front consonants gradually increase, while back consonants decrease.

Thus the final stanza contains most of the front consonants (labials) and least (none, in fact) of the back consonants, while the reverse picture emerges from the first stanza, containing the highest number of glottals and velars, and the lowest number of front consonants (labials, dentals and alveolars).

Concerning the metre of the poem, it should be observed that its base form is iambic tetrameter. There are two general variations to this norm. One is the reversed foot, e.g. *horseback* (line [1]), *flutes* (line [4]), *what* (line [13]) and *wildness* (line [15]). Sometimes whole lines are reversed and become trochaic. This is the case for lines [6], [11] and [13]. A second variation on the metrical base consists in a change to a ternary metre. This is quite obvious in line [3] in cases such as *and in comb* (x x /) and *of his foam* (also x x /). See also lines [10], [12], [14], and [16]. Tension between metre and rhythm occurs for the major verbs in the poem: *falls* (line [4]), *treads*, (line [10]) and *sits* (line [12]). In each of these cases the metrical system would withold primary stress from these full verbs, while ordinary speech rhythm would demand primary stress for them. Similarly the second syllable of *pitchblack* (line [7]) should, according to the metrics, be perceived as unstressed, while ordinary speech would have a high degree of stress on the second syllable too. A double stress may be observed in: *dew, dappled* in line [9] and in *long live* of line [16]. Notice that Hopkins' diacritic marks on *féll-frówning* (line [7]), and on *fáwn-fróth* (line [5]), indicate level stress on both words where this cannot normally be the case in everyday speech. In general it would appear that the metrical structure has enough variation to give it some intrinsic interest. It does not, however, appear to augment the patterns seen in the lexis, grammar and partly in the segmental phonetic structure, which mark off the final stanza from the rest of the poem.

3.8 COMPARISON OF THE STYLISTIC ANALYSIS AND THE PROTOCOLS

First of all, two general remarks are in order:

(i) it should be pointed out that the stylistic analysis was completed *after* the protocols were written (otherwise the protocols would not have contained the informants' first reactions);

(ii) the stylistic analysis was performed by the two authors/informants. In a sense this makes the whole exercise less objective than it might otherwise have been as the interpretative part of the stylistic analysis is bound to have been coloured by the first reaction to the poems as contained in the protocols. However, we have striven to make the analysis as objective and observable as possible. The reader may like to make a note of his own intuitions so far and compare them with the protocols and stylistic analysis we have produced.

In one obvious sense one of the purposes of the original experiment can be seen not to have been fulfilled. There are no major interpretative aspects contained in the protocols which stylistic analysis cannot explain reasonably well. This does not, of course, mean that the bounds of stylistic description are now clearly defined. It may well be that examination of reactions to a different text would have thrown up things for consideration which stylistic analysis cannot at present deal with. It could be argued from the evidence of the protocols, however, that stylistic analysis as at present practised does not give quite enough weight to the reading *process* and the ways in which readers deduce or infer meaning by correlating evidence from linguistic structure with world knowledge and contextual information of various kinds. The most clear-out feature which emerges from the stylistic analysis of the poem was to do with the relationship between the four stanzas. Firstly, it has been argued that the semantic structure of stanzas I–III led to the expectation of a fourth stanza in which HOPE and LIFE are expressed in conjunction. This 'prediction' is only met in the most general terms and correlates with the evaluative remarks which the informants indulge in when they read the last stanza. It is also the case that the informants appear throughout their protocols to be attempting to compare and contrast the stanzas with one another (see, for example, their comments on [8]; MHS [9], [12]; WVP [10]). Secondly, the stylistic analysis demonstrates very clearly that the last stanza is set off from the rest of the poem in semantic, syntactic and partly in phonetic terms. The two informants can clearly be seen to be reacting to this structural demarcation in their remarks on lines [13] and [16] especially.

The stylistic analysis notes heavy foregrounding in lines [8]–[9], and also in lines [2]–[3] to a lesser degree. There are certainly sections of the poem to which both readers give considerable attention. Lines [2]–[3] in particular get extensive comment. This is probably because in addition to being foregrounded they come at the beginning of the poem. Presumably the readers' interpretative schemas will not have settled down very much at this point in their reading processes.

The semantic analysis of the poem points out groupings of lexical items. The two informants also attempt to group items together as part of their interpretative strategies (see, for example, comments on lines [3], [7] & [8]). This grouping tendency appears to be part of a general wish on the part of readers, critics and stylisticians to find patterns in the text on the basis of linguistic evidence and then to use the semantic relations found as a result of the patterning to build up interpretations.

The two informants spend a considerable time puzzling out non-literal meanings of deviant expressions (e.g. comments on lines [2], [3], & [4]) and in general concentrate on *semantic* matters. They do also comment on syntax and phonetics (e.g. lines [4] & [5]), though to a lesser degree. Given their academic training as stylisticians it may be that they notice structural, as opposed to meaning, features more than other sensitive readers. It may well be, then, that stylistic analysis should weight evidence from different levels of structure in order to represent adequately the weighting that readers give to those levels. At present relatively little attempt is made to do this. The issue of how well stylistic analysis accounts for such psychological phenomena appears to be a fruitful area for future research.

3.9 EVALUATIVE STRATEGIES

One of the major difficulties with work on literary evaluation is that the concept of evaluation itself has a long and discouraging history, in which it has proved notoriously difficult to pin the notion down. A further problem lies in the fact that it appears extremely difficult to relate evaluation to descriptive statements about a work of art, in this case a poem. A third factor which complicates the issue is that until now hardly any insight has been gained into the relative importance of various factors influencing evaluations. As a result, little is known about what is most or least important in judging a literary work. We do not even have a crude taxonomy of evaluative factors. Hence the brief remarks below are in no sense an attempt to solve all the intricate problems involved in this area. Rather, they are preliminary remarks which are an attempt to account for the fact that the respondents made the evaluative remarks that they did, even though the original experimental design did not call for them to do so. They are made in the expectation that others, in reacting to what we say, may be able to improve upon our somewhat crude and tentative suggestions.

What this enquiry hopes to do, is to provide some insights into each of the three problem areas outlined here. First, we hope to show that evaluation is not a monolithic concept, and that several ways of evaluating exist. In this respect we prefer the term *evaluative stategies*, indicating that readers have a choice between various ways of evaluating a text. The choice that is made may be a function of personality, of mood, of the text-type, the task demands, etc. (At this stage it is not really possible to determine what the motivating factors are, but the point is that different strategies are available to readers, and that they do have recourse to them.) The fact that readers use different evaluative strategies does not necessarily imply that they arrive at different overall evaluations. The situation may be analogous to driving to the same town by partially different routes. Indeed, this appears to be what happens to some extent in the protocols in both evaluative and interpretative terms.

In the second place we hope to show that readers do base their evaluative strategies on the content and the structure of the text itself, and that therefore the *relation between evaluation and description* of the text may perhaps be less problematical than has often been assumed in literary studies. Thirdly, the link between such descriptive and evaluative statements may be clarified through the proposal of a *primitive taxonomy*, in which the psychological concept of *expectancy* plays a crucial role. This notion of expectancy may be understood as a principle unifying the various evaluative strategies open to a reader.

First of all, then, different strategies for evaulation are available to the reader when dealing with texts. In our experiment, this may be clearly seen in the protocols. So, for instance, MHS sometimes uses the notion of predictability in order to evaluate particular parts of the text (lines [11], [12], [15] & [16]): in these lines one finds instances of negative evaluations ascribed by MHS to too high a degree of predictability, caused by exact or too much repetition. At other times (e.g. lines [15] & [16]) MHS uses a strategy of basing evaluative statements on the success (or failure) to integrate particular text-parts into a general framework. WVP on the other hand uses a strategy of referring to discrepancy (or good fit) between different text-parts (e.g. lines [15] & [16]). At other times he seems to prefer a strategy that consists of matching the structure of the text and the purpose it supposedly serves (e.g. lines [12] & [16]). In general then, we find in the protocols a clear warrant for the notion of evaluative *strategy*: both readers use different ways to arrive at their evaluations. This is not to say that we can only detect differences in these strategies. Clearly there are also constants, as we shall try to demonstrate below. What we do want to propose is that, in the same way as readers may use different interpretative strategies in reading, they also have *potential recourse* to different strategies for evaluating a text. The precise nature of these strategies, the particular factors that trigger specific strategies to become operational and the connections between interpretative and evaluative strategies will only become clear when more investigation has been carried out in this area.

A second point concerning evaluation that emerges from the protocols is that in several instances they show a clear link between evaluative statements on the one hand and descriptive statements and the ongoing interpretation of the text on the other. (This may be clearly seen in lines [12], [13], [14], [15] & [16] for wvp and in lines [6], [10], [11], [12], [15] & [16] for mhs.) What we can notice about the occurrence of these evaluative statements is first that their number is about equal (i.e. five *vs* six) and that moreover they frequently occur in the protocols at almost identical text-locations. Clear examples are lines [12], [15] and [16]. What is most obvious in these cases is that the evaluative comments of both readers coincide with (and at particular points explicitly refer to) the shift in topic that occurs in stanza iv, a shift that was also picked out by the stylistic description (see section 3.7 above). We conjecture that this is due to the final stanza lacking any strong links with the patterning set up in previous stanzas. Hence the elements of this stanza cannot be systematically related to (or contrasted with) the elements of the other stanzas, and this causes 'Inversnaid' to be less successful than most of Hopkins' other poems. In terms of the descriptive categories employed by stylisticians this may be explained as a breach of the principle known as the 'cohesion of foregrounding' (see Leech 1965, 1970: 123). By this is meant the way in which separate instances of foregrounding are related to each other or to the text in its entirety. We suggest that the final stanza of 'Inversnaid' shows a marked drop in this respect: while the three initial stanzas form an extremely tight pattern of strong foregrounded features on all linguistic levels, the final stanza shows little cohesion with these patterns.

Such a conclusion, based on observations from both the stylistic analysis and the protocols, shows that readers do employ descriptive categories in their evaluative statements. The question then is, of course, in what precise way these descriptive and evaluative aspects are connected. (For an interesting philosophical discussion of this matter, see Sibley 1965.) That brings us to our third point, i.e. the relative importance of the various factors that are at work in evaluation. In this respect we propose that the protocols suggest a kind of *primitive taxonomy* of evaluative factors. Central (or topmost) in this hierarchical taxonomy stands the notion of *expectancy*. As the text unfolds, a number of expectancies are aroused, and readers respond to these. That this is so, can be clearly seen in quite a simple example. Suppose a story begins with the following sentence:

It is now 5.00 p.m. and Bill is *not yet* home.

This sentence generates a strong expectancy in the reader's mind. The phrase *not yet* leads to the assumption that Bill normally comes homes *at 5 o'clock or earlier*. But it also makes clear that something must have prevented him from being home by that time. It follows from this that the reader's attention in the unfolding story will be drawn, not so much to future, but on the contrary, to *past* events, i.e. what happened to prevent him. From there on the story may proceed in basically two different ways. Either some other character goes out to look for Bill, or the events preventing him from being on time are narrated. In both cases we expect a point in the story at which the previous events are provided as an explanation for the unexpected state of affairs. Hence the sentence calls for at least *some* a-chronological narration. Some kind of flashback will be expected, providing the desired explanation. This constitutes a clear example of how the concept of expectancy plays a crucial role in the evaluative process: the fulfilment of the expectancy in the following part of the story will make favourable evaluations more probable, whilst any failure to fulfil the expectancy may easily lead to unfavourable evaluations.

Of course one has to allow for the possibility that the latter may not be the case in certain instances (for example, some modern stories and plays have no real ending). It follows from this that the 'narrative law' involved is not an absolute one but a tendency. But even in such apparent counter-examples, there must be a pay-off of some kind for the reader. Note how in this case the expectancy was created through *linguistic* and *cognitive* (not personal and associative) means. It is here that evaluation and description may meet: concrete linguistic expressions create specific expectations in the mind of the reader, the fulfilment of which (or its artful frustration) plays a central role in the evaluative process.

Obviously many other kinds of expression are capable of creating such expectancies. One may think of such things as the use of deixis and anaphora, adverbs expressing spatial relationships, the choice of definite or indefinite articles, the use of proper names, etc. If one looks at the protocols from this perspective, one notices various references to such expectancies, especially in the comments on lines [9], [11], [12] & [16] for MHS, and in lines [12], [15] & [16] for WVP. These instances also reveal that expectancies may be created through other than purely linguistic means, for instance literary conventions, such as rhyme, rhythm, etc.

To summarize, then, evaluation crucially hinges on expectancies created by linguistic and other means in the text. Two aspects, subordinate to expectancy, may further be distinguished, i.e. *relevance* and *cohesion*, each contributing to the general expectancy in its own way. To take the latter first, *cohesion* consists of forward and backward pointing among linguistic elements occurring in the text. This may be brought about by a wide variety of means: e.g. verb tense, phoric expressions, repetition, syntactic parallelism, metre, rhyme, associations between lexical fields of meaning, etc. Because cohesion is a constitutive aspect of text-structure, it is projected into the reader's mind, thereby creating an expectation. The example given above, where *not yet* constrained the number and kind of potential cohesive ties, was such a case. The concept of cohesion is subordinate to that of expectancy, because it plays a subordinate role in the evaluative act, i.e. it only realizes its evaluative potency through and *via* the psychological mechanism of expectancy.

Cohesion is not the only device constributing to expectancy. There is at least one other such device, that of *relevance*. While cohesion is a *structural* notion, referring to the actual text-struc-

structure, relevance is a parallel *functional* notion, referring to the (reconstruction of) communicative meaning. We use the term *relevance* with reference to the conditions necessary for the global interpretation of different linguistic elements. For instance, if a speaker (S) addresses the utterance 'There's the dog' to a hearer (H), there are conditions operating in order that S may successfully (from a communicative point of view) use definite reference in speaking about the dog. If in a particular circumstance such conditions are not met, the result will be puzzlement and questioning on the part of H. The fact that the conditions involved are not explicitly supplied does not necessarily lead to a negative evaluation, because it is often possible for the reader to *infer* appropriate conditions. (This is often the case when stories start *in medias res*.) But if such inferences are difficult to make, or if too many possibilities can be inferred this is likely to lead to a negative evaluation, unless it is possible (perhaps later in the reading process) to relate this local processing difficulty to some higher-level strategic purpose on the part of the author (he may, for example, want to create confusion in the reader's mind at a particular point in order to enable some later effect dependent on that confusion). The notion of *relevance* refers to the existence of these conditions within the communicative situation and to the fact that language users generally try to meet these conditions. A writer is in a similar position to S, in that he addresses (a group of) readers.

In general, a writer may want to include in his text certain actions, events, descriptions, arguments, etc. – and he may want *not* to include others. In doing so, he will have to make such selections as relevant as possible, i.e. he will have to consider the conditions under which the selected items may be interpreted meaningfully together. Unmotivated violation of this principle of relevance may lead to negative evaluation on the part of the reader. Thus the second subordinating principle by which expectancy is constituted is that of *relevance*: the reader constantly interprets elements in the text and on the basis of this interpretation forms an *expectation* with respect to any newly read element. Incoming information is matched against previously formed expectations; any difficulty in integrating such incoming information into the expectation will make negative evaluation probable.

Fig. 3.4

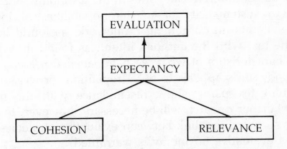

To summarize, then, our primitive taxonomy operating on evaluative acts hinges on the notion of expectancy, which itself consists of at least two subordinate concepts, i.e. relevance and cohesion. The taxonomy may be rendered schematically as in Fig. 3.4. We have indicated how each of the subordinate notions of cohesion and relevance may be described and analysed, i.e. by means of a structural description (in the case of cohesion) and of a pragmatic analysis (in the case of relevance). On the basis of such description one may deduce which cognitive and affective elements are activated in the reader's mind, thus forming the basis of his expectation. In its turn this expectation is linked to the evaluation activities in which the reader becomes involved.

If we now turn to the protocols again, we notice that the evaluative comments found there all hinge on the notion of expectancy, and that furthermore the subordinate concepts of cohesion and relevance are clearly at work. Hence MHS's evaluative comments on lines [11] & [12] and the references to exact repetition in lines [15] & [16] witness the cohesive warranty of the evaluation. The reference to the inappropriate associations of *tread* in line [10], and the questioning of systematicity in lines [15] & [16] are witness to the notion of relevance. In WVP's comments one notices the expectancy being stated in terms of cohesive devices in lines [15] & [16] and in terms of relevance in line [12]. As such the different evaluative strategies referred to before turn out to be really two sides of the same coin.

As a final note we may refer back to the evaluative *strategies* mentioned above; it now emerges that they display quite obvious similarities to the notions of cohesion and relevance, appealed to in previous paragraphs. We conjecture that the different evaluative strategies evolving from an analysis of the protocols result from the use of different categories in the taxonomy. For instance, appeals to systematicity or to the possibilities of integrating textual elements into a general framework, as found in MHS, or fitting the text with the author's intent, as found in WVP, clearly exhibit characteristics of what we have labelled *relevance*. On the other hand, MHS's appeals to exact repetition, or WVP's matching of different text-parts, show resemblance with the notion of *cohesion*. Further research will be necessary, however, to establish whether such a direct link between evaluative strategies and the proposed evaluative taxonomy is warranted.

3.10 CONCLUDING REMARKS

The main findings that emerged from the present study are:

(i) the high amount of inter-reader agreement and a comparatively low amount of disagreement between readers over matters of interpretation;

(ii) the strong permeation of interpretative and evaluative kinds of comments, in spite of the absence of any reference to the latter in the task demand;

(iii) the near-absence of idiosyncracies and the high correlation in responses (even in associations) to textual elements and structures;

(iv) the high degree of similarity in general reading strategies employed by the readers;

(v) the high agreement over text-locations to provide evaluative comments on;

(vi) a high correlation between a stylistic analysis of the text and reader responses;

(vii) the conjecture of a primitive taxonomy of evaluation, in which the psychological concept of *expectancy* may be realized by the structural properties of *cohesion* and by the functional aspects of *relevance*, or by a combination of these;

(viii) the manifestation of different evaluative strategies in the protocols, and their possible relationship to different concepts of the evaluative taxonomy.

In general the experiment and its results warrant the conclusion that more attention should be devoted to generalities and commonalities in the reading act than has often been professed in literary criticism and related areas of study. Further research in this direction may be profitable both to our insight into the act of reading in general, and to our understanding of the way particular authors, genres etc. may be studied.

The design of the experiment displays encouraging features. It throws up a lot of data, and is easy enough to administer. Its setting is also rather naturalistic and holistic, bearing a reasonably close correspondence to the reading process as it normally occurs. Its limits are set by the difficulty in quantifying the data, and in the decisions to be made over the relevance of particular comments in the protocols. The method also seems less suited to longer texts, and faces problems of what to treat as a unit (corresponding to the verse-line) in other genres than poetry. In any case, more reactions of different readers to the same and to different (kinds of) texts will be needed in the future in order to make the present findings more generalizable.

Concerning the general methodology adopted, it should be pointed out that one of its most interesting aspects is that it helps to guard against the experimenters' own biases, especially if work is carried out with subjects not trained within the field of literary studies. What will be needed, however, are thorough comparisons of written and spoken introspections, both for the same and different texts, preferably with trained introspectors, or at least with the help of introspectors whose cognitive styles are known. Concerning the editing of protocols a system of transcription is needed that allows for relatively easy reading while at the same time doing justice to the raw data.

Finally, in order to allow comparison between protocols obtained by different experimenters, some kind of uniformity in these transcriptions will be highly welcome. We are aware that the development of these areas of future research may only come about through close cooperation of researchers in different fields, such as stylistics, literary theory, aesthetics and psychology. This is no doubt a long and winding path, but perhaps one of the shortest ones that is at present left open to us.

FOUR

Reading literature
J. Charles Alderson and Mick Short

4.1 INTRODUCTION

It is frequently claimed (see, for example, Widdowson 1979b) that texts do not have one meaning, waiting to be extracted by the reader, but rather that they have meaning potential, which is only realized in the interaction between reader and writer. It is known that the reader's understanding of a text will be conditioned by what he already knows, and by the availability of that knowledge during the reading process (see Bransford *et al*. 1984). Given also that different purposes and motivations for reading result in different levels of processing and outcome (Fransson 1984), it is likely that different readers will to some extent interpret texts in varied ways. This, indeed, is notoriously the case for literary texts, where it is often said that there are as many interpretations as there are readers to interpret. Yet it is intuitively unsatisfying to claim that a text can mean anything to any reader. The text itself must to some extent condition the nature of the under-standing that a reader constructs. In an account of interpretation, there must be a place for discussion of the amount of agreement between readers, and between a particular reading and 'what the text says'. This would then lead to the notion of some interpret-ations being more correct than others, in the sense of 'more faithful to the text'.

Stylistic analysis is intended to help determine interpretation through the examination of what a text contains, by describing the linguistic devices an author has used, and the effects produced by such devices. Such analysis is predominantly text-based, and has tended to see texts as containing meanings, which a reader has to unearth. Psycholinguistic approaches to reading, on the other hand, tend to focus on the reader and the way in which individuals process language, in an attempt to describe the ways in which different reading outcomes are produced. Such an approach is more likely to see meaning as variable.

One of the aims of the study to be presented in this Chapter was to examine two approaches to reading to see the nature of agreements and disagreements about text meaning. Furthermore, it was hoped to discover not only what meanings were assigned to texts, but *how* those meanings were assigned: what sorts of strategies do readers use when reading literary texts?

Given the enormous amount of literature which is read, any theory of reading will have to take it into account. If interpretations of literary texts are notoriously individual, then the examination of such texts will test to the limit the claim that even though readers are bound to some extent to react differently there is still an element of control which the text exerts over the reader. It is often assumed by teachers and literary critics that literature is read in a different way from non-literary writing. However, evidence suggests that a *linguistic* distinction between literary and other kinds of text is difficult to sustain (Pratt 1977; Werth 1976). The last aim of this study was thus to discover whether the processing of literary texts was different from what is known to happen when people read non-literary texts.

After a brief discussion of the methodology of the study, this paper takes the following form:

  (i)   the reader is presented with the text which was the object of study and is requested to read it and introspect on that reading before proceeding;
 (ii)   a transcript of the protocols, the two introspections produced by the authors;
(iii)   a comparison and analysis of the two protocols (for ease of reading, more detailed comparative material is presented in appendices 1–3);
 (iv)   concluding remarks.

It should be noted that this study focuses upon areas of *agreement* between the protocols. Disagreement (cf. Kintgen 1983) is clearly also important for a complete account of reading, but beyond the scope of the present Chapter.

4.2. METHODOLOGY

In order that knowledge of a text's author, period, literary value (or preconceptions of its literary worth) might not influence the readers, the two authors of this Chapter, whose reading processes were to be the subject of the study, asked a colleague to provide a modern text (i.e. written in modern English) by a recognized author, but which they were unlikely to have read before. It was requested that the first printed page of a short story or novel be selected, so that understanding of the extract would not depend on previous portions of the text.

Each researcher read the text alone. Whilst reading they verbalized their thoughts about the text and what they were doing into a tape-recorder. This corresponds, roughly, to the 'think-aloud' technique (see Hosenfeld 1977, 1984). The tape-recordings were then transcribed to produce protocols for analysis and comparison. Subsequently retrospective discussion took place based upon the protocols. This acted as a memory-aid for the researchers and helped them to decide whether differing formulations in the two protocols constituted agreements or disagreements over meaning.

Reading is essentially a silent, private activity, and so presents particular problems for someone wanting to know what occurs in the reader's mind as he reads. Every methodology is likely to have its disadvantages, and the think-aloud technique is no exception:

(i) It distorts the reading process to have to verbalize one's thoughts because the verbalization slows the reading down and interferes with the process. Moreover some distortion is bound to occur if, as in this case, the introspector concentrates on the *process* of reading as well as trying to understand the text.

(ii) Because the process of reading is largely subconscious many aspects of understanding will still remain uncaptured by this method (although later discussion can bring some of these features to light).

(iii) Results may vary depending upon the skill and training of the introspector.

(iv) Having to talk 'on the spot' involves some sacrifice of accuracy and explicitness.

In spite of these disadvantages, the method has some benefits:

(i)   Because it takes place at the time of reading, the commentary is less likely to be marred by forgetfulness and *post hoc* rationalization than more leisured retrospection or analysis (see, for example, Kintgen's criticism of Stanley Fish, Kintgen 1983: 11–19).

(ii) It enables the recording of observations which might otherwise be forgotten.

(iii) It helps to capture the 'flow' of reading, changes of mind, etc.

(iv) More direct methods of observation are just not available.

(v)   The protocols form a useful aid for later discussion of the text as they help the recall of thoughts occurring during the reading process, something which is otherwise difficult to capture (cf. the 'talk-back' procedure in Harri-Augstein and Thomas 1984).

4.3 PROCEDURAL ADVICE TO THE READER

To facilitate understanding of the study the authors suggest that the reader replicates the order of events which the researchers followed. The reader is asked to read the text, and at the same time, to introspect on his general reading process, the meanings which he deduces and how he arrives at them.

[0]   **Markheim**

'Yes,' said the dealer, 'our windfalls are of various kinds. Some customers are ignorant, and then I touch a dividend on my superior knowledge. Some are dishonest,' and here he held up the candle, so that the light fell strongly on his visitor, 'and in

[5]   that case,' he continued, 'I profit by my virtue.'

Markheim had but just entered from the daylight streets, and his eyes had not yet grown familiar with the mingled shine and darkness in the shop. At these pointed words, and before the near presence of the flame, he blinked painfully and looked

[10]   aside.

The dealer chuckled. 'You come to see me on Christmas Day,' he resumed, 'when you know that I am alone in my house, put up my shutters, and make a point of refusing business. Well, you will have to pay for that; you will have to pay

[15]   for my loss of time, when I should be balancing my books; you
will have to pay, besides, for a kind of manner that I remark
in you today very strongly. I am the essence of discretion, and
ask no awkward questions; but when a customer cannot look
me in the eye, he has to pay for it.' The dealer once more chuc-
[20]   kled: and then, changing to his usual business voice, though
still with a note of irony, 'You can give, as usual, a clear account
of how you came into the possession of the object?' he
continued. 'Still your uncle's cabinet? A remarkable collector,
sir!'

[25]   And the little pale, round shouldered dealer stood almost on
tip-toe, looking over the top of his gold spectacles, and nodding
his head with every mark of disbelief. Markheim returned his
gaze with one of infinite pity, and a touch of horror.
'This time,' said he, 'you are in error. I have not come to sell,
[30]   but to buy. I have no curios to dispose of; my uncle's cabinet
is bare to the wainscot; even were it still intact, I have done well
on the Stock Exchange, and should more likely add to it than
otherwise, and my errand today is simplicity itself. I seek a
Christmas present for a lady,' he continued, waxing more fluent
[35]   as he struck into the speech he had prepared; 'and certainly
I owe you every excuse for thus disturbing you upon
so small a matter. But the thing was neglected yesterday; I

*What follows are the protocols produced by the researchers. The reader
is asked to read them and compare them with the results of his own
introspections. This will facilitate a fuller understanding of the method
and a more critical appraisal of the analysis which follows the protocols.*

4.4 THE PROTOCOLS

4.4.1 JCA's introspections

OK MARKHEIM. Name of a person, place. Person: as I glance
down, I see the second paragraph begins with Markheim . . .
OK I have no idea who this is by, what it's about. I assume
[5]   it's the beginning of a novel, since that's what we asked
David to do. And it begins with conversation. OK,
somehow reminds me of Dickens, for some reason. Perhaps
it's the sort of conversational interchange. OK well I haven't
started reading it yet I'm just glancing over it to get an idea
[10]   of what's happening and I see *dealer* I see *Markheim*, I see

dealer with glasses on, nodding his head in disbelief. And it is some conversation. OK I'm going to start reading . . . Hmm. *Windfalls of various kinds,* Markheim's just come into a shop, OK second paragraph tells me that. It's dark.

[15] There's a flame, there's a candle around, it's the dealer's candle, he's talking about windfalls. OK, he means a profit I suppose. So maybe he's dealing with, I don't know, second-hand goods or something like that. Because of this shine and darkness in the shop. *Our windfalls.* Why does

[20] he say *Our windfalls?* OUR *windfalls?* I mean, is this a sort of reference to MY *windfalls,* he's just being polite? And *Yes* suggests that he's already answered some . . . he's answering some question. But Markheim has only just come in. So maybe he's talking to somebody else. I look

[25] down and I don't see that he is. No. *Windfalls of various kinds. Some customers are ignorant, and then I touch a dividend on my superior knowledge.* OK so he makes money by knowing more than customers. Customers are buying because they don't know the true value of things?? Then

[30] they will pay less. Ah, unless he is selling mutton dressed as lamb, as it were. *Some are dishonest, and here he held up the candle, so that the light fell strongly on his visitor.* There's a suggestion here that in fact when erm Markheim, his visitor, I assume *his visitor* is Markheim, his visitor is

[35] dishonest because here he is making a point, he's emphasizing a point by casting light on the visitor, and it says *fell strongly on his visitor* like suspicion falls on somebody, then in that case, *I profit by my virtue.* If people are dishonest, how does he profit by his virtue if people who buy his stuff

[40] are dishonest? No maybe it's people selling him stuff. No I can't work out quite how he profits. I am going to read on. *Markheim had but just entered from the daylight streets, and his eyes had not yet grown familiar with the mingled shine and darkness in the shop. At these pointed words* . . . Yes, as I

[45] thought, that is, the ones about dishonesty, *and before the near presence of the flame, he blinked painfully.* OK *painfully.* There's a sense of guilt here. It's not just from the light in other words, *and looked aside.* Uh huh, a suggestion that he knows what the guy is talking about, and, of course, the

[50] dealer responds, he chuckles. *'You come to see me on*

Christmas Day.' he resumed, 'when you know that I am alone in my house, put up my shutters, and make a point of refusing business'. OK it's Christmas Day and the place is normally shut. Why has he come on Christmas Day? *Well, you will have to*
[55] *pay for that; you will have to pay for my loss of time, when I should be balancing my books.* The guy is balancing his books on Christmas Day? He had nothing better to do? *You will have to pay, besides, for a kind of manner that I remark in you today very strongly.* So the guy knows him, the dealer knows
[60] him, partly because he knows that Markheim knows that he's alone in the house and partly because he says *I remark in you today* very strongly some kind of manner. So other days he doesn't have that sort of manner. What is this manner? OK *you will have to pay for a kind of manner that I*
[65] *remark in you. I am the essence of discretion, and ask no awkward questions; but when a dealer [sic] cannot look me in the eye, he has to pay for it.* That refers to his looking aside, presumably, blinking painfully and looking aside, perhaps his . . . *The dealer once more chuckled, and then changing to his usual business*
[70] *voice* . . . [inaudible, but reading rest of paragraph] . . . *A remarkable collector, sir!* OK, right, so this dealer is actually buying goods from people who come in. So I can go back to that first sentence in a minute and make sense of that. I wouldn't normally actually, but I could. So he's asking in
[75] his business-like voice *You can give as usual a clear account. As usual* suggests he's a general customer, a long-standing customer and you have to, presumably, show that you didn't steal: *a clear account of how you came into possession of the object . . . Still your uncle's cabinet?* In other words, the
[80] uncle's cabinet has been the excuse for or been the source of objects that Markheim has come and sold to this dealer for some time. And he says *A remarkable collector, sir!* He's being ironic, of course, that's the touch of irony *with a note of irony* suggested earlier. He doesn't believe him. His uncle
[85] must have had an amazing cabinet to have had all these items in it. *And the little pale, round shouldered dealer stood almost on tip-toe, looking over the top of his gold spectacles, and nodding his head with every mark of disbelief.* OK, well, that's the irony. That emphasizes the *some are dishonest, the light*
[90] *falling strongly on his visitor,* the irony lower down,

Markheim's guilt, Markheim's eyes turning away, *pointed words* these all tie up together. *Markheim returned his gaze with one of infinite pity and a touch of horror.* Why should Markheim pity him? Because he is just a clerk? Because he
[95] is a dealer, because he looks down on him, because he has to sell stuff off *and a touch of horror?*
This time, said he, you are in error. He must refer to Markheim. Why? Because he says *I have not come to sell but to buy.* OK. *I have come.* The dealer hasn't come, so *he* must
[100] be Markheim. *I have no curios to dispose of; my uncle's cabinet is bare to the wainscot; even if it were still intact, I have done well on the Stock Exchange and should more likely add to it than otherwise, and my errand today is simplicity itself.* So he's going to buy stuff: he's done well on the Stock Exchange, he's
[105] made some money. He claims that his uncle's cabinet, which is the cabinet he referred to earlier, is *bare to the wainscot.* To the . . . I thought wainscot was panelling. At any rate. I don't see how a cabinet can be bare to the panelling of the wall against which it stands. I'm not too sure but it
[110] doesn't really matter. *Even if it were still intact* . . . [unintelligible] . . . *is simplicity itself. I seek a Christmas present for a lady.* Well, it is Christmas Day, after all. OK *he continued, waxing more fluent as he struck into the speech he had* PREPARED. OK, so that suggests it is not actually true, he's
[115] prepared a speech. Why has he prepared a speech? *And certainly I owe you every excuse for thus disturbing you upon so small a matter.* Why is it a small matter? Not necessarily, and he's disturbing him on Christmas Day, OK? *But the thing was neglected yesterday;* in other words he didn't buy a
[120] present yesterday. *I* . . . What is he going on to say? Well, that's interesting speculation. I had no time to do it, or I was out of the country, or some sort of excuse, anyway, some explanation, some reason for why the thing was neglected yesterday, is what I expect to come.

[125] OK what have I built up? A picture of a guy who's come into a shop on Christmas Day, a shop he comes to fairly regularly, normally to sell objects, objects that ostensibly come from his uncle's cabinet but which the dealer suggests, at least, and which Markheim by his own behav-

[130] iour suggests are ill-gotten objects – reference to the dishonest customers. Erm . . . the dealer makes fun of him, he's obviously sort of setting him up in order to make money out of him – profiting by his virtue. Against the dealer's expectations it appears that actually Markheim has

[135] come to buy, he's come to buy a present for a lady. Something that he couldn't do in the day before. But why he's buying the present on Christmas Day itself . . . ? That's unusual. But he's got a prepared speech, one wonders why this is prepared? Is there something behind his apparent

[140] errand? He's done well on the Stock Exchange, his uncle is obviously, apparently some sort of collector, a well-off person. OK, *Markheim* itself suggests a Jewish name, a German name. Something about it makes me think that it is sort of Victorian. I wonder whether it's the style, *had but*

[145] *just entered* strikes me as slightly archaic language. *The mingled shine and darkness* again sounds slightly old-fashioned. Let's have a look. What else? *I am the essence of discretion and ask no awkward questions.* There's something Dickensian about that phrase. *The little pale, round shouldered*

[150] *dealer*? No, not particularly. Why is he standing on tip-toe? Because he's short? Because he's looking over the counter? There's a sentence I'm not too sure about yet. *Markheim returned his gaze with one of infinite pity and a touch of horror.* Pity for whom? For the dealer in his job? Having to deal

[155] with . . . , buy and sell . . . , filthy money, suggests aristocratic disdain. The *touch of horror*. Horror at what? Being at the mercy of such a person, in the hands of such a person? Maybe.

This time you are in error. That's it. *You are in error* not 'You're

[160] wrong'. *You are in error.* Strange phrase, strangely formal. *Even were it still intact* rather than 'even if it were'. Again suggests a formality that is more appropriate to the nineteenth century than the twentieth. *Stock Exchange.* I don't know when the Stock Exchange started? I presume it was

[165] around in the nineteenth century. *I should more likely add to it than otherwise.* That presumably refers to the cabinet. *I would add to* IT *than otherwise*: cabinet, not the Stock Exchange. Well, why? Because you don't add to Stock

Exchanges, whereas cabinets . . . it's bare and you could
[170] presumably because of his windfall, the money he's got on
the Stock Exchange, he could actually buy some objects to
put into the cabinet. *My errand today is simplicity itself.* Why
should that be particularly simple? *I seek a Christmas present
for a lady, he continued, waxing more fluent as he struck into the*
[175] *speech he had prepared; and certainly I owe you every excuse for*
THUS *disturbing you upon so* SMALL *a matter.* Self-deprecation.
But the THING *was neglected yesterday.* Again a very depre-
cating tone: *the thing.*

Well, what do I make of this? Nothing very much. Let me
[180] go through it again and see if I can work out how I know
what I know. *Yes, said the dealer, our windfalls are of various
kinds.* In other words, the money we make. OK. *Some
customers are ignorant and then I touch a dividend on my superior
knowledge.* OK, what he means is 'when people come in,
[185] customers are ignorant.' What I half suspected at this point
before is that he's buying stuff, they don't know the value
of things and therefore he makes money because he DOES
know the value of things. I can see that. *Some are dishonest
. . . and in that case . . . profit by my virtue* [at this point JCA
[190] omitted the inserted prose]. Does that mean that people are
going to sell him stolen goods, hence *dishonest* and therefore
he profits by this because he bargains them down in price
knowing perfectly well that if he were to reveal to the police
they were stolen goods, then the seller . . . would accept
[195] a lower price, in other words, in case he were to reveal to
the police that it was stolen. It's an ironic sort of 'virtue'.
Markheim had but just entered from the daylight streets. The
streets are in daylight, it's in some city somewhere therefore. And during the daytime, Christmas daytime. *His eyes*
[200] *had not yet grown familiar with the mingled shine and darkness
in the shop.* It's not a dirty shop. *Mingled shine and darkness.*
Darkness because it's not lit? Because it's in contrast with
the daylight. *Shine* because of the objects: I mean brass objects, glass objects and so on, presumably, plus clean polish,
[205] polished furniture. *At these pointed words* – pointed. *Some
are honest*[sic], presumably . . . *and before the near presence of
the flame, he blinked painfully and looked aside.* So there's a

suggestion of guilt in past dealings, the notion that . . .
maybe that's the *horror* that's referred to later. He's horrified
[210] at being in this guy's knowing clutches: the guy knows
Markheim IS dishonest, has been dishonest in the past.
And he chuckles at this. Why does he chuckle? *The dealer
chuckled.* Presumably at Markheim's blinking painfully and
looking aside, recognition of his guilt. Now he shows that
[215] later on doesn't he? Erm Ah *when a customer cannot look me
in the eye, he has to pay for it.* Right, That's why he chuckled.
*You come to see me on Christmas Day, he resumed, when you
know that I am alone in my house put up my shutters and make
a point of refusing business,* Uhhuh *put up my shutters.* He
[220] means close the shutters, doesn't he? I mean, to me it's the
other way round. You put up shutters if you are opening
shop, but anyway. *Make a point of refusing business.* So why
should he come to see him on Christmas Day when
normally he doesn't do business? *Have to pay for that; you
[225] will have to pay for my loss of time, when I should be balancing
my books; you will have to pay, besides for a kind of manner that
I remark in you today very strongly. I am the essence of discretion
and ask no awkward questions.* Ah. OK. So why would he
have to pay for this manner that he remarks in him? Er, he
[230] looks like a guilty person, he's saying 'when a customer
cannot look me in the eye, he has to pay for it'. And since
I profit by my virtue when customers are dishonest I'm going
to profit by my virtue today, when you're going to have
done . . . you're probably going to sell me something that
[235] you have stolen. I know you've stolen it, you cannot even
look me in the eye, and therefore I'm going to make damn
sure that you accept the lowest possible price. *Once more
chuckled, and then, changing to his usual business voice, though
still with a note of irony, 'You can give, as usual, a clear account
[240] of how you came into possession of the object?' he continued. 'Still
your uncle's cabinet? A remarkable collector, sir!'.* He's giving
him the excuse, the reason he's been given in the past,
because of *still. And the little, pale round shouldered dealer stood.
Round shouldered.* What does that suggest? Stooping over
[245] money-bags? *Looking over the top of his gold spectacles.* Why
gold spectacles? Why should this guy be wearing them?
What image is conjured up by this? *Little, pale.* Jewish?

Round shouldered, hook-nosed? All he does on Christmas
Day is balance his books, receives stolen goods. *The little*
[250] *pale, round shouldered dealer stood almost on tip-toe.* He's small
– that's the little *looking over the top of his gold spectacles.* Spec-
tacles suggests 'bookish', *gold* suggests wealthy, *looking over*
the top of them suggests they are for reading, that is
balancing the books. *Nodding his head with every mark of dis-*
[255] *belief.* Disbelief presumably of the story. OK, not a very
sympathetic character. *Markheim returned his* GAZE *with one*
of infinite pity and a touch of horror. 'This time,' said he, 'you
are in error.' You are wrong. *I haven't come to sell but to buy.*
What had he come here on Christmas Day to buy, and why
[260] this particular place? Is he going to demand credit or what?
OK and then he explains that he doesn't have anything to
sell anyway, he's just after a Christmas present. *Waxing*
more fluent as he struck into the speech he had prepared. He
wouldn't normally prepare a speech in this situation. The
[265] fact that he has prepared a speech suggests that it is not
going to be the truth. *I owe you every excuse for thus disturbing*
you upon so small a matter. But the thing was neglected
yesterday. I wonder what sort of thing he was going to buy
and why he has come to disturb this guy on this particular
[270] day with it? OK, I've got a general picture, again, in my
mind. A guy coming into a shop, a dealer with whom he's
intimate, with whom he's already had shady dealings in the
past, and sounds like he's building up to a shady deal
again, although I must say, everything seems quite inno-
[275] cent, he just wants to buy a Christmas present for a lady.
The unusual nature of his call, time of his call, suggests that
it IS going to be something shady. I don't know whether
Markheim is old or young. I don't know. He talks of his
uncle's cabinet so . . . no, I'm not so sure . . . suggests a
[280] young, profligate man whose uncle is actually still alive. No
he can't be alive. It must be something he's inherited when
the uncle died otherwise he wouldn't have the right to be
selling things off from it, or at least using that as the legit-
imacy of his getting hold of the object he's selling off. I'm
[285] not sure there's anything else to say about this. The candle
. . . the candle the dealer has is obviously he's come out to
answer the door-bell with a candle. Maybe that's partly why

I think it's Dickensian: but why does he have the candle in the shop during the daytime? OK, well he wouldn't switch [290] the lights on because there's no electricity. Didn't exist in those days. He has a candle rather than oil lamps. That suggests it is temporary light, that he has been disturbed, because he is not normally open. Would it be normal: candlelight in there? Why candle? Hm, OK, I'm quite happy [295] with that I think I'll stop at that point.

Perhaps I should just add, it seems to me that I've taken much less time over this. I haven't concentrated on every word in the way that I did with the poem. The poem I felt was self-contained and therefore there was a lot of meaning [300] condensed in there that I had to get out, there was nowhere else to go for meaning. The beginning of this novel, I mean I feel I could just read on. I wouldn't normally in any case pore over it over the page trying to milk it for meaning, as it were. So the sort of speculations I would engage upon [305] about the candle, for example, I'm not sure I would do even subconsciously, let alone consciously. I think I'd just read on and then IF it proved to be significant later that this guy was being mean by having a candle or the fact that he was beaten up and the candle falls to the floor and sets fire to [310] the building, then the significance of the candle would in any case be revealed. If it is not revealed explicitly later on, then I would perhaps, I mean, perhaps it would help me build up a picture of what's happening: darkness, and so on erm, but perhaps it wouldn't. On the other hand, it has [315] been CHOSEN by the author, the word *candle*, so there must be some reason for it. I wouldn't spend time normally speculating on that, though. I'd just read on. And then come back, maybe with a knowledge of the text, to see how I had arrived at that particular interpretation. So it is more signifi- [320] cant, actually, that I have . . . I mean there are far more words in this, yet I've spent much less time on it. Normally I would just read on, actually, not delving into these para- graphs for more and more meaning creation, or the creation of hypotheses about which I could speculate when reading [325] on, to see if they were confirmed or disconfirmed in the text. I mean I've no idea whether from here this dealer is going to be significant or whether it's simply the fact that Markheim has come to a dealer that will prove to be significant. I don't know whether that will make any difference. [330] I have no way of knowing whether the action will continue to take place in this shop or whether it'll just be the opening incident and in fact it'll go on for several years outside the shop and this may or may not be referred to again. It may be a sort of crux point at the beginning which is referred [335] to again and again like, say, the Kirks' party in *The History Man*. It may be just a scene-setter, atmosphere-setter, to throw light on Markheim's shadiness, his wealth, his lack of honesty, and so on. It's rather hard to tell. I could probably speculate on that a little more. I wouldn't normally do [340] that. I don't know to what extent that would be helpful.

4.4.2 MHS's *introspections*

Markheim German? Name of place or person

yes . . . dealer. An agreement. The definite article means the narrator is assuming we know who the dealer is – 'close' point of view.

[5]   *our windfalls . . . kinds . . .* Previous speaker has made some statement about windfalls? – that is things which have *happened* which are good.

some . . . knowledge. I touch a dividend is odd. The customers are ignorant, and because of what the dealer tells them they [10]   favour him in some way.

some . . . dishonest relates to the previous bit *via* parallelism and Maxim of Relation. The first set of customers are innocent and don't know. The second lot are opposite and so might be testing him in some way. A parallelism between [15]   *ig*norant and *dis*honest?

and here . . . visitor. Here marks closeness of viewpoint. We don't yet know whether the narration is first- or third-person. But if we assume the third person norm, the *here* must mark the narrator's point of view, not speech or [20]   thought presentation. *The* for *the candle* is assumed information on the narrator's part, so again close point of view. The fact that the light is held above the customer and falls *strongly* on him indicates the dealer is in command.

[25] *and in that case . . . virtue.* Some kind of parallel. The dealer always comes out on top. If the customer is ignorant he wins. If the customer is not ignorant but not honest he wins.

Markheim . . . shop. Markheim is a man and the person the dealer is talking to. *Had but just* is a little archaic. *Daylight*
[30] *streets – daylight* is a non-delimiting adjective here to contrast with the dark of the shop (might, up till now, have assumed both were light). *Mingled shine and darkness* is vaguely poetic. The light in the shop comes partly from outside and partly from the candle (so it's pretty dark
[35] inside). Possible symbolic meaning? Markheim coming in from the light (=good) to the darkness of the shop (=bad). Likely with the dishonest/honest references.

At these . . . looked aside. The words are *pointed* and so he blinks *painfully.* So the lexis makes the cause and effect
[40] relation between the dealer's words and Markheim's discomfort more obvious. He looks aside, presumably to avoid the dealer and therefore pain/embarrassment (note the word *dealer* is consistently used, but it is a shop – a bit odd? possibly Germanness?). The dealer is on top.

[45] *The dealer . . . business.* An unusual day to come. The dealer chuckles and so is on top and happy with the situation in spite of being disturbed on Christmas Day. He is alone in the house and so vulnerable? The time and the vulnerability are two indications of him not wanting to do business.

[50] *Well . . . very strongly.* It is reasonable that Markheim should pay for disturbing the dealer but odd (because impolite) that the dealer *says so.* Odd also that he is balancing his books on Christmas Day unless he is a Jew, which is possible as it has to do with money. But then the last bit – customers
[55] do not usually have to pay for their manner. *Remark* and *besides* (its position?) gives a vaguely archaic flavour (late-nineteenth- or early-twentieth-century?).

I am . . . questions. The Maxim of Quantity is broken as the two bits say more or less the same thing. Emphasis?

[60]   *But . . . pay for it.* Obviously refers back to *blinked painfully and looked aside* – because we know that *aside* must mean from the dealer (general world knowledge?). But again, what is odd is that the customer is paying for . . . well, his feelings.

[65]   *The dealer . . . chuckled.* Back to *chuckled* – repetition. Dealer on top.

And the . . . business voice. We now know the previous bit was said in a different, non-business tone of voice. Did not know this at the time.

[70]   *Though . . . irony.* So he has gone back to his business voice ON PURPOSE (note the intentional verb) to make some kind of ironic point, and, so, had NOT been using it before (friendship?).

You can . . . continued. As usual indicates Markheim has
[75]   been often before (we knew this already because he disturbs the dealer on Christmas Day?). Certainly made clear now. *The object* is interesting. They know what it is and so it is odd that they refer to it with such an uninformative noun (what about that *Journal of Linguistics* article on marked and
[80]   unmarked lexis?) – effect on reader? Evasiveness? Formality? Some formal vocabulary (*possession, account*) – to do with the time when it was written?

Still . . . collector, sir! We infer that he infers that Markheim will say that the object has come from his uncle's cabinet
[85]   and that it is an excuse for Markheim having it, but the dealer doesn't really believe the putative excuse – because of the *remarkable collector* remark in an ironic tone of voice. Presumably Markheim has brought in so many things in the past that it is unreasonable to assume that they all come
[90]   from the same cabinet – because of the number or quality of items.

And . . . spectacles. Long NP referring to the dealer (first one like this). Non-delimiting material. Indicates he is *physically*

defenceless, even though he is tactically on top (note the
[95] 'threat' context somehow brings out this latent possible
meaning). *Spectacles* – dealerishness, wealth (*gold*), defenceless.

nodding . . . disbelief. What are the marks of disbelief? They
are either nods that go with the remarks the dealer has
[100] made before or, more likely, Markheim sees waves of disbelief coming over the dealer (so Markheim's point of view?)
and he nods with each one (is this a general rule? – if two
characters and external view of x, then viewpoint of y
unless specifically marked otherwise?). The first time we
[105] have had Markheim's point of view.

Markheim . . . horror. Markheim now looking DIRECTLY at the
dealer and his reactions are opposed to one another. So
Markheim must be a good man (likely as he is the title
person) as he is pitying the dealer with a lot of pity (*infinite*
[110] *pity* is not literally true, so hyperbole) in a situation where
the dealer appears to be screwing Markheim.

This time . . . error. Direct Speech again. Markheim speaks
for the first time, and tells him he is wrong.

I have . . . to buy. Coordination, parallelism, short sentence.
[115] Opposes all the assumptions the dealer, and we, have built
up before.

I . . . dispose of. Backs up previous part of sentence. Note
no *object* after all – presumably that is why the dealer was
being so vague.

[120] *my uncle's . . . wainscot*. Assuming the previous curios have
supposedly come from the uncle's cabinet, this backs up the
previous statement and makes it stronger.

even . . . Exchange. So he doesn't NEED to raid the *cabinet*.

and . . . otherwise. Says roughly the same thing (I should
[125] work out how we know all these different statements
amount to the same thing). So, his good financial standing
is very emphasized.

and . . . lady. Presumably the pity was because the old man
was not going to get what he wanted. No, because he will

[130] gain from the transaction anyway (why do I assume he is
old? – his position and spectacles?). What is odd, of course,
is that Markheim comes for the present now. He should
have thought of it before, and is UNLIKELY to have forgotten.

he continued . . . prepared. *Waxing more fluent* tells us about
[135] tone of voice, manner of delivery and so on. By implication,
before he must have been more hesitant. He is fluent now
because he has worked out his speech beforehand (cf. the
word *speech*).

and . . . yesterday. *Certainly* and *every excuse* opposed to *so*
[140] *small a matter.* A passive structure, note, and certainly some
formality about it – goes with the prepared quality of the
speech. *This thing* instead of 'it'. A bit like *the object* (though
now we know the dealer COULDN'T specify – there was no
object for him to refer to).

[145] So, what we have at the end of the passage is a situation
where the roles are reversed from what we and the dealer
expected (so we have been kept outside Markheim at the
beginning of the page for strategic reasons – as he is the
main figure we would expect to get things from his view-
[150] point, knowledge, etc.). Markheim is buying, not selling.
And it is Christmas Day, which is unusual and strange. So
we still want to know why he has to buy on Christmas Day
(and what he will buy, and who he will give it to and why).
So the dealer may still have some kind of advantage/hold
[155] over Markheim (yet Markheim *pities* him, and why is still
not clear) and we'll be looking for that to develop.

SECOND RUN-THROUGH

Yes . . . kinds. Why *our* instead of 'my'? Royal *we* or more
than one of them in the business?

some are dishonest. It is now clear that when the dealer holds
[160] up the candle over Markheim he is implying that Markheim
is dishonest (and that is why he profits by his virtue – this
explains why the look on his face is going to cost him
money – though note the dealer's virtue is of rather an odd
kind. In any case, presumably much of this goes by the
[165] board when Markheim says he is buying. So this is mainly

scene setting stuff?). So the *here* is important as it makes the connection more obvious. This is reinforced by the fact that Markheim looks aside not just because of the word but also because of the flame. So he does feel guilty about *something* [170] either generally or about this particular errand.

Christmas Day. Presumably the dealer deals from his house or lives over the shop. Note the repetition of '*you will have to pay for* (xyz)' – stressing *the kind of manner I remark in you.* *Remark* is an unusual perception verb. A bit odd – period?

[175] *I am the essence . . . pay for it. But* suggests opposition, and presumably indicates indirectness versus directness.

the dealer once more chuckled at . . . irony. Verb of locution omitted.

you can give a clear account . . . object. The business voice is [180] formal – *the possession* – definite article and nominalization.

still your uncle's cabinet. Indicates that Markheim must have given that reason before – so in the dealer's eyes, Markheim is disreputable, of course. Will he turn out to be? We have conflicting information on it so far – apparent previous [185] knowledge versus the 'hero' of the story and the fact that he pities the dealer.

Sir. A marker of politeness because the dealer is inferior socially? Or a nineteenth-century term between equals? Or ironic?

[190] *And the little . . . disbelief.* Markheim is bigger than the dealer. Not described as little, does not have to stand on tiptoe. Presumably Markheim is not pale or round-shouldered either. So Markheim is a fitter (and younger, if he gives Christmas presents to ladies?) man than the dealer. [195] Markheim now DOES return the gaze. Markheim's speech is short sentences and clauses – directness (goes with youth etc. – and honesty?).

a lady. Indefinite article – Markheim not letting the dealer have any information if he can help it.

[200] *Excuse* is odd. *Apology* would be more normal today – a change in the use of the word?

Does Markheim feel pity for the dealer because of the sort of man he is?

4.5 PROTOCOL ANALYSIS

4.5.1 *Reading strategies*

(i) There are some obvious differences in the reading behaviours: where MHS processes more or less linearly, JCA moves backwards and forwards in the text, expecially at the beginning of the reading, apparently sampling and selecting. In addition, JCA reads through the text several times, whereas MHS simply reads it twice. In the case of JCA, the protocol includes a number of questions about parts of the text. Sometimes these questions are answered and sometimes not. MHS, on the other hand, tends to comment by making statements. The third obvious difference is that MHS, despite the intended use of the 'think-aloud' technique, has a tendency to read a chunk of text silently, and then to comment, semi-retrospectively, whereas JCA appears to try to capture the flow of thoughts concurrently.

(ii) Nevertheless, despite the obvious differences, there are many similarities. In particular, both readers tend to comment on or to question similar parts of the text, and to come up with not very different interpretations of meaning. Although there are differences in interpretation, some of these disappear as the readers progress through the text and one or the other revises his interpretations. Thus, despite surface differences, both readers can be seen to be engaged in establishing a generally similar line of meaning for the text, building up a picture of what the text is about, and trying to fit the textual evidence into that picture.

(iii) When either reader goes back over the text, in a re-read, he selects particular parts, and does not pay attention to every-thing in the text. The focus in the re-read seems to be upon obscure parts of the text, the 'understood' parts being ignored. Thus a re-read is an attempt to puzzle out or create further meaning in the light of what has been read *since* that problematic piece. JCA shows an awareness that this is likely to be the case in JCA 72–3 'So I can go back to the first sentence in a minute and make sense of it', and he actually reinterprets the second sentence of the first paragraph, on his second reading, in the light of subsequent knowledge (JCA 182–8), having already explicitly noted the connections among the items in the text in JCA 89–96. See also MHS 159–64.

(iv) JCA engages in a pre-read which is selective. He identifies words and phrases, in a content sampling process, to get a general idea of what the text is about (JCA 0–12). This is a conscious attempt to establish a framework, or context, within which his outside knowledge can operate to interact with the text and create meaning.

(v) Each reader refers to assumptions he has been making up to a given point in the text, which have had to be revised in the light of new information. In other words, the reader is carrying information 'in his head' as he goes through the text, and refers to it when new information confirms or contradicts this 'in-head' information. Both readers are thus creating what might be called an 'internal text' – their interpretation, constantly revised, of the 'external' text. This internal text is held on to, and checked against the external text. Hence the reading process can be seen as a process of integration of the incoming external text with the internal text. This internal text is produced by a continuing process of fusion of what is already in the reader's head (which is itself a combination of pre-existent knowledge and assumptions and meaning arrived at from the text so far), and what is outside it – i.e. the part of the external text being processed at that moment.

(vi) While reading linearly, both readers refer back (either covertly or overtly, through comments or questions) to the previous text, which has become part of the internal text. Sometimes this process can be seen explicitly in the protocols; sometimes it is inferrable from the sort of comments or questions that appear (JCA 72–3 and MHS 159–64).

(vii) The internal text is continually being modified, partly on the basis of the incoming external text, partly on the basis of speculations, judgements about logic, plausibility and the like. The internal text is compared with the external text, and either confirmed or contradicted. If congruence is found, then the internal text is confirmed, reinforced and added to, from the new incoming external texts (MHS 60–1, 65, 120–2; JCA 83–4, 89–92). If, however, there is incongruence between the two texts, various things may happen:

(a) the external text may be re-examined, perhaps with a comment (e.g. 'that's odd'), or a question (JCA 152–8);
(b) the oddity may merely be noted and held in store for possible later use (MHS 43–4, 62–4);
(c) the internal text may be modified in the light of the external text (MHS 31–2, 68–9, 115–16, 136–7; JCA 72–3);
(d) the external text may be revised, i.e. mis-read.

(viii) Often incongruities occur, and 'errors' are detected; yet no revision takes place in either text. MHS infers both friendship between the dealer and Markheim (MHS 71–3) and supremacy of the dealer. He also notes that the dealer is happy ('chuckles'), yet suggests that he might not want to do business (MHS 48–9). This frequently happens when the reader feels that the main thread of meaning is not being disturbed by the incongruity. In other words, the reader makes a decision on whether to revise or not, based upon a judgement as to the relevance and importance of new information. Thus, reading involves judging and deciding, as well as comparing, matching, noting and 'perceiving'. JCA shows himself to be consciously aware of this process towards the end of his protocol (JCA 301–29).

(ix) The readers infer information that is not explicitly stated. These inferences are at times very similar between the readers, and at others quite different (see appendices 1 and 2 for a list of agreements). This seems to depend in part upon a judgement by the reader on what part of the text to focus upon: where does he need to infer something in order to satisfy his need for a congruent internal text? There appear to be a number of motivations for readers to infer:

(a) the writer cannot be totally explicit;
(b) in order to justify what the writer has produced (for example, both readers feel the need to work out why the author states that the dealer's spectacles are *gold* (MHS 96; JCA 245–6, 252);

(c)   in order to get at hidden meanings that the reader expects or knows to be present (MHS 32–7).

Inferencing appears to be an essential part of human comprehension, since texts, spoken or written, are never fully explicit. The subject of inferencing is taken up in section 4.5.3.

(x) Both readers speculate, not only about the reasons for the mention of an idea or word (MHS 154–6) but also about what is to come in the text. See JCA's comments on what he expects to appear on the next page of the story (JCA 120–4) and MHS's more general comments on what he expects to develop later in the story (MHS 151–6). As part of this speculative process readers set up conceivable alternatives in order to examine them (e.g. JCA's 'So maybe he's talking to somebody else?' (JCA 24)). This may be due to the reader's wishing to avoid making false interpretations by ruling out other conceivable alternatives. A particularly clear example of this is seen in JCA's protocol (JCA 162 ff.), where he hypothesizes that the text dates from the nineteenth century, on the basis of several 'odd-sounding' phrases. He then focuses on the phrase *Stock Exchange*, and asks himself whether the mention of the institution is consistent with the hypothesis that the text is a nineteenth-century one. If the Stock Exchange was not in existence then, the text could not date from that time. He is sampling different parts of the text and relating them to his knowledge of the world, in order to determine whether his hypothesis is consistent with the text.

(xi) Both readers constantly use background knowledge:

(a)   in order to create the internal text. For example JCA (27–9, 71–2) assumes that if the man entering the shop is a customer he must be a buyer;
(b)   in order to infer, or as the basis for inference. For example MHS (130–1) assumes the man is old because he wears spectacles and because he appears to be the owner of the shop. Similarly JCA (17–19) infers, because the shop is dark and yet has shiny objects in it, that the dealer trades in second-hand goods;
(c)   in order to check hypotheses and speculations. The *Stock Exchange* example in (x) above is a clear case. MHS (52–3,

171–2) develops the hypothesis that the dealer is a Jew based upon the fact that he is balancing his books on Christmas Day, which MHS knows from his background knowledge is an unusual thing to do. He then confirms the plausibility of the hypothesis, again from his background knowledge, by saying 'which is possible, as it has to do with money' (MHS 53–4). Although no explicit mention is made in MHS 171–2 of the hypothesis that the dealer is a Jew it would appear that the remark about this man living over the shop is a further example of the checking of this hypothesis against a cultural stereotype.

(xii) Readers use their awareness of period style, stylistic devices (which are not necessarily explicitly perceived, or referred to in the metalanguage of stylistics), etc. in order to create settings for events, times and expectations. Both readers comment on what they call the 'archaic' quality of the language (e.g. MHS 29, 55–7, 188–9, 200; JCA 144 ff.). In both cases they identify the passage as being probably a nineteenth-century one on similar evidence (for example *had but just entered*), by calling on their knowledge of current English syntax. JCA even specifies the archaic quality as Victorian or even Dickensian, consciously searches the text for confirmatory evidence of his impression, and wonders about the author, and time of the passage. Not surprisingly, the stylistician is more analytic in his introspections about the text, using a particular metalanguage to express his thoughts.

(xiii) It is interesting to note that no value judgements were made about the text, and no indication was given of enjoyment of the experience of reading literature. This may be in part due to the research methodology and in part to the fragmentary nature of the text. But it may also be the case that even when reading literature, readers do not make value judgements constantly: they first attempt to create meaning (internal texts); they establish and follow the story line. The judgement of literary worth (which is often said to be the goal of reading literature critically) may be a retrospective one; something done later in the reading process or after reading altogether, once the internal text has been established. Perhaps it is a separate process from the reading process (see Short and Van Peer, this volume).

4.5.2 *The role of questions and comments in the reading process*

In section 4.5.1 (i) reference has been made to the fact that one of the readers makes statements whilst the other tends to ask questions. In 4.5.1 (vii) it could be seen that these comments play an important part in the process of creating the internal text. Often the reader appears to engage in a 'dialogue' with himself. He asks questions and speculates about possible answers to them. Of course 'questioning' of this kind does not necessarily have to have a surface interrogative form. A comment followed by a later comment which confirms or negates the first remark can be seen as a declarative equivalent. These speculations can be seen as hypotheses which are available for the reader to confirm, disconfirm or abandon as he sees fit. Below (appendix 3) we examine in more detail the role of questions in the reading process. As JCA is the interrogative questioner we use his questions as the starting point for discussion. Appendix 3 is a list of questions asked in the protocols along with retrospective descriptive comment on the part of the analysts. The reader may therefore find it useful to familiarize himself with appendix 3 before he proceeds farther.

4.5.3 *Methods of inferencing*

In our discussion of the general strategies involved in the reading process we have often attended to the fact that readers deduce meanings from texts which are felt to be *implicit* rather than *explicit*. Many of these implicit meanings are arrived at *via* a process which has come to be generally known as *inferencing* (e.g. Carton 1971; Dillon 1978; Clark 1977). At present, discussions of inferencing seem to lack a systematic taxonomy. As a contribution towards remedying this situation we list below kinds of inferencing which we have found ourselves involved in. Most of the types and examples come from the protocols on the *Markheim* text. More particularly, we limit ourselves almost entirely to examples where we as readers have *agreed* upon a meaning inferred from the text (see appendices 1 and 2). But as the text is limiting in that it may not contain examples of certain inferencing processes we have added other kinds to the list. We doubt that the list is exhaustive and the categories which we suggest may well not be the most useful. Instead, they are put forward to provide an impetus for more systematic work in this area.

A note on the categories

It would appear that inferences in spoken discourse could be made from a number of different knowledge bases:

(i)   general background knowledge of the real world and the way it works;
(ii) knowledge of a particular situation in which the discourse takes place;
(iii) knowledge gained from kinesic and paralinguistic phenomena, e.g. eyebrow raising, tone of voice;
(iv) linguistic knowledge;
(v)   a combination of two or more of these bases.

In *written* discourse, in one sense all the information deduced must be from a linguistic base, because the only thing the reader has to go on is the text in front of him and the rules, procedures and knowledge 'inside his head' which he uses to interpret the text. However, the categories distinguished above allow us to keep the commonsense distinction between the fictional world the author sets up and the way he describes it (cf. Leech and Short 1981: Ch. 5). A similar kind of division can be seen to be useful in understanding newspaper reports, advertising, etc. This general distinction between linguistic and other kinds of knowledge applies for any discourse, and as there are two discourses in this text (that between the two characters and that between the narrator and the reader, in which the narrator describes the characters, comments on them and so on) it is useful to remember that the reader will be inferencing on two different levels. He will be deducing what, for example, the dealer implies to Markheim when he talks to him, and also what the narrator is suggesting to him about the characters, the situation and so on (for more extended remarks on the discourse structure of prose fiction see Leech and Short 1981: Ch. 8).

(i) REAL WORLD INFERENCE

There are no really clear cut examples of this kind of inference in our text, but a good constructed example would be, 'It was raining and the car skidded into a lamp-post', where we would infer that a probable reason for the car skidding was the slippery condition of the road. An example of real-world inferencing in JCA's protocol is his initial belief that Markheim must have entered the shop in order to buy rather than to sell something. This is based on his knowledge of what usually goes on in shops (JCA 28 ff.). The first item in appendix 1 might also count as an example of this category. We infer that Markheim is probably German from our general knowledge, namely that many Germans have names ending in -heim (JCA 1, MHS 1). This piece of real-world knowledge happens to be knowledge about language. It is likely that real-world inferencing is open to sub-categorization in the same way that linguistic inferencing is. (See (iv) below.)

(ii) KINESIC INFERENCING

An example of inferencing from kinesic information would be our interpretation of someone's raised eyebrows at a colleague's remarks. We would take this to imply some surprise at or maybe disagreement with the views that had been expressed. The most clear-cut example in the text (see appendix 1, text-line 5) is when Markheim averts his gaze as a result of the dealer's words and actions. Both readers understand this to mean that Markheim is avoiding eye-to-eye contact as a result of his guilt (JCA 47–9; MHS 38–42).

(iii) INFERENCES BASED ON KNOWLEDGE OF THE PARTICULAR SITUATION

These inferences may be based on knowledge of people or circumstances. One which the dealer makes in the passage (based on his previous knowledge of Markheim) is that he has come to the shop to sell him something. This inference turns out to be a false one. An interesting point about JCA's reaction to the text mentioned in (i) above is that at the beginning, from his real-world knowledge, he decides that as Markheim is a customer in a shop he must be coming to buy something. Then, as he observes the dealer's 'particular situation' inferences based on his knowledge of Markheim, JCA revises his opinion (JCA 72–4), only to discover that his original assumption was right all the time and that the dealer, the 'insider' turns out to be mistaken.

(iv) LINGUISTIC INFERENCING

(a) INFERENCING THE MEANING OF WORDS

Carton (1971) discusses how the meanings of unknown or coined words can be retrieved from the contexts in which they occur. Alderson and Alvarez (1977) offer a partial categorization of the way in which structural–semantic relations can be used as an aid to inferring the meaning of words in context. There are no really difficult words in the Markheim passage, although both readers were somewhat unfamiliar with the word *wainscot*, which JCA mentions in his protocol (JCA 105–7). It gave him some difficulty as he assumed that it referred to the panelling round the walls of a room. He worried for a little about what *bare to the wainscot* meant as he assumed that the cupboard would have a back. But very quickly he decided that it did not much matter whether the cupboard had a back or was fixed directly on to the wall as the important part of the meaning of the expression was that the cupboard was completely empty. It is apparent from this that readers do not just infer word meaning from context; they also decide whether the amount of meaning they have deduced is specific or detailed enough (see section 4.5.1 (viii)).

(b) *INFERENCING FACTS FROM THE MEANING OF LEXICAL ITEMS*
An obvious example of this is the phrase *as usual* in *You can give, as usual, a clear account of how you came into possession of the object?* The inference (see appendix 1, text-line 21), clearly, is that Markheim has given such accounts in the past and so by impli- cation is a long-standing customer. In this particular case the inference is strengthened in speech act terms because of the declarative structure of the question. It follows that the dealer is sure that he knows the answer to the question he is asking. This inference is confirmed when he goes on to suggest what the account might be – *Still your uncle's cabinet?*

(c) *INFERENCES VIA GRICEAN IMPLICATURE*
The effect of the declarative-structured question above is presum- ably explicable *via* a mechanism like Grice's (1975) Maxim of Manner. In normal circumstances speakers are expected to avoid obscurity and be as direct as possible. Since it is more direct to ask questions by using interrogatives, it is inferrable that the dealer is not asking a question but demonstrating his knowledge of Markheim, for a reason which might not yet be clear in the narrative. It follows that the breaking of other Gricean maxims can give rise to inferences on the part of the reader. We will not

give examples of each maxim, but it should be obvious that part of the complex ironic meaning of *Still your uncle's cabinet? A remarkable collection, sir!* comes from applying the Maxim of Relation (see appendix 1, text-line 23). Both readers first infer, *via* this maxim, that the reason for Markheim's uncle being a remarkable collector is that his cabinet must have contained a large number of items. The further, ironic, meaning is then deduced by deciding that Markheim has brought too many things for them to have come from one source. A special case of the Maxim of Relation to which we return in section 4.5.3 (v) below, is that of the relation between some linguistic utterance and some action (see appendix 1, text-lines 3–4 and 8–10). In written texts actions are also, and necessarily, conveyed through language.

(d) *INFERENCES FROM SPEECH ACTS*

A clear example of this would be if a character at the beginning of a text issues a command to some other character. The reader can infer from the set of felicity conditions for the speech act that the character must be in a position to issue the command. Thus it is possible, as long as the speech act can be identified with certainty, to deduce social relations between the characters (see Short 1981). A somewhat more difficult example in the data is when the dealer tells Markheim that he will have to pay for disturbing him on Christmas Day. MHS (51) comments on the dealer's lack of politeness in saying this, but JCA does not refer to it. There is no easy speech act label for this kind of action, but it could be called 'charging'. Part of the felicity conditions for 'charging' would appear to be that the utterer must have provided some goods or service. He must also be capable of extracting the fee. Hence the dealer would appear to think that he is in a position of some supremacy over Markheim, a possible reason for MHS's remarks about the dealer being 'on top' (MHS 65–6).

(e) *INFERENCES FROM DISCOURSE STRUCTURE*

A clear example of this category can be seen in appendix 1, text-line 1. *Yes* cannot be discourse-initial, and so the fact that it comes at the beginning of this text allows the reader to infer that the story starts in the middle of an interchange between Markheim and the dealer (MHS 2–4; JCA 21–3).

(f) *INFERENCES AS A RESULT OF PARALLELISM*

A good example of this is appendix 1, text-lines 27–8. Items turning up in parallel constructions are often conceived by the reader as invitations to code them as being semantically related in one of two ways – as quasi-synonyms or quasi-antonyms (see Leech 1966b & 1969). In this case Markheim's pity is seen as contrasting with his horror, in spite of the fact that *contempt* is more likely to be given as an opposite to *pity* in English.

(g) *INFERENCES AS A RESULT OF LINGUISTIC CHOICE*

The most obvious kind of example in this category is that where a speaker chooses one word rather than another. In appendix 1, text-line 1, we note the interest that both readers had in the dealer's choice of *our* instead of the unmarked *my*. The markedness is obvious here because the choice of terms comes from within a closed system. Another example is the use of the phrase *the thing* (appendix 1, text-line 37). This is more interesting as the noun chosen is not from a closed set. Both readers assumed that Markheim could easily and normally have used some more specific locution (e.g. *I neglected to buy something yesterday*) to indicate that he had not carried out an action he should have. In the context of phrases like *so small a matter* this vagueness is interpreted (MHS 131–3; JCA 174–6) as Markheim being offhand, or playing down the importance of the present. Another example is MHS's remarks (MHS 77–82) over the dealer's use of *the object*. He assumes (wrongly, it turns out) that Markheim has something to sell which the dealer can see. He therefore perceives *the object* as being too vague in the circumstances and goes on to interpret this as evasiveness, a significance very similar to that arrived at for the vagueness of *the thing* mentioned above.

(h) *INFERENCES BASED ON THE FACT THAT THE AUTHOR BOTHERS TO MENTION SOMETHING AT ALL*

The clearest example of this category is in appendix 1, text-line 24, *gold spectacles*. It is clear that the adjective *gold* is a non-limiting adjective, and is therefore not needed to disambiguate some reference to an object being described in the situation. As a result, both readers interpreted the presence of the adjective as an attempt on the part of the narrator to tell them something about the wearer (MHS 92–7; JCA 245–52). Given the obvious associations for *gold*, they both infer that he is wealthy. It would seem, then, that readers assume, for each situation that is being described, some baseline of essential information. Other information is perceived as additional in some way and therefore has to be ascribed to some authorial intention. This baseline would appear to be very difficult to tie down formally. Nevertheless, further support for its existence is provided by the fact that both readers also make reference to the spectacles themselves. MHS perceives them as indicating that the author wants the reader to see the dealer as defenceless and as an archetypal man in a shop ('dealer-ishness'). JCA interprets the spectacles as indicating 'bookishness'.

(v) INFERENCE FROM A COMBINATION OF BASES

As with any set of categories this prospective taxonomy has the problem of items which appear to sit on the borderline or share features from more than one category. For example, the infer-ences over the word *Markheim* could be seen as involving both real-world and linguistic knowledge; we have assumed that real-world knowledge can include some very general linguistic infor-mation. However, we reserve this category for clear cases where inferences are made as a result of correlating matter from different informational bases. Appendix 1, text-lines 3–4 is a good example, where a character's actions and words have to be related in order to infer that the dealer is indicating to Markheim that he knows that he is dishonest. The agreement noticed in appendix 1, text-line 11 involves relating linguistic, situational and kinesic knowledge in order to understand the significance of the dealer's chuckle.

4.5.4 Inference versus assumptions

So far we have talked about inferences which are felt by readers to be important for the understanding of the text in front of them. We also noticed, in our discussion of linguistic inferencing, that the level of specification at which readers infer appears in some way to be related to the textual purposes which they feel to be at work. Another aspect of this phenomenon would appear to be the inferences which one *could* make but which one is unlikely to. An example of this would be that the two characters are dressed. This inference could easily be made by using real-world knowledge. In fact information of this kind appears to be so basic that to talk of inferring or deducing it seems over-powerful. Instead, we will call this kind of implied knowledge part of our *assumptions* about a text. Unless the text is markedly unusual (e.g. a science-fiction story) the reader assumes that basic general facts about his world pertain. He typically enters into a process of inference when an item in the external text is foregrounded in some way and therefore becomes noticed. If the item can be fitted in some patterned way into the internal text it becomes textually salient. An interesting example of this in the data, because it is marginal, is the fact that the dealer is described as *little*. JCA notices the dealer's smallness and tries to understand it, presumably because it seems marked as a result of being mentioned at all – '*The little pale, round shouldered dealer* . . . Why is he standing on tip-toe? Because he's short? Because he's looking over the counter?' (JCA 149–51). He then forgets about it, and so it becomes an example of what is referred to above in section 4.5.1 (vii) and (viii) as a question which is raised in the reader's mind, only to be forgotten unless it becomes salient at some later stage. MHS, on the other hand (MHS 92–6, 190–4), sees the smallness of the dealer as one of a series of contrasts which the author is trying to build up between the two characters, tall *vs* short, young *vs* old, virtuous *vs* dishonest, etc. He thus infers that Markheim is tall, and an unspecified assumption, namely that the dealer and Markheim are of some size or other, becomes specified and so potentially salient. Both readers ponder over the inclusion of the word. But then, because one reader thinks he sees a pattern, it becomes salient for him, whereas the other, not perceiving such a pattern, stores the information just in case it turns out to be relevant later.

4.6 CONCLUSION

This discussion of inferences and assumptions brings us back full circle in that inferencing in relation to pattern is one example of the large-scale strategies which readers engage in. To summarize, it is possible to characterize the process of both readers as being the creation of an internal, ongoing text, the establishment of a general picture, to which details and further general elements are added as the reader progresses through the text. However, this additive process is mediated by a monitoring one where the reader tests the internal text for its fit with the external one. Inferencing is an important part of the reading process. In order to facilitate further research in this area we have attempted to describe and categorize the kinds of inferencing that readers engage in. The categories that we have set up here are, of course, open to discussion and rearrangement. It is likely that there are alternative modes of categorization and more examples of kinds of inference than the ones we have noted. Very similar remarks also apply to our description of the general reading process. In order for work in this field to become more ordered and systematic it will be necessary to set up a working taxonomy based on observations of what happens when people read. The work described here is inadequate in that it only deals with one text and the reactions of two informants. However, given the admitted inadequacies in our experimental design and the difficulties involved in verbal introspection as a way of gaining information about reading processes, we feel that the measure of our agreement over what to comment on, what the relevant meaning was and how that meaning was arrived at indicates that the text plays a considerable role in limiting the meanings that readers create.

An important aspect not fully covered in this study is the amount and kind of disagreement between the readers. Any complete account of text interpretation will have to consider the nature and sources(s) of disagreements among readers, the proportion of agreement and disagreement, and how to weight the importance of these conflicting tendencies in arriving at judgements over whether two or more 'interpretations' count as equivalent. It is only when questions such as these have been resolved that proper consideration can be given to the issue of competing interpretations and the status of mis-interpretation.

APPENDIX 1 – AGREEMENTS IN THE PROTOCOLS

There is some difficulty as to what exactly counts as an agreement or a disagreement as the readers used different lexical characterizations in coming to their conclusions. Some of these ambiguities were resolved in discussion of the protocols.

Text-line

Line 0
Markheim – the name of a person or place, which is quickly resolved to be a person. General knowledge of the world allows two obvious possibilities (there are others, which both readers chose to ignore). The ambiguity is resolved when Markheim turns up as subject to a verb of movement at the beginning of paragraph 2 (line 6). Both readers are also agreed that the name was German, presumably because of its ending.

Line 1
Yes. Indicates that the story starts in the middle of a conversation. This is a result of linguistic knowledge, what readers know about the function of *yes* in discourse. It is usually an agreement response or a mechanism for continuing talking. It cannot be the very first element in an interchange.

Line 1
Our windfalls. Both readers chose to comment on *our* presumably because it is *marked* in terms of the correlation between linguistic form and situation. The dealer is an individual, and so the unmarked pronoun would be *my.* The two readers then arrived at different reasons for the oddity. JCA saw it as a politeness marker (JCA 21) and MHS thought that the dealer was being grandiose ('the royal we') or that he was indicating that he was a representative of a group of people (MHS 157–8). This disagreement was not resolved within the text portion.

Lines 3–4
'Some are dishonest', and here he held up the candle so that the light fell strongly on his visitor. Both readers agreed that at this point the dealer was indicating that he knows Markheim is dishonest. Both comment on the dealer's action with the candle at this point, and so the inference appears to come *via* a correlation between what the dealer says and what he does. MHS also

notes that the use of *here* makes the fact of correlation more noticeable (MHS 16–20). JCA makes a connection between light and suspicion falling on Markheim (JCA 35–7).

Line 5   MHS (163) and JCA (197) both note that the 'virtue' that the dealer ascribes to himself is of an ironic kind.

Lines 8–10   *At these pointed words, and before the near presence of the flame, he blinked and looked aside.* Markheim is shown to feel guilty at this point. The possible reasons for inferring this are various. It could be because the text says that he blinked at the words as well as at the light. From this the readers can infer that the author wants them to know that Markheim has correlated word and action under 3–4 above in much the same way as JCA and MHS. It might also be because Markheim looks aside as, in kinesic terms, dishonesty is often correlated with the refusal to make eye-to-eye contact.

Line 11   *The dealer chuckled.* Both readers chose to comment on the fact that the dealer chuckled, and MHS explicitly interprets it as evidence of the fact that the dealer feels he has some kind of hold over Markheim (MHS 45–7). JCA sees the chuckling as an indication that the dealer knows of Markheim's feeling of guilt (JCA 48–50). These remarks look like different versions of the same thing. The inferencing appears to be based on knowledge of kinesics correlated with situation.

Line 21   *As usual.* Both readers noted that this indicated that Markheim was a long-standing customer of the dealer. MHS also noted that this information is deducible in other ways: e.g. the fact that Markheim disturbs the dealer on Christmas Day (MHS 74–6). JCA deduced the same information from a combination of Markheim knowing that the dealer is alone and his saying *I remark in you today* (JCA 59–64).

Lines 23–4   *Still your uncle's cabinet? A remarkable collector, sir!* Both readers took this to mean that Markheim had sold a number of things to the dealer before, claiming his uncle's collection as source. It was also apparent that the dealer did not believe the explanation and was indicating his disbelief. Both assumed that Markheim had brought in so many things that it was not reasonable to believe that they all came from the same source. Both also commented on the fact that the dealer says this with a note of irony. This confirms that the dealer means something different from what he apparently says.

Line 26   *Gold spectacles.* Both readers commented on the spectacles as indicating the wealth of the dealer. There is no obvious reason why the possession of such spectacles should indicate wealth. Instead MHS and JCA were reacting to the fact that the author bothered to put in the adjective. It is non-limiting and therefore unnecessary in a 'basic' description of the dealer's action at this point. They thus inferred an intention on the part of the author. It was the fact that gold was *mentioned*, especially given the situational frame, that was deemed significant. It brings to the fore a piece of knowledge which might be considered to be deducible from general background knowledge (dealers have to have money in order to be able to buy things) but which would not necessarily be considered significant. Mention of the word *spectacles* becomes noticeable in the same way, and JCA and MHS infer different but similar meanings from its occurrence – 'bookishness' and 'dealerishness' (JCA 251–2; MHS 96–7).

Lines 27–8   *Markheim returned his gaze with one of infinite pity and a touch of horror*. Both readers considered this sentence significant, JCA returning to it after some time because his attempt at explanation for it was not satisfactory to him (JCA 152 ff.). The sentence is foregrounded by the parallelism in the reduced coordinated phrases. This makes the reader notice that horror and pity are roughly opposed. Both readers set up reasons for the horror and the pity, but do not come to hard and fast conclusions. This therefore looks like an example of something which readers will be looking for later in the text.

Lines 11 & 33–7   The fact that Markheim comes to buy the present on Christmas Day is noted by both readers as being odd and therefore as needing explanation at some point later in the story (MHS 45–7, 151–3; JCA 53–4, 117–24, 222–4).

Line 37   *The thing*. Both notice this because it is marked for its vagueness (cf. also MHS's comments over *the object* (MHS 77–9). JCA sees it as self-deprecation. MHS relates it to the fact that Markheim is playing down the object's importance. These look like closely related if not identical interpretations.

General   Both readers indicate that the text is not modern. This has to do with situational information (e.g. the candle as opposed to electric light) and also with linguistic information, in particular the presence of lexical items which might now be considered too formal to turn up in the contexts that they do (e.g. *regarded, wainscot*) and slightly archaic constructions (e.g. *had but just entered*). JCA (7) attributes a Dickensian flavour to the passage on these grounds, and MHS places it as late nineteenth or early twentieth century (MHS 55–7).

APPENDIX 2 – THINGS NOT MENTIONED IN ONE OR BOTH OF THE PROTOCOLS BUT WHICH THE READERS AGREED UPON WHEN THEY DISCUSSED THEM

(i) Both readers agreed that Markheim was probably young, although they deduced the information in different ways, from the fact that he has an uncle, from the fact that he is buying a present for a lady (though note that neither of these are *necessary* inferences), and perhaps from a desire to contrast the two characters (the gold spectacles probably identifying the dealer as older).

(ii) Both readers agreed that they were intended to sympathize with Markheim, rather than the dealer, in spite of the fact that he appears to be involved in shady dealing. The bases for this were various. He is named, whereas the dealer is never given a name and is therefore distanced from the reader. The reader is given direct authorial information about Markheim's inner feelings, but he does not get such information about the dealer. This suggests two patterns of contrast for which the reader will be scanning the later portions of the text – Markheim *vs* the dealer and Markheim's apparent shadiness *vs* the reader's sympathy for him.

(iii) The fact that Markheim's speech is prepared indicates that he is probably not telling the truth. People do not prepare speeches unless it is important that they get what they want to say exactly right. Given the frame of shady dealing, both readers infer that Markheim is keeping the truth from the dealer.

(iv) *Changing to his usual business voice* (line 20) presupposes that when the dealer was talking before, he was not talking in his business voice, but a more informal, friendly one.

(v) *At these pointed words* (line 8) refers back to the dealer's direct speech because of the use of *words*. But *these pointed* indicates that it is the latter portion of the speech which is being referred to – because *these* indicates a relation to some of the words which are 'nearer' than others and because it is only the latter part of the speech which can be characterized as pointed.

(vi) *'This time'*, *said he* (line 29). The *he* refers to Markheim because of the inversion of *he* and *said*. This indicates that tonic placement would have to be on *he* as it normally occurs on the last lexically significant word in a tone group. This makes *he* contrastive, from which the reader can infer that the speaker has changed. The information within the accompanying direct speech then confirms this inference.

(vii) *A remarkable collector, sir!* (lines 23–4). Both readers agreed that this was said in an ironic manner, as well as the preceding speech, which is described as having a note of irony. The exclamation mark shows that the speech must be phonetically marked in some way. An obvious assumption is that it is uttered in an ironic tone. Both readers also agreed that as *collector* is assumed information in the discourse, the tonic would have to fall on *remarkable* and thus be in an unusual position in the tone group. The combination of these features indicates that the tonic itself would be marked in some way, probably by having a wide pitch range, as this is one obvious way of making the sentence sound ironic. In any case, *remarkable* is, by definition, marked.

APPENDIX 3 – LIST OF THE QUESTIONS THE READERS ASKED, WITH COMMENTS

JCA 20 'Why does he say *Our windfalls?* OUR windfalls? I mean, is this a sort of reference to "My windfalls" – he's just being polite?'

Our is presumably unexpected. (*My* would be unmarked, because there is only one speaker, at this point.) The reference to *my* suggests JCA recognizes this markedness. Note how he then produces a possible answer but does not follow it up: 'What are the consequences of a dealer being polite? Is this plausible?' JCA leaves this open, yet there is no evidence that the notion of politeness or formality is part of his ongoing internal text.

JCA 29 'Customers are buying because they don't know the true value of things? Then they will pay less.'

Here JCA is assuming that customers *buy*, and thus finds a discrepancy between his internal text and plausible interpretations of the external text. He draws a conclusion from the question which leads to an absurdity: the *logical* deduction results in a contradictory relation between paying less and the dealer touching a dividend. Having monitored these 'inferences' JCA then rejects his account and comes up with interpretations of the dealer's activities which have him selling cheap goods as expensive ones. But as this interpretation itself does not fit comfortably with the prior assumption, JCA is forced to modify his internal text (JCA 40): 'Maybe it's people selling him stuff.'

JCA 39   'If people are dishonest, how does he profit by his virtue if people who buy his stuff are dishonest. No, maybe it's people, selling him stuff.'

JCA detects a contradiction between the assumption that customers buy – this assumption must come from everyday experience with what goes on in shops – and what the dealer has been perceived to be saying; i.e. it does not make sense to see a dealer profiting by having dishonest buyers. JCA then answers the contradiction by questioning and changing the original assumption to fit the external text. This customer is selling. The contradiction is still not resolved to JCA's satisfaction; but rather than continue to wrestle with it, he reads on, perhaps expecting that the text will resolve the dilemma. Note that later he returns to this point (JCA 41 and particularly 71 ff. See also JCA 133–5 & 190–5 for an extensive glossing).

What is being questioned does not seem to be the reason for inclusion of a word, or odd detail, but possibly an unexpected action. Note that JCA is trying to relate what is being said to what he has understood so far.

JCA 54   'Why has he come on Christmas Day?'

JCA questions the reason for an action (rather than the author's reason for including the phrase). He notes a contradiction between expected behaviour – expected from cultural knowledge that shops are shut on Christmas Day – and Markheim's action. The dealer himself is commenting on this unusual behaviour, so JCA's comment is an echo of the text as well as a question about it. Note, moreover, that JCA does not at this point provide an answer overtly. He may have done so internally but did not report it, e.g. by saying that it must be an important errand, shady, urgent, etc. Evidence of this is suggested by JCA 222–4, where he comments that the *time* of Markheim's call suggests a shady deal.

However, later in the protocol (JCA 112 & particularly 117 ff.) JCA seems to show that he is aware that by coming on Christmas Day, Markheim has done something odd, which suggests an important errand. In JCA 136–7 the question recurs: 'But why he's buying the present on Christmas Day itself . . . , that's unusual.' Again, in JCA 222–4: 'So why should he come to see him on Christmas Day when normally he doesn't do business?' The puzzle remains unresolved, and it is the focus of more questions: 'What had he come here on Christmas Day to buy, and why this particular place? Is he going to demand credit or what?' (JCA 260) and 'I wonder what sort of thing he was going to buy and why he has come to disturb this guy on this particular day with it?' (JCA 268–70).

Obviously JCA is holding his question about reasons and motives in store, and seeking answers to what is for him a crucial point. Note that MHS does not ask questions at this point, but he does comment on the oddity: 'An unusual day to come' (MHS 45); 'we knew this already because he disturbs the dealer on Christmas Day?' (MHS 75–6). Most importantly (MHS 151 ff.): 'And it is Christmas Day, which is unusual and strange. So we still want to know why he has to buy on Christmas Day (and what he will buy and who he will give it to and why).'

Thus JCA and MHS agree on the oddness and importance of this piece of text: but indicate this in different ways: JCA by questions, MHS by statements.

JCA's later questions, especially JCA 222–4, spell out the assumption from cultural knowledge that shops are shut on Christmas Day. The later questions, especially JCA 259 ff., also incorporate new information; that is, information that was not available when the question was asked in JCA 54.

JCA 56   'The guy is balancing his books on Christmas Day? He had nothing better to do?'

This relates to the previous question on the oddity of certain behaviours on a day when one would not expect them; cultural expectations are violated, and are commented on and accounted for tentatively. A possible reason for the dealer's working on Christmas Day is simply that he had nothing else to do. Again, this reason is formed only tentatively, and not referred to again. However, he does later refer to the fact that the dealer is balancing his books (JCA 248–9), commenting that 'all he does on Christmas Day is . . .', which is reminiscent of the earlier question.

It is interesting to note that the comment in JCA 248–9 is made in connection with a suggestion that the dealer may be Jewish, which corresponds to MHS's comment (MHS 52–3) that it is odd 'that he is balancing his books on Christmas Day unless he is a Jew'. Once more, MHS's comment on oddness relates to JCA's question on the same point. There is also a suggestion that JCA (JCA 247–9) suspects that the reason for the dealer working on Christmas Day is his religion.

One further interesting point is that although MHS does not return to comment on the balancing of books, he *does* comment (MHS 171–2): '*Christmas Day.* Presumably the dealer deals from his house or lives over the shop.' This inference conceivably comes from noting the oddness of the dealer's activities on Christmas Day, and concluding that he must live close to the shop in order to be working there on such a day.

JCA 63   'What is this manner?'

JCA asks a question, presumably because the nature of the *manner* is hinted at in *a kind of manner* (line 16), but he does not provide his own answer to the question since it is answered by the next sentence. In JCA 228–9 JCA returns to this point, and shows that the manner has been interpreted as a sign of guilt.

JCA 93   'Why should Markheim pity him? Because he is just a clerk? Because he is a dealer, because he looks down on him, because he has to sell stuff off *and a touch of horror*?'

The amount of speculation at this point indicates that JCA thinks this to be an important point in the text. He does not decide on one answer, but continues, perhaps in the hope that the text will provide an answer. It does not, however, as is shown by JCA 152 ff.: 'There's a sentence I'm not too sure about yet. *Markheim returned his gaze with one of infinite pity and a touch of horror.* Pity for whom? For the dealer in his job? Having to deal with . . . buy and sell . . . filthy money, suggests aristocratic disdain. The *touch of horror.* Horror at what? Being at the mercy of such a person, in the hands of such a person? Maybe.'

JCA does not provide an answer to his question, but continues, accepting the uncertainty of not knowing the reason for an apparently significant mention of Markheim's emotions – the only one, in fact, apart from the guilt, which appears to be so significant. The possible reasons for the pity and horror that JCA has put forward in JCA 93–6 recur in the second set of questions. JCA has held on to them as plausible, or at least has not rejected them; they form part of his ongoing internal text. Presumably, however, because JCA still indicates doubt, they are available to be revised in the light of incoming external text.

MHS (MHS 202–3) explicitly asks the question: 'Does Markheim feel pity for the dealer because of the sort of man he is?' which echoes JCA's own speculations. He has previously also commented on the pity – although not at the point in the text where pity and horror are mentioned (MHS 107–11), but later (MHS 128–30): 'Presumably the pity was because the old man was not going to get what he wanted. No, because he will gain from the transaction anyway.' Clearly MHS has noted the emotions Markheim is apparently experiencing, and incorporated them into his internal text. This is particularly apparent in his summary at the end of the first reading (MHS 154–6): 'So the dealer may have some kind of advantage/hold over Markheim (yet Markheim pities him and why is still not clear) and we'll be looking for that to develop.' Note that MHS is commenting at this point on the reasons for Markheim's pity (but not his horror). He also appears to have noticed a conflict between that pity and the dominant position of the dealer, something JCA has not commented on because he has not created a picture of the dealer as being 'on top'.

In JCA 209–11, JCA makes a forward connection with *horror*: 'He is horrified at being in this guy's knowing clutches': i.e. JCA is trying to answer an unanswered question by reference to the 'story-line'. (This is based on empathy perhaps – how would the reader feel if *he* were in Markheim's place?)

JCA 97   '*He* must refer to Markheim. Why? Because he says *I have not come to sell but to buy.*'

The question here focuses on the anaphoric reference, but more interestingly on the issue of how JCA knows what he (thinks he) knows. This question has a monitoring function similar to the embedded question in JCA 179–81: 'Let me go through it again and see if I can work out how I know what I know.' JCA shows an awareness of his processing, in that he has made the correct assignment of referent but then steps back, as it were, to ask himself how he knows this. He is also conceivably checking that there is no ambiguity in the reference. It is unlikely that he would normally do this in undisturbed reading. Note that MHS comments at this point: 'Markheim speaks for the first time' (MHS 112–13).

JCA 115   'Why has he prepared a speech?'

Presumably the notion of preparing a speech strikes JCA as odd or unexpected. He assumes there must be a reason for the author mentioning this fact, and so wonders what that reason might be. He does not provide an answer. It could be that those questions to which he provides tentative answers are thereby marked as being more important than those where he simply reads on. However, in JCA 138–40 he comes back to the preparedness of the speech to infer that preparation may indicate premeditation or hidden motives: 'But he's got a prepared speech, one wonders why this is prepared? Is there something behind his apparent errand?' This is spelled out in JCA 263–6: 'He wouldn't normally prepare a speech in this situation. The fact that he has prepared a speech suggests that it is not going to be the truth.' Yet again, although the protocol did not show JCA answering his question, later evidence suggests that at some point he has developed an answer that is sufficiently plausible for his purposes. MHS, on the other hand, does not speculate about the reasons for Markheim's having prepared a speech, but merely notes that it has been prepared (MHS 137): 'he has worked out his speech beforehand'. Unlike JCA, he comments on how Markheim must have been delivering his speech up to this point. In other words, MHS revises the impression he has of Markheim's speech – his internal text – in the light of new information.

JCA 117   'Why is it a small matter?'

JCA is questioning the reason for the inclusion of certain words; since they have been included they must be assumed to be significant. JCA doubts Markheim's sincerity at this point ('not necessarily'), by relating what Markheim describes as a trivial affair to the fact that he has unusually appeared in the shop on Christmas Day. In other words, the question arises because JCA has detected an apparent incongruence between incoming and internal text. Later (JCA 176), he qualifies this as indicating 'self-deprecation', which presumably means that this is not really a small matter after all.

JCA 120   'I . . . What is he going on to say?'

JCA is speculating on what might come next. It is interesting that he predicts an answer to an implicit question; namely, 'Why didn't he buy the present yesterday?'

The questions that follow relate to second or subsequent readings and might therefore be regarded as somewhat different from those above. Most of the questions that JCA asked are contained in the above discussions, as they relate to previously raised issues. What follows concerns new information.

JCA 150–1   'Why is he standing on tip-toe? Because he's short? Because he's looking over the counter?'

This question must be taken to refer to the significance of the author's mention of this physical fact. It is not clear what the second tentative reason refers to. However, it is clear that JCA does not reach a conclusion. Indeed, he does not refer to the question again. MHS also only comments on *tiptoe* in his second reading. In this case (MHS 190–2) MHS deduces from the fact that the dealer has to stand on tiptoe that 'Markheim is bigger than the dealer. Not described as little, does not have to stand on tiptoe.' That is, he infers from the absence of a description of Markheim the opposite of what is said about the dealer.

JCA 167 '*I would add to IT than otherwise* [sic]: cabinet, not the Stock Exchange. Well, why? Because you don't add to Stock Exchanges.'

This question indicates monitoring taking place – JCA asking himself how he knows the anaphoric referent (cf. the question in JCA 98). The answer comes from JCA's knowledge of the world, and arguably his knowledge of the meaning of *Stock Exchange*.

JCA 172 '*My errand today is simplicity itself.* Why should that be particularly simple?'

JCA does not suggest an answer, but the question itself casts doubt on the truth of Markheim's utterance, in the same way as did the question in JCA 117.

JCA 201 '*Mingled shine and darkness.* Darkness because it's not lit? Because it's in contrast with the daylight.'

JCA answers his own question, presumably to his own satisfaction as this issue does not recur. He may have arrived at the answer through noting the implicit contrast between the streets and the shop, and therefore daylight and darkness; or, conceivably, he rejected the 'not lit' interpretation as being inconsistent with the (internalized) fact that the dealer has a candle and therefore the shop *is* lit. MHS also comments extensively on this point, without questioning: 'daylight . . . contrasts with the dark of the shop (might, up till now, have assumed both were light). *Mingled shine and darkness* is vaguely poetic. The light in the shop comes partly from outside and partly from the candle (so pretty dark inside). Possible symbolic meaning? Markheim coming from the light (=good) to the darkness of the shop (=bad)' (MHS 29 ff.).

JCA 212 'Why does he chuckle? *The dealer chuckled.* Presumably at Markheim's blinking painfully and looking aside, recognition of his guilt. Now he shows that later on, doesn't he? Erm Ah. *When a customer cannot look me in the eye, he has to pay for it.* Right. That's why he chuckled.

JCA speculates on the reason for an action, and hypothesizes an interpretation based on the text – that is, he makes connections across the text based on the assumption that the chuckling is at

Markheim's recognition of guilt. He then actively seeks to confirm the hypothesis by finding a section of the text he vaguely remembers. However, he still has not made the connection explicit even though it has satisfied him. Presumably the argumentation goes like this: Markheim cannot look the dealer in the eye. When this happens the customer pays for it. Customers pay for being dishonest. Not being able to look somebody in the eye is therefore a sign of dishonesty (which JCA knows anyway from his knowledge of the language and his experience of guilty people). Thus the dealer is chuckling at (in anticipation of) the fact that Markheim will have to pay. MHS's reading is similar: 'dealer chuckles and so is on top and happy with the situation in spite of being disturbed on Christmas Day' (MHS 45–7) and 'The dealer chuckled. Back to chuckled – repetition. Dealer on top' (MHS 65–6). MHS laconically relates the chuckling directly to the dealer's superior position, whereas JCA does this more circuitously through anticipation of payment and recognition of guilt. MHS comments explicitly on the fact that the author has repeated a phrase, showing an awareness of the linguistic structuring of the text.

JCA 244   'Round shouldered? What does that suggest? Stooping over money-bags? Looking over the top of his gold spectacles. Why gold spectacles? Why should this guy be wearing them? What image is conjured up by this? Little, pale? Jewish? Round shouldered, hook-nosed?

JCA wonders why the author included certain modifiers and not others, and tries to determine the associations that such descriptions are intended to evoke, or do evoke. What seems to be going on here is a conscious process of association: 'Spectacles suggests bookish, gold suggests wealthy, looking over the top of them suggests they are for reading' (JCA 251–3). Thus JCA provides answers to his own questions to create a picture of the dealer, and in particular his character, that fits the internal text he has created about him. Indeed, JCA ends his description with: 'OK, not a very sympathetic character.' MHS engages in the same sort of free association over precisely these items, without explicitly asking himself questions: 'Spectacles – dealerishness, wealth (gold) – defenceless' (MHS 96).

JCA 288   'Why does he have a candle in the shop during the
daytime? OK, well he wouldn't switch the lights on
because there's no electricity. Didn't exist in those days.
He has a candle rather than oil lamps. That suggests it
is temporary light, that he has been disturbed, because
he is not normally open. Would it be normal: candlelight in there? Why candle?'

Even here JCA is relating the part of the text in question to his
ongoing internal text – to his notion of the time the events took
place, to the fact that the dealer is not working as normal, that
it is Christmas Day, and so on. Moreover, he relates one piece
of information to another piece of perceivedly relevant information; he does not relate it to the dealer's spectacles or size, for
example. These last questions relate to a detail that JCA recognizes
is probably unimportant, and so he quickly desists from trying
to provide an answer. There would appear to be a law of diminishing returns in operation over the number of questions one can
usefully ask, certainly explicitly. It is as if there is a need to
suspend questioning and simply hold the information mentioned
in the text in store, in case it proves to be significant (see JCA
304–19).

FIVE

Speech presentations in fiction with reference to *The Tiger Moth* by H. E. Bates

Tom Hutchinson

5.1 INTRODUCTION

How to represent speech in a medium that is not speech: this is
the fundamental problem of speech presentation in fiction, and
the means that authors have used to represent speech have been
the subject of much debate.

The reason for the problem is easy to understand if we
consider some of the constraints that the written medium imposes
on the spoken word. Speech in fiction has after all to be
represented using the same means as all other parts of the novel
or short story, such as descriptions of scenes or narrative. And
yet there are a number of features of speech which cannot be
directly expressed in writing. The written medium can, for
example, show only crudely such features as intonation, stress
and tone and the other paralinguistic features which accompany
speech – gesture, facial expression and eye contact (see e.g.
Brown and Yule 1983: Ch. 1). Similarly the hesitations, false starts
and dialect idiosyncracies of natural speech would soon become
tiresome for the reader if fully presented. The Negro speech in
Gone with the Wind, for example, makes for very slow reading, and
Shaw soon abandons the attempt to give a phonetic rendering of
Eliza Doolittle's Cockney in *Pygmalion*. These are extreme examples, but the basic principle holds true for all speech presentation.
Whereas the ear is very competent in filtering out the anomalies
of speech, the eyes are far less tolerant. Any representation of
speech in fiction, therefore, is necessarily idealized for the sake
of reading fluency. Indeed, so strong is this concept of idealization in the written mode that the use of features which deviate
from the written norm are seen as being marked for some
particular purpose (Leech and Short 1981: Ch. 5).

It is, then, not difficult to see why the question of speech presentations in fiction has attracted so much debate. This debate has mostly centred around the question of how varieties of speech presentation can be usefully classified and described. In this paper, however, I wish to take a different perspective and to look at how the variety of speech forms can be exploited by the author to create particular effects. While recognizing the need for some kind of classificatory framework of speech types, the aim of this paper is to show how the author's use of the variety of speech presentations contributes to the total communicative effect of the novel, or, in this case, short story.

The analysis is based on *The Tiger Moth*, a short story by H. E. Bates. (All quotations are from *The Tiger Moth*, unless indicated otherwise. Page references refer to the Penguin 1974 edition.)

5.2 A FRAMEWORK FOR ANALYSIS

McHale (1978) provides a very thorough review of the various attempts that have been made to classify speech presentations. He outlines first of all, the traditional syntax-based system of three categories: Direct Speech (DS), Indirect Speech (IS) and Free Indirect Speech (FIS). These can be identified, as follows:

DS: This presents the actual words spoken. The speech is marked off from the rest of the text by quotation marks or some similar device. Usually there is an introductory verb of saying, unless it is obvious from the context who is speaking.

IS: Indirect speech does not present the actual words spoken, but a report of them. A number of features can be identified by which IS is generally characterized:

(i) Quotation marks are removed and the speech clause becomes syntactically dependent on the reporting clause. This dependence may be made more overt by the use of *that*.

(ii) Personal and possessive adjectives and pronouns change from first- or second-person to third-person. This is not a defining feature of all IS. Leech and Short (1981) point out that it is only a feature of third-person narrative – the commonest form of IS.

(iii)   When the reporting verb is in the past tense, the verb tenses in the speech clauses are backshifted (e.g. present becomes past).

(iv)   Deictic elements are 'distanced', e.g. *here* becomes *there*, *now* becomes *then*.

(v)   Direct questions take statement word order.

(vi)   Direct imperatives become statements introduced by *that* or infinitive nominal clauses.

(vii) Certain features, such as interjections, are suppressed.

FIS: Free Indirect Speech combines some of the features of IS and DS. Generally it retains the back-shifting of verbs and the shift of person, but the remaining five characteristics of IS noted above seem to be completely optional. FIS can as a result appear very close to the DS form or to the IS form, depending on which features of the original DS are retained, e.g.

> As for himself he spoke a lot of the future. Did she know what he longed for more than anything? Two things.

> (p. 115)

This example has the backshifted verbs and third-person pronouns associated with IS, but it keeps the interrogative word order and the incomplete syntax (*Two things.*) of DS.

FDS: To the three-category system outlined so far, we might add the fourth category of Free Direct Speech (FDS). In FDS the actual words spoken are presented but they are not marked off by quotation marks from the remainder of the text e.g.

> 'More like a dream.'
> No, no, he insisted, a miracle.
> (p. 116)

The problem with this traditional system lies with the two Indirect Speech categories. They have been felt by some authors to be too broad. As McHale comments with regard to FIS, 'its range of formal possibilities is extremely large' (ibid.). The degree and nature of indirectness can vary considerably. IS and FIS as a result have to serve for a spectrum of speech presentations which extends from a literal transposition of the actual words spoken to a summary hardly distinguishable from the narrative. Attempts have consequently been made to construct more precise and revealing categories.

Hernadi (1971) sets aside the syntax-based categories in favour of one based on 'categories of literary representation'. This produces seven categories on a scale running from diegetic summary to Free Direct Discourse.

Page (1973) similarly sets up a system in which he identifies eight categories based on the permutation of four variables:

(i)   whether there is an introductory verb of saying;
(ii) whether the subordinate clause is in the past tense;
(iii) whether the lexical features of the speech are represented as neutral, i.e. 'undifferentiated with regard to the individual speaker' (ibid.) or idiosyncratic;
(iv) whether the phonological qualities of the original speech are indicated.

With these variables Page establishes the eight categories of Direct, Submerged, Indirect, Parallel Indirect, Coloured Indirect, Free Indirect, Free Direct and Slipping (from Indirect to Direct in mid-utterance). Having established the categories, however, Page sounds a note of caution:

> In the whole question of forms of speech presentation, indeed, what is encountered is not so much a set of rigid categories, each with its own exclusive and unmistakeable identifying features, as a merging of one form with another and with narrative style (ibid.).

Unfortunately, even the categorization that Page sets out is difficult to apply in practice. Let us look in more detail at the finer distinctions introduced by the Submerged, Parallel Indirect, Coloured Indirect and Slipping.

(a) 'Slipping' is a useful concept, since it frees us from the boundaries imposed by the sentence. Bates makes use of this strategy to move from one form of speech presentation to another in mid-sentence, as we can see in the following examples:

> 'Far away?' she said and he said yes, he was far away.
> (p. 107)

The fireplace of the cottage sitting-room was filled with pine cones. She murmured something about gathering them in the woods on her way home from school and should she light the fire?

(p. 113)

In the first of these two extracts, Bates slips from DS to FDS in order to provide a contrast between the two speakers. In the second example, he slips from the narrative through IS to FIS: *should she light the fire?*

These two examples illustrate two important features about Slipping. Firstly, there is no need to restrict it to Slipping from IS to DS. It can, as we have seen, be used to move through the various forms of speech presentation. Secondly, and more importantly, Slipping cannot really be regarded as a category. It is rather a *strategy* which enables the author to move from one category to another within a sentence.

(b) To illustrate the Submerged category in his classification Page takes a sentence from Dickens and gives examples of how each of the speech types would express it:

'There are some happy creeturs,' Mrs Gamp observed, 'as time runs back'ards with and you are one, Mrs Mould.' (DS)

The Submerged form of the quotation Page gives as:

Mrs Gamp complimented Mrs Mould on her youthful appearance.
(Submerged)

This contrasts with the Indirect form which would be:

Mrs Gamp observed that some fortunate people, of whom Mrs Mould was one, seem to be unaffected by time. (IS)

Page's description of the Submerged form, to distinguish it from the Indirect form is: 'This [i.e. the Submerged version] indicates that speech has taken place but retains none of the idiosyncracies of the original: lexically it is formal and literary; grammatically it is beyond reproach; and there is no implication of non-standard speech.' (ibid., my brackets)

But this description probably fits the Indirect version equally well. Neither form is particularly faithful to the original: *unaffected by time* is as much an interpretation of the DS phrase *as time runs back'ards with* as the so-called Submerged expression, *youthful.* How far does the Indirect form have to differ from the DS to become Submerged? It is difficult to see how one can distinguish the two varieties consistently.

Having said this, however, there does seem to be a need for a category which is so far removed from the actual words spoken as to almost merge into the narrative. Leech and Short (1981) propose a category which they call a 'narrative report of a speech act' (NRSA). NRSAs 'merely report that a speech act (or number of speech acts) has occurred, but . . . the narrator does not have to commit himself entirely to giving the sense of what was said, let alone the form of words in which they were uttered' (ibid.). The following are examples of NRSA:

> As for himself he spoke a lot of the future.
> (p. 115)

> In a long night of passionate farewell he again spoke a great deal of boats and apple blossom.
> (p. 116)

The second example illustrates the fuzzy edges of the NRSA category. It gives more detail about the actual content of the conversation than the first example and seems by the end of the sentence to be slipping towards IS.

Both Page's Submerged and Leech and Short's NRSA illustrate the need for a category which, so to speak, marks the boundary between speech presentation and narrative. NRSA is based on the communicative function of the speech presentation rather than the distance from the original DS, as Page's Submerged category is. NRSA, therefore, seems to be a more useful means of identifying the category.

(c) Page's remaining categories – Parallel Indirect and Coloured Indirect – prove, however, to be rather less useful. These categories represent attempts to come to terms with the problem noted in section 5.1 of representing features of dialect and idiolect. In the versions of the sentence from Dickens above the Parallel form would retain the non- standard lexical features of Mrs Gamp's speech; the Coloured category would include in addition the orthographic representation of the dialect. This raises two issues.

Firstly, it seems to imply that there is some special significance attached to dialectal and phonological forms. But if we are to isolate Coloured and Parallel versions of Indirect Speech why not also of Direct Speech, which is, as we have noted above, also usually idealized?

Secondly, such a categorization assumes the possibility (and indeed the usefulness) of distinguishing standard from non-standard speech. But this is no simple matter, as the following passage from *The Tiger Moth* illustrates:

> Well, *it wouldn't be long* now. *A matter of a few months*, he thought. The invasion *had gone pretty well* so far and *for the life of him* he didn't see how the Germans could last another winter. We were *giving them hell* with the bombing too.
>
> (p. 116)

Are the five italicized expressions standard or non-standard? They are not unusual expressions in spoken English; they are not marked as any particular slang, jargon or dialect. But presumably they do represent the class and regional dialect of the speaker. This speech also presumably represents the accent of the character: with standard spellings, we assume he is a speaker of a form fairly close to Received Pronunciation.

Since this example represents the actual expressions used and by default the character's accent, this is Coloured Indirect Speech. But as the accent is unmarked it could be Parallel, or as the expressions are not strikingly idiosyncratic it could be just Free Indirect. In other words, all speech must represent a dialect, idiolect and accent of some sort, so there can be no neutral forms against which the Coloured and Parallel forms can be matched. The categories of Coloured and Parallel speech, therefore, seem to be relevant only to works involving speakers of non-standard English.

While recognizing that the traditional categories of IS and FIS cover a very wide range of content, attempts to produce a more precise terminology have, with the exception of the addition of the NRSA category, not succeeded in producing a useful system.

This inevitably leads us to ask why it should be so difficult to define more precise categories. The answer probably lies in the fact that descriptions of speech presentations have implicitly operated from the starting point of the actual words spoken. In other words, the various forms are seen as some kind of linguistic 'transformation' of the original DS. But in what sense are they transformations? If we pursue the concept of transformation, we will find that it can be a misleading basis from which to operate.

The first problem with the concept of transformation is highlighted by McHale (1978). He observes that 'in fiction . . . there is no direct "original" prior to or behind an instance of IS or FIS; the supposedly "derived" utterances are not versions of anything, but are themselves the "originals"'. In fiction, in other words, the DS form of an IS or FIS never existed. We obviously cannot take this argument too far. We must necessarily look to the DS form as a reference point. But McHale's observation sounds a note of caution about the explanatory potential of viewing speech presentations as some kind of transformation of a spoken original.

A second attack on the concept of transformation can be made from the point of view of syntax. This is an important consideration given the fact that IS is traditionally described largely in terms of syntactic transformations from DS (see above p. 121). But Banfield (1973) uses Transformational Generative principles to illustrate very convincingly that syntactic transformations cannot account for many of the significant features of IS. Examples of DS from *The Tiger Moth* will illustrate some of the points she makes.

(a) Some verbs can only be used with DS, e.g.

'Will you have it with milk,' she called, 'or black?'
(p. 113)

A simple transformation would give us the deviant sentence: 'She called whether he would have it with milk or black.' A correct rendering in IS requires a fuller explanation of the activity of the verb, e.g. 'She called out to see whether he would have his coffee with milk or black.'

(b) Grammatical rules cannot convert expressions used in spoken language into a written register, e.g.

'By the way,' he said, 'you haven't told me your name.'

(p. 108)

He said by the way she hadn't told him her name.

(c) The grammar alone cannot generate elements which were not present in the original speech, e.g.

'Sounds pretty dull though. Still, fun and gossip in the common room I've no doubt.'

(p. 107)

What form would be needed to express this indirectly?

He said it sounded pretty dull but he had no doubt
(there must be   )
(there would be   )
(there was   ) fun and gossip . . .
(she could listen to)
(she could join in   )
(etc.   )

These examples all require the transformational rules to supply elements which are not presented in the original DS form. Such elements could only be derived from the context in which the original speech occurred.

(d) The syntax-based description, restricted as it is to the level of the sentence, cannot account for meanings conveyed at the level of discourse, e.g.

In the mile drive to the cottage a pool actually formed in the lap of the mackintosh. He apologised and she said:
'I suppose you wouldn't care to come in for coffee?'
With icy brevity he merely said, 'Thank you.'

(pp. 112–13)

The woman's utterance, although it has statement word order, is in fact a question. In the spoken form the intonation would indicate this. The illocutionary force of the utterance is an offer. The man's reply is an acceptance of this offer. A straightforward grammatical transformation to IS would produce:

> He apologized and she said that she supposed he wouldn't care to go in for coffee. With icy brevity he merely thanked her.

The woman's statement has now lost its interrogative form and can no longer be construed as an offer (that is unless one wishes to argue that grammatical rules can account for changing intonation into lexical features). The statement now comes across as an observation on his willingness to go in for coffee. In which case his thanking her is nonsense.

It is thus not enough to make a series of syntactic transformations to produce coherent discourse. The reporter must interpret the DS utterances in such a way as to maintain the meaning conveyed by the original discourse structure.

In this example the whole exchange must be reformulated in order to capture the *meanings* as well as the *forms* of the original. This might produce something like this:

> He apologized and she asked him tentatively whether he would like to go in for coffee. With icy brevity he accepted her invitation.

Syntactic transformation, then, does not provide a very sound basis for understanding variation in speech presentations. As we have seen, it cannot properly handle factors which relate to meaning. This is not to say that syntactic transformations are unimportant. Quite clearly there are distinct patterns that can be observed, such as the back-shifting of verbs. But these are best seen as the surface realizations of a much deeper change. They are symptoms of a transformation rather than the essence of the transformation itself.

From both a literary and a syntactic point of view, then, the concept of transformation from the DS form provides a shaky basis for observing and explaining speech presentations. And yet, surely the whole nature of speech presentations is based on the fact of some speech having taken place, or at least of creating the illusion that this is so. How can we realistically explain the nature of speech presentations without the initial premise of an actual or fictional communicative event?

One way in which we might come to terms with this paradox is to look at speech presentations not so much in terms of transformation of language, but rather in terms of the transformation of the relationship between author, characters and reader. In other words we should look not at the forms of the speech itself but rather address ourselves more to the question of why the author at any particular point chooses a particular way of representing the characters' thoughts or words to the reader. This approach may help to get closer to the real dynamic of speech presentations, which lies not in the forms of the words themselves but in the purpose behind the author's choice of those particular forms. In the next section we shall look at this explanation in greater detail.

5.3 THE AUTHOR'S PURPOSE AS A BASIS FOR VIEWING SPEECH PRESENTATIONS

An author has two purposes in choosing a particular form of speech presentation: the communicative purpose of the speech event and the stylistic purpose. The communicative purpose refers to the choice of linguistic features within the context of a particular utterance. It is concerned with the micro-level question: what information is the author trying to convey in this utterance? The stylistic purpose is concerned with the choice of a particular form of speech presentation in relation to the other utterances in the discourse. It is concerned with the macro-level of choice and answers the question: why has the author at this particular point in the discourse chosen this particular way of presenting speech?

These two levels of choice are, of course, interdependent, but for the purposes of analysis, it is convenient to consider them separately. We shall look first at the communicative purpose, as this provides a basis for an analysis of the stylistic purpose.

5.3.1 Communicative purpose

To understand the nature of speech presentations we need to see the novel or short story in terms of the triangular relationship between author, characters and reader (cf. Leech and Short 1981, 8.5). This relationship is manipulated by the author. In the example from *The Tiger Moth* below we shall see how the linguistic forms of the speech presentation are a result of the relationship the author creates.

In DS the author, though present, is apparently dissociated from what is said: the words are the characters' own. The relationships and references used in the speech of the characters will be those relevant to their own situation, e.g.

> Presently Mrs. Forbes said from behind the bar:
> 'Will you be staying to eat tonight, Mr. Williamson? I've got a little –'
> 'No, not tonight, Mrs. Forbes. I ate at the Mess. Thank you all the same.'
> 'I see. Would Mr. Thomas be coming in?'
> 'I'm afraid not. Mr. Thomas bought it yesterday.'
> 'Bought it? Bought what? Oh! I see – I'm terribly sorry.'
>
> (pp. 110–11)

(i) The author and reader are not considered in the references used by the characters. They refer to themselves as *I* and to each other as *you*. The time references operate from the time of speaking. This applies to the adverbs *tonight* and *yesterday* as well as to the verb tenses. The place reference is similarly fixed to the location of the characters at the time of speaking. The implicit inference of *Will you be staying?* and *Would Mr Thomas be coming in?* is 'here'.

(ii) Personal relationships are treated in the same way. Both characters know who Mr Thomas is and know that the other knows who he is. The name, therefore, requires no explanation. The identification of Mr Thomas is the polite form appropriate to the relationship between Messrs Williamson and Thomas on the one hand and Mrs Forbes on the other. Williamson knows Mr Thomas as *Maxie*, but this name is not appropriate to the situation in which the person is being discussed.

(iii) Williamson's interruption of Mrs Forbes's utterance is shown simply by the fact that she stops in mid-sentence.

In DS the narrator tries to give the impression of simply relaying what was said. Thus the references are those of the world of the characters. As readers we are made to believe that our world does not impinge upon the nature or content of the speech. This is quite clearly not the reality, since we must use our real-world knowledge to understand what the characters say and the author must take account of that state of knowledge. Nevertheless, the illusion is created that no such concessions to the readers' knowledge are made by the characters directly. We are meant to feel as no more than eavesdroppers on the dialogue.

In IS, by contrast, narrator and reader influence what is said directly. The reader is no longer given direct access to the world of the characters, but instead receives a report. Being for the benefit of the reader, this report must be cast in terms which will enable the reader to understand what happened. It must, therefore, take account of the reader's reference situation *vis-à-vis* the speech situation. We can see what effect this has if we re-cast the passage above in IS.

> Presently Mrs. Forbes, who was behind the bar, asked him whether he would be staying to eat. She was just saying what she had to offer, when he interrupted her to say that he had already eaten at the Mess. He thanked her all the same. She then asked whether his friend, Mr. Thomas, would be coming in, but he replied that unfortunately Mr. Thomas had 'bought it' the day before. At first Mrs. Forbes didn't understand what he meant by the expression 'bought it'. When she suddenly realised what he meant she was a bit embarassed and she said she was very sorry to hear it.

Even a short passage like this may require a substantial amount of paraphrase and explanation from the narrator. It is not enough just to operate certain formal shifts: the whole speech event must be re-cast to take account of the reference situation of the reader:

(a) Although Mrs Forbes calls the man Mr Williamson, he is known to the readers as *he*; the pronoun is therefore sufficient in the IS form. Indeed, if 'Mr Williamson' was used, it would appear as being marked for some reason. In contrast Mr Thomas is only known as *Mr. Thomas*, so this form is retained. In a later passage of IS in the actual story, he is referred to as *Maxie*, the readers having meanwhile come to know him as such: 'His mind went back to the first meeting with her, his impression of an innocuous, moth-like quietness, and then the second, his almost suicidal bitterness about Maxie . . .' Personal references, therefore, are expressed in terms of the relationship with the characters which the author has created for the readers; the references will change as this relationship develops.

(b) Mrs Forbes' questions are re-formulated as statements in the IS passage, because the roles of addressor and addressee have changed. In DS the interrogative form signals to the addressee (Williamson) that the addressor (Mrs Forbes) requires certain information. In the reporting situation, however, the roles have changed; the addressor is now the narrator, and the addressee is the reader. The reported question is not trying to elicit information from the new addressee (the reader), but is reporting the fact that Mrs Forbes wanted some information from Williamson. In other words it is a statement about a speech act. The appropriate form for the IS situation, therefore, is a statement. Its orginal interrogative force is described in the introductory verb: 'she asked him whether . . .'.

(c) Just as the question form is inappropriate for the IS situation so too are the emotive elements of DS. Emotions felt by the original speaker are not those of the speaker in the reported form. Emotive elements, therefore, must be re-formulated as the narrator's interpretation of what feelings the expressions represent. Thus the expression *Oh, I see* cannot simply be represented as: 'Oh, she saw'. It has to be reformulated in order to capture the emotion of sudden and slightly embarrassing realization.

(d) The time and place references in the passage cannot be dealt with by a simple 'distancing' rule. The expression *tonight* (or 'that evening' as it would become) is quite redundant in the IS form. The meaning is clear without it. By a distancing rule, also, the word *come* in *Would Mr. Thomas be coming in?* should be changed to 'go'. This would, however, change the meaning, implying that Mr Thomas was going somewhere other than Mrs Forbes' bar. *Come* must, therefore, be retained (or a longer paraphrase used).

(e) There are several points in the extract where the author must make explicit the meanings conveyed by the discourse structure of the DS. When Williamson interrupts Mrs Forbes and, as noted in (c), when Mrs Forbes fails to understand the expression *bought it*, the author must explain what happens.

Direct and Indirect Speech, then, are not just different realizations of the same utterance. They fulfil different functions. DS conveys the actual words spoken. IS is a report for the benefit of another who has no access to the actual interaction (whether real or imagined). The forms chosen for IS will be those appropriate to fulfilling this function and will, therefore, vary according to what the narrator considers appropriate to the field of reference available to the reader.

But what of FIS? How are we to account for this? We have seen that the nature of DS and IS are characterized by the different reference systems within which they operate. But this is not a clear-cut distinction. By its very nature a report operates between two worlds. Whereas DS operates solely within the world of the characters, IS does NOT. But how far it is distanced from that world is a variable which the author can manipulate to suit particular purposes. Thus FIS forms can draw on the reference systems of the two worlds to produce a variety of permutations.

Speech presentations, then, are best understood in terms of the author's communicative purpose. How the author chooses to show what the characters say will lead to choices as to which reference system the speech presentation operates within.

On this basis it is possible to identify only four meaningful categories of speech presentation:

(i) Direct Speech: easily identifiable because it is marked off by punctuation.

(ii) Free Direct Speech: this is like DS in that the terms of reference are those of the character. But the speech has no graphological marking. The reader has to infer from other signals whether this represents the exact words spoken or not.

(iii) Free Indirect Speech: the basic reference framework is that of the reporting situation: the verbs are usually backshifted and the pronouns take the third-person form. But into this basic framework may be inserted time, place and personal references taken from the characters' world. This enables the author to utilize the advantages of the reporting form, but at the same time to allow the voice of the character to come across, e.g.:

'Far away?' she said *and he said yes, he was far away.* (my italics)
(p. 107)

(iv) Indirect Speech: in the full indirect form both the structure and the references are those relevant to the reporting situation. There is no attempt to disguise the presence of the author.

To these four categories of speech presentation we can add the NRSA (Leech and Short 1981) category, which acts as a bridge between speech presentation and narrative. This, then, provides a scale of five categories for the analysis of speech presentations.

Of these five categories only the DS form can be regarded as a discrete, readily identifiable type. The other varieties form a cline (Jones 1968) ranging from FDS to narrative, with each type merging into the next. With so many features involved – time and place references, personal relationships, emotive expressions, etc. – there are obviously many possible permutations available to the author.

The crucial element in defining speech types is thus the degree of authorial involvement; the surface realization of this is the field of reference employed. Categories of speech presentation based on this factor offer the most constructive basis for the analysis of speech presentations in fiction.

5.3.2 *Stylistic purpose*

Setting up a system of categories of speech presentations is an essential prerequisite to analysing a literary text, but the ultimate purpose of a framework of categories is to reveal how the author uses the variety of forms to create particular effects. We have seen that the author will have a communicative purpose in the use of a particular language form. He will choose those forms which are meaningful and appropriate in the chosen context. But we need to look also at the question of why any particular variety of speech presentation should be chosen in the first place. Why in short should DS be preferred to FIS or IS or FDS in any given situation? For the answer to this we need to look at the wider context, to what we might call the author's stylistic purpose, i.e. the use of particular forms or a mixture of forms to create stylistic effects and so contribute to the overall communicative force of the work. In the following analysis we shall see how H. E. Bates uses the variety of speech presentations to achieve certain effects.

In *The Tiger Moth* Bates uses permutations of DS, IS, FDS, FIS and NRSA forms for the following purposes:

(a)   summarizing;
(b)   blending;
(c)   contrasting;
(d)   distancing;
(e)   taking a viewpoint.

(a) Summarizing

One of the greatest advantages of reported speech is its ability
to summarize – to distil the essence of what was communicated
from the mass of the actual conversation. But, in summarizing,
the presence of the narrator may be too obvious, the liveliness
of the actual speech can be suppressed and the character's own
voice lost. Bates remedies this by employing FIS: the narrator's
voice is masked by that of the character, as these two examples
show:

> (i) As for himself he spoke a lot of the future. Did she know what
> he longed for more than anything? Two things. He wanted to grow
> apples and buy himself a boat. Somewhere in the West Country.
> Something like thirty or forty acres. The boat a twenty-five footer.
> There was no sight in the world like an apple orchard in full blossom
> and no feeling like that you got when you saw a sail at full stretch
> in a good wind.
> 'No feeling? Not even with me?'
> It was something like the same thing, he said. The curve of a sail
> or an apple always reminded him of the curve of a woman's breasts.
> 'Does that explain Adam and Eve or why men hanker after
> possessing boats?'
> Could be, he said. But what did she feel? About the apples and
> sailing, he meant. It didn't sound too impossibly dull for words?
> 'On the contrary.'
>
> (p. 115)
>
> (ii) Driving back east Williamson could only repeat, over and over
> again:
> 'It's a bloody miracle. It's a bloody miracle.'
> 'More like a dream.'
> He loved her for saying that, he said. Well, it wouldn't be long
> now. A matter of a few months, he thought. The invasion had gone
> pretty well so far and for the life of him he didn't see how the
> Germans could last another winter. We were giving them hell with
> the bombing too.
> 'I'll be able to give up teaching. That'll be a relief.'

How she'd brightened up his war, he said. God, he could hardly wait for the peace.

(p. 116)

These paragraphs summarize long and intermittent conversations: in the first example it is a summary of many different conversations over a period of two months; in the second, it encompasses only one conversation, but one lasting the several hours of a journey from the West Country to Norfolk.

The tense and pronoun systems indicate that what Williamson says is not being given *verbatim*; but the references and forms are those the character might use in DS. Thus we find elements which in true IS would be altered:

(a)   Interrogative word order:

Did she know what he longed for more than anything? (p. 115)

But what did she feel? (p. 115)

(b)   Exclamations:

God, he could hardly wait for the peace. (p. 116)

How she'd brightened up his war, he said. (p. 116)

(c)   In complete syntax:

He wanted to grow apples and buy himself a boat.
Somewhere in the West Country. Something like thirty or forty acres. The boat a twenty-five footer. (p. 115)

(d)   Present time references:

Well, it wouldn't be long now. (p. 116)

The invasion had gone pretty well so far. (p. 116)

(e)   Colloquial expressions:

. . . and for the life of him he didn't see how . . . (p. 116)

We were giving them hell with the bombing, too. (p. 116)

FIS, then, enables Bates to summarize the main points of the speech but still keep up the effect of actual conversation; this is heightened by the use of DS for the woman's role.

The second passage above is ambiguous in that it is not clear whether this is a representation of his actual speech or of his thoughts. The significance of this will be discussed below.

Bates uses the summarizing capacity of FIS on several occasions. One striking example is when Williamson first tells the woman about Maxie:

> Tensely, gloomily, he went on to try to enlighten her lack of understanding. Very bad type, Maxie. Whistled most of the time when not on ops. For ever unfaithful to the popsies. Born liar. Occupations: seduction, alpine-climbing and collecting shells. Cashed dud cheques, borrowed money right, left and centre. None returned.
> 'Devious character.'
> 'I loved the bastard.' He laughed briefly, his voice brittle.
>
> (p. 111)

Using the impersonal framework reminiscent of an official cord form combined with the references derived from Williamson's friendship with another pilot, Bates not only summarizes the conversation, but also produces an effect of bitter irony on Williamson's part. The FIS highlights the contrast between the death of just another airman, as represented by the terse list of phrases, and the death of Williamson's friend, as represented by Williamson's own voice – *ops, dud cheques, right, left and centre, popsies.*

(b) Blending

We noted above the fact that the categories of speech presentation are not discrete. This factor creates the second important feature of IS, which is its ability to blend into the narrative, by the selection of features more closely associated with DS or with the indirect forms. Bates uses this ability of the indirect forms to blend into the narrative as a means of 'fading' from one scene to another, or as a way of directing the focus of the reader's attention.

narrative
The fireplace of the cottage sitting-room was filled

NRSA
with pine cones.| She murmured something about gathering
(IS)
them in the woods on her way home from school| and should
FIS   (FDS)
she light the fire?| It would be more cheerful.|
   'Let me light it.'
        DS
'I'll start the coffee. There are lots more pine cones. They burn well.'|
(p. 113)

The scene begins with straight narrative. It then moves into what looks as if it will be NRSA, but as the sentence progresses more detail is added, so that it slips into a form which could be an IS version of what she actually said. From IS it moves to FIS and then to a sentence (*It would be more cheerful*) which could be either FIS or FDS and concludes in clear DS. The effect of this progression is almost cinematographic in the way that it introduces the reader to the scene as gradually as Williamson himself is introduced. On first entering the room his mind would be taking in many aspects; he then focuses on the fire and the cones, and tunes in to what the woman is saying.

We might note also that we are quite clearly seeing these scenes through Williamson's eyes. Thus the progression of speech forms also serves to identify the reader with Williamson's viewpoint (see below).

The fading technique is used for similar effect in Williamson's later conversation with the farmer's wife about the purchase of the farm:

narrative
In due course he got a week-end's leave. They drove to the West Country, staying for two nights at a farmhouse as man and wife. Apples still glowed crimson in the October orchards. There was good rough cider to drink and home-cured bacon and home-baked bread for breakfast. The farmer had injured his spine in a fall from a hay-rick that summer and hobbled about on two sticks.| He
(IS)
seemed unlikely ever to work again, so that now the wife made a few pennies by taking in guests.
        DS   narrative
'Ever think of selling the farm?'| Williamson said.|
           FIS
   It wasn't a question of thinking, the wife said. If things didn't improve they'd have to.

'They say if you want a thing passionately enough you'll get it in the end. You name the price and I'll pay you a ten per cent deposit. The war won't last more than a few more months and the deposit'll keep you going that far.'

DS

'We'll talk it over and let you know in the morning.'

(pp. 115–16)

The wife's part in this conversation goes through a progression of forms. The passage begins with narrative, but then starts to change into what could be an IS version of what the wife actually said (*He seemed unlikely ever to work again, so that now the wife made a few pennies by taking in guests.*) The expression *made a few pennies* suggests the wife's own voice. Her next contribution is in FIS (*It wasn't a question of thinking, the wife said. If things didn't improve they'd have to.*) The past tense and third-person pronouns indicate that it is indirect, but the colloquial expression (*a question of thinking*) and the elliptical form (*have to*) suggest the wife's own words. Finally the wife moves into DS (*'We'll talk it over and let you know in the morning.'*)

Thus the speech of the wife emerges from the narrative, becoming more and more personalized and concluding in a direct statement. In the same way we might imagine that the subject of selling the farm would have emerged from casual conversation, gradually formulated itself, becoming the focus of the conversation and concluding in a specific offer by Williamson and a specific reply by the wife.

In a later example the technique is employed to fade into a crucial interchange:

NRSA

In a long night of passionate farewell he again spoke a

(IS)

great deal of boats and apple blossom.| She wouldn't let

FIS

him down? God, he knew he kept on saying it – but it was all a miracle.|

DS

'More like a dream.'

FDS

No, no, he insisted, a miracle.

(p. 116)

Here the pattern again begins with narrative. It then moves to NRSA, which, as before, starts to slip into a kind of IS. We are not given Williamson's actual words, but the items *boats and apple blossom* refer us back to the previous conversation about these matters. Bates, so to speak, makes us imagine what Williamson probably said. The next sentence is in FIS, which with the FDS form of Williamson's next utterance provides the background to the woman's DS statement.

This complex 'fade-in and fade-out' sequence highlights the one line of DS (*More like a dream*). This, the woman's only contribution to the whole sequence, is a *verbatim* repetition of a previous remark. It is thus doubly emphasized; the point being, of course, that dreams don't come true.

(c) Contrast

We have seen in the last extract how the use of different forms of speech presentation enables the author not only to blend a series of utterances into a connected sequence, but also to contrast one utterance with another. Bates makes extensive use of FIS to provide contrasts between speakers. The only patterns of conversation in this story are DS–DS as in normal conversation and DS–FIS (several examples of the latter have already been quoted and others can be seen in the later extracts). As McHale (1978) remarks: 'The reader is more likely to interpret a sentence as FIS when it appears in the immediate neighbourhood of DS or IS sentences'. Thus having two patterns available enables Bates to highlight certain passages which are important for the story.

A good example of the use of a DS–FIS contrast is in the sequence where the woman's cottage is discussed:

> She rested her fork on the edge of her plate and he noticed for the first time that she was wearing no wedding ring. He immediately changed the subject.
> 'Are you in one of the services?' he said.
> No, she said, she was teaching literature and history in St. Anne's High School for Girls. They had been evacuated from London to a mansion called Clifton Court. Did he know it?
> 'I see it from the air. Sounds pretty dull though. Still, fun and gossip in the common-room I've no doubt.'

No, she was free of all that, she said, thank God. She'd managed to buy a small cottage of her own.
'Sounds cosy. Perhaps I might invite myself over some time?'
'The garden's a mass of weeds.'
This enigmatic answer of hers had the effect of changing his interest into a certain excitement.

(p. 107)

In this sequence Bates sets up a pattern of DS for Williamson and FIS for the woman (see (d) below). But the final exchange breaks this regularity and we get the internally deviant DS sentence: 'The garden's a mass of weeds.' This deviation highlights the statement; the garden's weediness comes up again in the final scene as the background for Williamson's disillusionment. This answer both produces his desire for the woman and sets the scene for his losing her. It also gives the impression that it is the one utterance of the whole conversation which sticks as a *verbatim* imprint in Williamson's mind. A similar effect is created by the '*More like a dream*' utterance discussed above. This highlighting is achieved through the contrast of the speech forms.

(d) Distancing

The term 'distancing' is often employed when referring to indirect forms; the reader is, so to speak, set at a distance from what was actually said and receives only a report from the narrator. In the last extract Bates creates this effect of 'distance' with the use of FIS for the woman. In the interchange Williamson is the one making all the running; the woman by contrast is more cautious, Williamson's DS therefore expresses the directness of his role in the conversation. It is clear, in other words, what he is trying to achieve. Her aims and motives, by contrast, are not obvious. The FIS helps to create the air of uncertainty. The sudden change to DS in the woman's final remark can thus be seen as suddenly removing the uncertainty from Williamson's mind. The following example of a DS–FIS conversation creates similar effects. The woman's conversation is set in FIS to produce the effect of 'seeing her with a distant rosiness'.

. . . three glasses of wine had already given his vision some haziness and he now found himself looking at her rather as he had looked at the field of oats, seeing her with a distant rosiness.

'Cottage far away?'
About a mile down the road, she said.
'What about running you home? I've got a gallon of juice in the old banger.'
Well, she said, she wasn't sure about that –
'Don't tell me you're shy.'
Not exactly, she said, but she supposed it would sound stiffish or something if she said it was all so sudden?
'It has to be. Tomorrow night I'll most likely be on duty. And perhaps the night after that. Sorry if it sounds like the old line.'

(p. 108)

In a later passage Bates again creates a distancing effect through the use of FIS for the woman's utterances, but this time in order to report a piece of speech, in which the time-reference is non-specific:

Thereafter, for the remaining two months of summer, except when operations made it impossible, he saw her night after night and sometimes in the afternoons. She was, she told him once, particularly addicted to things of an amorous sort in the afternoons. It was odd, but somehow it gave her a lovely feeling of guilt. That made it all the more exciting.

(p. 115)

The time (*once*) being unspecified, it would be incongruous to report the specific words she used. Yet, at the same time, a full IS form would destroy the sensuousness of the woman's remarks. The FIS form fulfils both requirements.

(e) Establishing a viewpoint

The discussion so far has been concerned largely with the local effects which Bates achieves. There is also an overall strategy in his use of speech types, by which he manipulates the reader's view of the characters.

From the very first sentence the story is seen from Williamson's point of view. There are several passages (many already quoted) which represent his thoughts, but we never see into the woman's mind. The reader has no more idea of what she is thinking than Williamson does, and she remains always distant. The strength of this effect can be seen in the language of this analysis. It may have been noticed that although the woman's name is used quite early on in the story, I have referred to her consistently as *the woman*. Using her name seems too intimate somehow: we never get to know her well enough.

Bates helps to create this effect by his selective use of indirect forms. The selection, however, is very complex, since, as we have seen, he uses both direct and indirect forms for both Williamson and the woman. But they are used in a different way for the two characters.

The IS forms used for Williamson's contributions are blended into the narrative of the story, with the result that it is not always clear whether we are reading part of the narrative, Williamson's speech or his thoughts. The following passage illustrates this ambiguity:

> Then at last came a day when he was obliged to tell her that his squadron was moving. He couldn't tell her where, of course, but only that he had just one more day.
> In a long night of passionate farewell he again spoke a great deal of boats and apple blossom. She wouldn't let him down? God, he knew he kept on saying it – but it was all a miracle.
> 'More like a dream.'
> No, no, he insisted, a miracle. His mind went back to the first meeting with her, his impression of an innocuous, moth-like quietness, and then the second, his almost suicidal bitterness about Maxie and then his final discovery that the moth, if it were moth at all, was at least, in its flaming affections, a tiger moth.
>
> (p. 116)

Does the first paragraph of this extract represent Williamson's thoughts? Is it narrative? Or is it an FIS representation of what he said to the woman? Bates seems to be making the distinction deliberately obscure with the result that Williamson's speech and thoughts are integrated into the narrative. The effect is to make us see the story through Williamson's eyes.

By contrast, the woman's thoughts are never represented. On the four occasions when FIS is used for her, it is made perfectly clear that it is her speech not her thoughts that are being represented, either by setting it in contrast to Williamson's DS in dialogue or by explicitly stating that it is speech (see the examples in (d) above). Beyond these four occasions, her speech is always in DS.

Thus by the application of the blending and contrasting strategies, Bates is able to create completely different effects with FIS forms for the two characters. The use of FIS forms blended into the narrative and often indistinguishable from thought for Williamson's part serves to identify the reader, through the narrator, with his point of view. We see the story through Williamson's eyes. The FIS for the woman's part by contrast serves to distance us from her. We, like Williamson, never know the truth of what she says.

5.4 CONCLUSION

I have argued in this paper that the soundest basis for categorizing speech presentations is the field of reference within which the utterances operate. This produces a spectrum of forms ranging from narrative through NRSA, IS and FIS to DS and FDS. The author can choose where along this range he wishes to pitch the representation of any specific piece of speech. He has, in fact, an extraordinarily large range of choice, because so many language features play a part in creating the spectrum. I have tried to show through the analysis of *The Tiger Moth* how the linguistic forms chosen depend in the first instance on the communicative purpose of the speech event and secondly on the stylistic effects that the author wishes to create. In so doing I hope to have shown the insights into speech presentations that can be gained from looking at how the author's choice of particular forms within their particular context contributes to the telling of the tale.

SIX

'Vers de Société': Towards some society

Graham Trengove

This essay is in part an interpretative account of Philip Larkin's poem 'Vers de Société' (its title grossly mistranslated, it would appear, as 'towards some society'). What may give it interest in the present context is that it was generated in seminar discussions at various courses for overseas teachers of English arranged by the British Council in the United Kingdom and abroad. The participants for the most part regarded themselves as professionally concerned with the teaching of language rather than literature. However acute and well-informed their personal interest in English literature may have been, the majority felt themselves obliged, by practical considerations of time and the linguistic competence of their students, to treat literary texts as at best peripheral or ancillary in their teaching. Nevertheless, when they were gradually led into a close linguistic examination of the poem, they found the experience an engrossing one, which rewarded them with an enhanced understanding of much more English than that employed in the poem itself, and which they were keen to share with their own students.

6.1 INTRODUCING VARIETIES OF ENGLISH

My ultimate but undeclared object in discussing the poem was to encourage the participants to re-open the question of what place literature might have in their own courses. My immediate and acknowledged aim was to get them to apply the consciousness of the varieties of English which was awakened or at least heightened by an earlier part of the course they were attending. That languages are not uniform and monolithic has been a commonplace notion amongst linguists for some time, long enough for particular instances of it to have been extensively treated in descriptive accounts (e.g. Crystal and Davy 1969; Leech 1966a), for introductory textbooks to have been devoted to it (e.g. O'Donnell and Todd 1980; Gregory and Carroll 1978) and also for syllabuses accommodating it to have been developed for language teachers both in Britain and abroad. Nevertheless there remain teachers in post overseas to whom the notion can profitably be introduced at summer schools and the like. Those attending the courses who were already familiar with it in principle were usually happy to extend their acquaintance with the diversity of English varieties.

What emerged as the most useful starting point for this activity was to look at the way modes of address are adjusted to take account of the relative age, authority, social standing, temper and so on of the parties to a conversation. This was so because participants from different countries immediately had comparative comments which they could contribute. Their practices in addressing colleagues, superiors, and students often varied considerably from those of British teachers, whose habits are anyway by no means uniform in this respect. Depending on the group, it was sometimes worthwhile examining Susan Ervin-Tripp's (1973) diagrammatic analysis of the systems of choice in mode of address for Americans and working towards the adjustments of the diagram necessary to account for British usage. Beginning at this point also allowed an early reminder (by contrasting *good morning* with *g'morning*) that phonology is a dimension of language which varies not only according to social and regional background, but also to the relative standing and conversational intentions of the participants. Again depending on the group, reference to research work on this topic, as for example that of Peter Trudgill (1974b), was sometimes thought appropriate. But what gave animation to the discussion was the immediately engaging practical application of the theory.

Thereafter we commonly discussed a wide range of varieties chosen to diverge as far as possible from discursive written and colloquial spoken English. These have included knitting patterns, notices in public parks, travel tickets, indexes to books, mail-order catalogues, newspaper small-ads for property and accommodation, sports and financial reports, holiday brochures, wedding invitations, and official forms requiring completion by applicants for sundry state benefits or documents. All these were examined through the prism of linguistics so that the participants' existing knowledge of the different levels on which language is organized could be used to identify the precise features which, in aggregate, identify a variety. The method employed may be briefly described as that of *Investigating English Style* (Crystal and Davy 1969) adapted and diluted to suit the oral exchanges of a seminar discussion. This worked well enough and to some degree they all emerged from the experience with an enhanced awareness of the intimate connexions between some varieties of English and the contexts in which they are characteristically employed, and which on occasions they actually create.

6.2 RECOGNIZING VARIETIES OF ENGLISH IN LITERATURE

However, despite their goodwill and their commitment to professional improvement, once we had got beyond the topic of modes of address they found that the exercise remained just that, an exercise. None of the varieties had any immediate relevance to their corporate presence in the seminar room, where they were neither knitting, replying to a wedding invitation, nor applying for a student grant. It seemed that it would be pedagogically useful to create a situation in which they would need to be aware or be made aware of some varieties if they were themselves to function appropriately. Asking them to engage in the creative process of reading a literary text, preferably a complete one, in which the meaning arose in part from the author's choice of particular varieties offered a means to this end.

So it was that we came to read 'Vers de Société' together, to create a meaning for the poem through discussion to and fro. This had ranged by the end over many disparate linguistic and cultural questions, which usually uncovered stimuli to meaning, but it was given a coherence additional to that provided by the poem itself by our constant reference to the notion of varieties of English. The poem was indeed chosen precisely because it offered points of entry from the immediately preceding instruction. The commentary on it which now follows faithfully reflects the content, if not the order, of the discussions.

Vers de Société

My wife and I have asked a crowd of craps
To come and waste their time and ours: perhaps
You'd care to join us? In a pig's arse, friend.
Day comes to an end.
[5]   The gas fire breathes, the trees are darkly swayed.
And so *Dear Warlock-Williams: I'm afraid –*

Funny how hard it is to be alone.
I could spend half my evenings, if I wanted,
Holding a glass of washing sherry, canted
[10]   Over to catch the drivel of some bitch
Who's read nothing but *Which*;
Just think of all the spare time that has flown

Straight into nothingness by being filled
With forks and faces, rather than repaid
[15]   Under a lamp, hearing the noise of wind,
And looking out to see the moon thinned
To an air-sharpened blade.
A life, and yet how sternly it's instilled

All solitude is selfish. No one now
[20]   Believes the hermit with his gown and dish
Talking to God (who's gone too); the big wish
Is to have people nice to you, which means
Doing it back somehow.
Virtue is social. Are, then, these routines

[25]   Playing at goodness, like going to church?
Something that bores us, something we don't do well
(Asking that ass about his fool research)
But try to feel, because, however crudely,
It shows us what should be?
[30]   Too subtle, that. Too decent, too. Oh hell,

Only the young can be alone freely.
The time is shorter now for company,
And sitting by a lamp more often brings
Not peace, but other things.
[35]   Beyond the light stand failure and remorse
Whispering *Dear Warlock-Williams: Why, of course –*
                    (reprinted from Larkin 1974: p. 35–6)

6.2.1 *The formulae of social discourse*

'Vers de Société' represents the thought processes of someone
who changes his mind about how he will respond to an invitation

to a sherry party or the like. The starting and finishing points of his internal debate are marked by the fragmentary presence of the formulae used for replying to invitations, which the participants in the seminars readily recognized. Italicized to demarcate the imagined reply, *'Dear Warlock-Williams: I'm afraid –* ' is sufficient indication that the persona's first thought is to decline the invitation politely. The familiarity of the pattern is such that it could only continue in some such fashion as 'I shall be unable to accept . . .'. Similarly, the revised response begun in the poem's last line, *'Dear Warlock-Williams: Why, of course –* ', could only continue 'I shall be delighted to join you . . .' or the like. The adoption of either formula itself argues a certain social background for its user, and on this basis we can begin to create the persona, the thinker of the thoughts which form the poem. He is evidently of the upper-middle class. Additional information is to be found in the mode of address employed. In these circumstances where the writer is clearly familiar with the addressee and intends at least outward politeness to him, the choice of surname without title indicates an upper-middle-class setting for the episode and suggests that the persona is relatively old, and certainly conservative in his linguistic habits. Appropriately for this setting, the addressee has a compound or 'double-barrelled' surname, a kind most frequently encountered, it is popularly believed, in the higher reaches of British society. (Noted in passing is *Warlock*, which occurs only rarely as a family name in Britain, though it does occur as a common, rather than a proper noun with the sense 'male witch'. This is probably a piece of playfulness in keeping with the genre of the poem.)

However, while our recognition of these formulae and the social clues they offer is essential to our understanding of the poem because they enable us to create the world of the poem, we are on first reading most immediately confronted with a challenge to our linguistic expectations. 'My wife and I have asked a few friends to spend the evening with us; perhaps you'd care to join us' is a likely style of invitation to an informal social gathering. Something close to this appears in the opening sentence, which is italicized to distinguish it, as an apparently quoted written text, from the thoughts which constitute most of the poem. However, someone has amended the customary phrases, introducing the offensive and collocationally intrusive *crowd of craps* and *waste their time and ours*. The first of these phrases is made even more markedly intrusive by the dense alliteration on velar stops, which here reinforces the note of biting contempt carried by the colloquialism. While it is not inconceivable that such an invitation might be sent in the real world for ironic purposes, within the created world of the poem it is better to regard these sardonic amendments as being the immediate, imagined response of the persona to some more conventionally worded letter. This reading is preferable because it does not require speculation about his correspondent and therefore maintains the focus on the persona. This early indication of his views on social gatherings is followed, in the standard lower case in which his musings are recorded, by the lively vulgarity of his imagined internal response, *In a pig's arse, friend*. This coarse suggestion that the persona would as soon meet his would-be hosts in that improbable venue as in their house is very much a piece of colloquial, slang English. It is so totally at variance with what the 'rules' of invitation giving and accepting allow that we perceive it as a measure of the violence of the persona's distaste for socializing.

The conventions of social communication used in the first stanza, whether by being observed or flouted, are placed in creative contrast with lines 4–5. These look more like traditional lyric poetry, partly because of the similarity of length and syntactic structure of the three sentences they contain. The topic also changes to one traditionally treated in lyric fashion, the sounds and movements of the close of day, which are suggestive of solitary reflection because we become conscious of them only when otherwise undistracted. The sentence *Day comes to an end* simply places the moment without comment, but the two sentences parallel with it suggest more than at first appears. *The gas fire*, a common comforter of private study in Britain, is said to breathe; because it is thus made the subject of a verb which normally has an animate subject, it is invested with a degree of independent life. *The trees are darkly swayed*. First we need to note that the word *darkly* is collocationally odd here because it does not commonly occur with verbs denoting movement. The *Oxford English Dictionary* offers as potential meanings for it 'in the dark', 'mysteriously', 'gloomily', or even 'ominously'. Perhaps some combination of these offers the best interpretation. But the structure in which the word is placed is itself a little odd too. While 'trees' and 'sway' form a familiar collocation in English, it is normally with 'tree' as subject of the intransitive verb 'sway', as 'the tree sways in the wind'. The use of the passive construction here suggests a corresponding active sentence in which *the trees* is the object of a transitive verb 'sway'. This opens the question of who, or what swayed the trees. Perhaps simply the wind? Perhaps something more? These speculative responses seem appropriate to what look at first sight simple sentences recording simple physical observations, and in making them the reader recognizes or creates a substantially different dimension for the persona's character from that which can be derived from the opening lines. It is this newly perceived dimension which accounts for (hence the phrase *and so*) the persona's willingness to conform to normal social conventions so far as to adopt the polite formula for declining the invitation.

6.2.2 *Colloquial and lyrical entangled*

The development of the second and third stanzas hinges similarly on a contrast between two kinds of English, this time between everyday colloquial English and, after line 15, what might again be called the lyrical. An informal conversational voice is established for the persona in *funny*, elliptical for 'it is funny' (that is, remarkable), and in the injunction *just think*. In this voice he presents a comically contemptuous picture of the kind of gathering he is declining to attend but to which he is all too frequently invited. He imagines himself at such a party. His glass, which it appears he prefers to hold rather than sip from, contains an inferior drink which he scornfully labels *washing sherry*. This expression the persona, or ultimately Larkin, has invented on the model of the more familiar phrase 'cooking sherry', which describes a cheap variety intended for culinary purposes but reputedly served by mean hosts; its implication for the drink so labelled is that it is fit only for washing dishes in. *Canted over* admirably captures the awkwardness of stance required of a tall man in order for him to listen to the conversation of a shorter, female fellow guest; commonly used of cranes and masts, it suggests tilting to the point of toppling. Particularly as that

conversation is limited to the topic of consumer goods, it is possible that 'cant' in the sense of meaningless chatter works as an
additional resonance at this point. If so, it may be triggered by
the word *drivel*. The primary sense of *drivel* in contemporary
English is 'foolish talk'; *catch* is regularly used in colloquial
English as synonymous with 'hear', as in 'I didn't quite catch
what you said'. But when we meet them in construction with
each other we are reminded of their literal, non-metaphoric
meanings, and are presented in consequence with the disconcerting image of a hand or glass held out to receive *the drivel*,
slaver or dribble, falling from the lips of the woman he dislikes.
Because dogs literally drivel, the word *bitch* is here no longer
merely a commonplace abusive term for a woman but a revital-
ized metaphor in which the perceived likeness of woman to
female dog is once again sharply disconcerting.

Another expression of his unfriendly view of these incursions
on his time is the metonym *forks and faces*. This takes two
disparate components from the sherry party scene, one inanimate, forks, one animate, faces, and by linking them syntactically
and alliteratively places them in an equivalence which can only
dehumanize the *faces* which stand metonymically for his
companions at parties. The phrase *forks and faces* is also linked
alliteratively to *filled*, to which verb it serves as object. In this
position it disappoints the expectations of plenitude and
completeness aroused by *filled* and left momentarily suspended
by the placing of the verb at the end of the line. It is *time* that
is thus *filled*. There is nothing unsurprising in this collocation, and
at first sight lines 12–13 seem to reflect the tired, unthinking
English of casual conversation. This is also echoed in the equally
familiar collocations 'spare time' and 'time flies'. But to combine
them thus runs counter to colloquial English; 'spare time flies' is
decidedly not a familiar phrase. The addition of a locative
expression 'straight into x' further upsets the expectations that
arise from our constant exposure to the spoken language. Finally,
having been led to consider as never before that time might fly
somewhere rather than just fly, we find disappointingly that that
somewhere is *nothingness*, and we are left with an increased
insight into the barrenness of social intercourse, at least as experienced by the persona. Our reading of the second stanza thus

depends on our ability to hear in the background a familiar variety of English and to recognize certain crucial amendments to it.

The colloquial gives way to the lyrical in line 15 in the description of his preferred use for spare time. He likes to sit alone, reading (*under a lamp*), and occasionally looking through his window at night, with leisure and silence enough to allow such a sensitive perception of the moon as his metaphor records. The vehicle here is a curved knife; its tenor is the waning and therefore thinly curved moon. A much used, frequently sharpened knife wears into a hollow curve. This simple metaphor is enriched by the additional metaphor in the epithet *air-sharpened*, a compound of the form agent noun and verb meaning that the blade is made keener by the air; the moon's image is clarified, made sharper in the visual sense, by that condition of the air characteristic of frosty nights, the absence from it of light-diffusing moisture. Responding to these metaphors, we are likely to feel sympathetic to the mode of life that encourages the quiet contemplation that engendered them. We can then more completely understand the persona's distaste for constant company.

Line 18 marks a return to conversational English. In the elliptical phrase *A life*, the persona acknowledges that such a mode of life is attractive. But the presence of the indefinite article *a* gives us pause, makes us aware that the ellipsis is reduced from 'It is a life of a kind', rather than 'This is the life for me.' It implies the existence of alternatives. This voicing of his inclination is less strident, more hesitant and apologetic than his earlier expressions of contempt for society have led us to expect. It strikes a defensive note in the face of the opinions that *All solitude is selfish* and *Virtue is social*. By now the italics indicate to us quite clearly that he is quoting words which do not necessarily reflect his own feelings. Both sentences are given the weight of maxims by their brevity. The first is also made to sound substantial by its being in effect the subject of the passive verb 'is instilled', which suggests that those who instil it are so much in the majority that they need not be identified. The word 'instilled' itself, particularly when modified by 'sternly', hints at an unremitting pressure to conform. The alliterative linking of *sternly it's instilled* and *solitude is selfish* adds to the syntactic coherence of these words and thus to the apparent authority of the message they carry.

Doing his best to resist the dictum, the persona recalls that those committed solitaries of the past, the hermits, with gown and bowl their sole possessions, symbolic of their humility and mendicancy, communed only with God; he recalls too that they no longer attract awe or admiration. Much hinges in line 21 on *too*. Its use here exemplifies the compression of statement constantly sought in poetry. In normal discourse 'too' occurs to make a 'cohesive tie' (Halliday and Hasan 1976: 3) drawing attention to the reiteration of an action overtly referred to in a preceding clause. We would not normally expect to hear 'God has gone too' unless an earlier clause had announced that someone else had already gone. Here, we are left to read by implication, founded on this feature of normal usage, that the decay of popular belief in the efficacy of hermits' practices has led to their disappearance from the scene. This is then linked to a more general decline in religious faith by the addition of the casually colloquial *who's gone too*. That this observation should be placed thus in a parenthesis, that it can be mentioned as an afterthought, itself constitutes an indirect and sardonic comment from the persona on the apparent unimportance to the world of the disappearance from it of God, or belief in God.

The historical awareness thus obliquely drawn on by the persona is then contrasted in the immediately following lines 21–3: *the big wish / Is to have people nice to you, which means / Doing it back somehow.* Here he offers an ironic preparatory gloss on the second of the italicized dicta. It is ironic because he couches it in the banal and undiscriminating vocabulary of the man-in-the-street attempting abstractions and generalizations. Once again the persona is seen to be peculiarly aware of language variation. He is especially so in the choice of *doing it back.* At first the phrase seems merely in keeping with *the big wish* and *nice*, but closer consideration of the way it is used in the real world reveals that it adds to the density of our picture of the speaker here. Because in the language of the common man it usually describes not the reciprocation of gifts or hospitality but rather of blows or a bad turn, it works here to suggest the sourness of the persona's distaste for the prevailing modern conceptions of social obligation.

In the penultimate stanza the persona asks himself if the

routine social gatherings exist just as opportunities for us to prac-
tise behaving in an ideal way which we, being imperfect, cannot
attain, though we may try. While recognizing this as a serious
philosophical question, we should not lose sight of its again being
cast in imprecise, all-purpose terms, *Something that bores us*. The
behaviour the question is asked about is exemplified in the yet
more colloquial *Asking that ass about his fool research*, expressive of
contempt rather than benign interest. In his elliptical responses
to his own questions, *Too subtle that*. *Too decent, too*, acknowl-
edging that acts of this kind cannot with honesty be thus favour-
ably explained, he maintains this colloquial note, as also in the
exasperated abandonment of this line of thought in the ejacu-
lation, *Oh hell*. Nevertheless, the more philosophical turn taken in
the development of the poem is reflected linguistically in the
several occurrences of the first-person plural pronoun with
generic reference.

In the final stanza, his rather different response to the prospect
of company clearly reveals him as more complicated than a
would-be solitary at odds with the age. Now it becomes apparent
that it is hard to be alone, not only because of the external social
pressures described in the second stanza, but also for internal
psychological reasons. In *Only the young can be alone freely*, the
line-end position gives *freely* a prominence which makes us look
for the most fitting of its range of potential meanings. That the
young can be alone 'readily, without constraint from external
agency or internal inhibition, by independent, individual choice'
(as one definition has it), and perhaps also 'generously' points to
a contrast between them and the persona. For the older man,
solitude brings instead unwelcome reflections on the passing of
time and his own inadequate use of it, from which company
offers him an escape. But, as the next line tells us, *Time is shorter
now for company*. Here we read *time* to refer, as in everyday usage,
to his crowded schedule, but then recognize, because *time* is
modified by the definite article, that it also refers to that part of
his own life-span remaining to him. The lyric note of the first and
third stanzas is re-introduced here, recognizable in the now-
familiar metonym for solitary study in *sitting by a lamp*, and also
in the absence of colloquialisms. Here, though, the tranquillity
that it formerly signified is disrupted by the presence of *failure and*

remorse, words which are foregrounded by the re-ordering of the sentence from the more usual 'failure and remorse stand beyond the light'. Here they are preceded by a verb which in non-figurative usage occurs most frequently with an animate subject, and by an adverbial construction which unambiguously refers to a physical location. This strongly predisposes us to see them as having some degree of animacy, that is to personify them. We find confirmation of this reading in their being also the subject of *Whispering*, which similarly requires an animate subject. All this underlines the importance these two emotions have in the final design of the poem. We see them as tempering the earlier vigorous denunciations of the social whirl, and investing with a new seriousness the moral and religious questions lightly, ironically or mockingly touched on in the later stanzas. Finally, in his spuriously enthusiastic acceptance of the invitation, the persona reluctantly acquiesces in his role as a social animal by adopting the linguistic formula appropriate to it.

6.2.3 The implications of the title

One last, or more properly first, language variety remains to be noted, that of the title (never to be overlooked in Larkin's work), and not simply because it is in French. Translated at sight by someone more competent than was envisaged at the beginning of this essay, it appears to mean 'social verse' or 'verse about society'. The appropriateness of this to what follows is plain. However, *vers de société* also serves as a term of English literary criticism, denoting a category of light verse which usually considers aspects of conventional social relationships. Frederick Locker-Lampson, the editor of an early anthology of the genre, said that it

> should be short, graceful, refined, and fanciful, not seldom distinguished by chastened sentiment, and often playful. The tone should not be pitched high; it should be terse and idiomatic, and rather in the conversational key. The rhythm should be crisp and sparkling, the rhyme frequent and never forced, while the entire poem should be marked by tasteful moderation, high finish and completeness.
>
> (Preminger 1974: 446)

It is clear that Larkin deliberately wrote his poem within the conventions of the genre whose name it shares, although in the self-revelatory persona it is also reminiscent of Browning's dramatic monologues. In his use of colloquial vulgarisms here, Larkin shows a willingness to echo the reality of modern speech which is characteristic of his poetry but which might not have been entirely to the taste of the mid-Victorian editor quoted above. This apart, he meets with notable success all the requirements of the genre.

The 'playfulness' and 'high finish' have already been observed in the juggling with language varieties. It may be seen in other technical features of the poem, as for example the changes which are rung on the rhyme pattern. It begins with simple pairs (aabbcc), but these are varied in stanzas 2–5 so that pairs come less frequently together (abbcca, abccba, abbcac, abaccb). In the final stanza, the original pattern is repeated, as is the topic, the reply to the invitation. Another aspect of the technical virtuosity at work in the poem is the use of the short line. Each stanza includes a variant from the dominant five-stress line, usually the fifth line but, in the first and last stanzas, the fourth line, thus reinforcing the framing effect of their shared rhyme scheme. The observations made in these short lines are all the sharper and more prominent for their being carried on only three stresses and for being composed largely of monosyllabic words. In each case, the line end coincides with the end of a major syntactic unit. These circumstances are likely to induce a natural pause in our reading, allowing us to dwell momentarily on the meaning of these lines.

Finally, in the loose matching of sentence structure to the formal stanzas, we should recognize poetic adroitness rather than flawed achievement. The play on the collocations of *time* already remarked is made the more effective by its placing in relation to the stanza form. Our feeling that 'time has flown' is a complete construction is confirmed by its coinciding with the end of the second stanza. That its new grammatical extension should be in the next stanza delays and makes more prominent this linguistic disruption of our normal perceptions. A similar effect is achieved in the last line of the third stanza, which appears to be syntactically complete. We first read *it* as anaphoric (Halliday & Hasan

1976: 14), and only discover it to be cataphoric when we find its referent in the first line of the following stanza. All these devices help to make reading the poem a linguistically challenging and entertaining experience.

Yet to recognize the poem as an example of light verse is not to imply that it is without seriousness. Larkin's insights into human sentiments and psychology are not less valid for being presented in this relatively playful way. As readers we may first be pleasurably engaged in the game of picking up the linguistic trail, but we come soon enough to perceive the humanity of the persona, and the reality and delicacy of his feelings. We may reasonably feel encouraged to identify such themes in this poem when we observe a pattern of being more serious than is immediately suggested by the surface of his writing in, for example, 'Church Going', 'An Arundel Tomb' and 'The Whitsun Weddings'.

6.3 CONCLUSIONS

In thus glancing at generalizations that might be made about Larkin's poetry we have moved some distance from the discussion of knitting patterns and the like, but not out of sight of the unifying theme, the necessity for all users of English to be alert to the existence of many varieties of that language. Developing a meaning for 'Vers de Société' required constructing a coherent character for the persona in the poem. The contributors to the discussion had constantly to attend to shifts in varieties, to identify and respond to these and other linguistic stimuli to the recognition of a context which made sense of his behaviour. In doing this they were not engaged in an exercise at some remove from the reality of communicative exchange, as they were when deciphering knitting patterns with not a ball of wool in sight. On the contrary, they were entering as fully as they were able into the real and present activity of reading a poem creatively and sharing their perceptions of that process with others. They were in fact moving 'towards some society', albeit ephemeral, whose membership was identified by their interest in the poem, and by their pressing and felt need for enhanced competence in the

English language so that they might refine and express their understanding of it. Their experience thus offers some justification for the title of this essay, and perhaps has stimulated them to consider undertaking a similar approach to literature with their own students.

SEVEN

What is stylistics and why can we teach it in different ways?

Ronald Carter

7.1 INTRODUCTION

In this article I[1] want to argue for a more comprehensive definition of stylistics as a discipline and to demonstrate that different kinds of teaching strategies need to be accommodated within this broader framework. A short and linguistically 'simple' poem is then taken and analysed. Here I hope to show that the poem affords considerable possibilities for integrated language and literature work and that much that is of pedagogical benefit can be derived from not limiting the nature of this integration either to any one mode of interpretation of the text or to any one model of stylistics as an activity and discipline.

7.2 THE NATURE OF STYLISTICS

Given that stylistics is essentially a bridge discipline between linguistics and literature it is inevitable that there will be arguments about the design of the bridge, its purpose, the nature of the materials and about the side it should be built from. Some would even claim it is unnecessary to build the bridge at all. In such a situation there is always a danger that stylistics can become blinkered by too close an affiliation to a single mode of operation or to any one ideological position. There is already a considerable division in the subject between literary stylistics (which is in many respects an extension of practical criticism) and linguistic stylistics (which seeks the creation of linguistic models for the analysis of texts – including those conventionally thought 'literary' and 'non-literary'). Such divisions can be valuable in the process of clarifying objectives as well as related analytical and pedagogic strategies, but one result can be the narrowing of classroom options and/or the consequent reduction in the number and kinds of academic levels at which stylistics to literature students can operate. For example, literary stylistics can be more accessible to literature students because it models itself on critical assumptions and procedures already fairly well established in the literature classes of upper forms in schools, whereas the practice of linguistic stylistics tends to require a more thorough acquaintance with linguistic methodology and argumentation.

I thus wish to claim here more comprehensive ground for stylistics as a discipline and to argue that it can be effectively taught at a wider range of levels. A helpful starting point may be to suggest that the practice of stylistics comes about *at any point of intersection of the language of a text with the elements which constitute the literariness of that text.* This is not to say that literariness is an absolute; rather there are degrees of literariness which operate along a cline which includes texts not conventionally assumed to be literary. (See Carter and Nash 1983.) One danger inherent in a purely literary stylistics is that the selection of texts for analysis can reveal certain unexamined presuppositions about what constitutes literature and can lead to statements that features such as, say, allusiveness or semantic play characterize the domain of literature. A linguistic stylistician may rightly point to examples from advertising copy such as those for Guinness and the British Leyland Mini below:

You can't see through a Guinness (semantic play)

Nips in and out like Ronald Biggs (semantic play and allusion)

and argue for more precise analytical models for determining the nature of literature or 'literariness' although, conversely, he or she may not be interested in a detailed interpretation of what a text means for them or how exactly it produces the responses it does. In reality, there is more overlap between linguistic and literary stylistics (and their sub-varieties) than I give credit for here; but, for the purposes of the development of linguistic and literary competence in the classroom, divisions must be highlighted in order that an argument for greater catholicity can be advanced.

I shall now work through this short text and point to some ways in which it might be explored in the classroom from within an expanded framework for stylistics. I shall outline eight main approaches (see 7.3.1–7.3.8 below). 'Eight' is no magic number, of course; there can be more and, alternatively, different approaches can be conflated in different ways. The purpose here is to point to some distinct ways in which a literary text can be taught by integrating its study with a consideration of its properties of language and to explore the different pedagogical purposes of the different approaches. The points are ordered but that should not mean that one is necessarily prior, either logically or procedurally, to another:

Off Course

[1] the golden flood   the weightless seat
      the cabin song   the pitch black
      the growing beard   the floating crumb
      the shining rendezvous   the orbit wisecrack
[5] the hot spacesuit   the smuggled mouth-organ
      the imaginary somersault   the visionary sunrise
      the turning continents   the space debris
      the golden lifeline   the space walk
      the crawling deltas   the camera moon
[10] the pitch velvet   the rough sleep
      the crackling headphone   the space silence
      the turning earth   the lifeline continents
      the cabin sunrise   the hot flood
      the shining spacesuit   the growing moon
[15] the crackling somersault   the smuggled orbit
      the rough moon   the visionary rendezvous
      the weightless headphone   the cabin debris
      the floating lifeline   the pitch sleep
      the crawling camera   the turning silence
[20] the space crumb   the crackling beard
      the orbit mouth-organ   the floating song

                                               Edwin Morgan (1966)

7.3 APPROACHES TO STUDY AND TEACHING

7.3.1 Teaching the grammar

Most striking here is the consistent pattern of nominal groups across the whole text. In each case the structure is that of d m h where d = definite article, m = modifier and h = headword. The predominant modifier of the headwords in the nominal groups of this poem is an epithet. But they are not all of the same type. We distinguish in English (though by no means exhaustively) between three main types of epithet:

e^a = qualitative epithet; e.g. marvellous, interesting, strong

e^b = colours; e.g. red, blue

e^c = classifying epithet; e.g. classical, wooden.

The usual order for these is **a b c**; so that you cannot normally have 'a red, classical, wonderful vase' but you can have 'a wonderful, red, classical vase'. In addition to these epithets English allows numerals, past and present participles (e.g. *shining* line [14] and *smuggled* line [15]) and other nouns (e.g. *the* **space** *walk* line [8] – sometimes called nominators) to act as modifiers in the nominal group. What kind of exploitation of these features is made in the text?

Epithet ordering rules do not really surface since only *one* modifier occurs at any one time. Morgan employs a *mixture* of modifiers including colours (*the golden lifeline* line [8]), nominal modifiers (*the cabin debris* line [17]) and participles (e.g. lines 3 & 5). In terms of classes of epithet classifying epithets (e^c) seem to predominate: e.g. *the weightless headphone* (line [17]); *the floating lifeline* (line [18]); *the imaginary somersault* (line [16]), even to the extent that the majority of participles are of a classifying kind. In fact, *the* **golden** *lifeline* may be seen to describe a characteristic of the lifeline as much as it does its colour. Thus, one cumulative effect of the use of this structure is that a number of objects are classified and re-classified. Occasionally, a particular qualitative contour is imparted to the things seen but the predominantly defining procedure suggests something more in the nature of an inventory (the run of articles reinforces this) or, more specifically, a ship's log with only occasionally the kind of qualitative reaction allowed in line [6] *the visionary sunrise*. I shall return to a discussion and fuller 'interpretation' of these features in another section.

Other key structural features which must be noted are the absence of a verb and the particular use to which the participles are put. One main result of the omission of a verb is that there are no clear relations between objects. Objects either do not seem to act upon each other or have no particular 'action' of their own. Verbs generally work to establish a clear differentiation between subject and object and to indicate the processes contracted between them; a resultant effect here is that processes between things become suspended. The poet's suspension of some of the normal rules of grammar can be seen in part, at least, to contribute to this effect.

Yet this observation can be countered by a recognition that there *are* verbs in the poem; for example, the participles already observed (e.g. *crawling* lines [9] & [19]; *floating* lines [3] & [21]; *growing* lines [3] & [14]) are *formed* from verbs. The difference between the two verbal items in the following sentences:

(i)   the world turns
(ii) the turning world

illustrates the point that in the participial form the 'verbs' work both with a more defining or classificatory function and to underline a sense of continuing, if suspended, action. The present participles convey a feeling of things continuing endlessly or, at least, without any clear end.

From a teaching or classroom viewpoint there is much that can be done with the above observations. They can be used in the service of fuller interpretation of the text; they can form the basis of discussion of the function of different parts of speech; and, more specifically, the text can be used to introduce and form the basis of teaching some key structural features of English syntax such as nominal group organization, participles, verbal relations, etc. There is no reason why a literary text cannot be used to illustrate such features. In fact, one real advantage of such a framework is that grammatical forms are not learned in a rote or abstract way or in relation to made-up examples; instead, grammar is taught in action and in terms of its communicative features (cf. Widdowson 1975). We are made to ask both what is grammatical *and*, practically, what specific job a grammatical form can do in addition to what the semantic relations are which underlie noun–phrase sequences. This can be of direct value to both native English language students and foreign-language learners of English.

7.3.2 Teaching the lexis

One procedure here involves discussion and definition of what the individual words mean; it is a conventional and time-honoured procedure and is clearly of most practicable use to foreign students. However, the introduction of the notion of lexical collocation can be rather more instructive. Here we are asking more direct questions about 'the company words keep' and exploring the different degrees of acceptability in the semantic fit between lexical items – in this case, between modifier and headword. Such exploration can teach more to foreign students about the meaning of words than dictionary-type definitions; we are forced in relation to this text into explaining, precisely, why *crackling headphone* (line [11]) contains items which sit more comfortably alongside each other than *crackling beard* (line [20]) or why *smuggled* has a greater degree of semantic compatibility with *mouth-organ* (line [5]) than with *orbit* (line [15]). Idioms are explained, e.g. *pitch black* (line [2]), as well as the extent of convertibility of idioms, e.g. *the pitch sleep* (line [18]) or *the pitch velvet* (line [10]); the range of meanings or associations carried by particular words can be discussed in relation to collocations such as *the rough sleep* (line [10]); *the rough moon* (line [16]); and the possibilities of metaphoric extension can also be investigated through the uses to which items like 'crawling' or 'crackling' are put e.g. *the crawling deltas* (line [9]); *the crackling somersault* (line [15]); *the crawling camera* (line [19]); *the crackling beard* (line [20]).

One central insight into the structure of the poem which should emerge as a result of such lexico-semantic analysis concerns the concentration of metaphoric extensions, semantic incompatibilities and generally unusual collocational relations in the last six lines of the poem. It is almost as if the typographic inlay at line [15] signals a markedly changed set of relationships between objects and their classifications even though both object and attribute remain fixed and finite. There is thus a basis laid for further interpretative investigation and for conjunction with the syntactic analysis above. From a linguistic point of view students start to appreciate the interpenetration of different levels of language organization in the creation of meanings; they can also learn about how words work, the network of relations they can contract, and something of the nature of figurative language. Foreign students of English can be engaged in more basic lexicographic work and may, indeed, be asked to write dictionary entries for some of the key words in the text. Again the emphasis throughout is on *how* the words mean and on their particular communicative values. Such strategies are given a particular focus by the kinds of dispositions of words found in many literary texts.

The orientation of the first two approaches has thus been on the uses of literary text for language teaching. Literary text can be a 'way-in' for the teaching of structures of the language. It would not be an overt aim of this approach to explore the literary meanings released by the text, although I would hope that a sound basis has been prepared. But by varying degrees of indirectness students can learn something of the nature of the exploitation of the rules of language involved in the creation of a literary text; they are being encouraged to recognize linguistic patterns and changes to those patterns and to ask what the functions are of the features they observe. They are at one point of the intersection of language and literature study and are engaged in a rudimentary form of stylistic analysis.

7.3.3 The teaching of text as discourse

The point of this area of work in stylistics and its teaching is to invite recognition of how a text works as a whole. It involves an investigation of the discoursal properties of a text. There are many ways in which textual discourse can be defined but for our purposes here it should consist of a notation of the ways in which smaller units of language (such as the **d m h** structure here) combine with other linguistic semiotic properties to make up, cumulatively, the elements of a whole text. The notation or definition should be able to account for our ability to discern and respond to such various discourses from a set of instructions for opening a can, to a novel – although some units of discourse are rather easier to specify than others. Correspondingly, such description should provide the basis for a differentiation of different kinds of discourse.

From a classroom viewpoint one of the most instructive and helpful means of distinguishing textual discourse is analysis through a juxtaposition of one discourse with another. In the case of 'Off Course' it may be useful to set it alongside texts containing instructions, or inventories, or lists of participants at a meeting, or even perhaps a recipe. In other words, texts which can be shown to contain linguistic conventions of a similar nature to the poem under consideration. One main aim here should be to focus attention on the nature of the textual organization of 'Off Course'; as a result, the following features should be discerned:

(i)   readers should be uncertain as to how they are to read it. Across? Or down? The typography is not a reliable guide in this respect.

(ii)   the lineation is unusual. There is an unexplained indentation at line [15]. The second column lacks the order and patterning of the first column although there is an equal space between noun phrases in both columns.

(iii) repetition of words is a marked feature although there is never repetition with the same collocational partner. A criss-cross patterning occurs across columns, with modifiers sometimes turning up elsewhere as headwords (e.g. *camera* lines [9] & [19]).

(iv)   the relation of the title to the text is not a direct one. Compare this with: 'Chicken and Vegetable Broth'; 'How to Use the Pump'; 'Shopping List' etc.

(v)   the poem has no punctuation.

Once again the discernment of features such as these can be used to augment an interpretation of the text. But it can also be stylistic analysis of the kind that aids recognition of different styles of discourse and their different functions. Such work can be of particular use to the foreign-language learner who in some cases may have to learn totally new sets of conventions for different discourses. How *explicitly* he or she needs to learn this depends on the teacher's assessment of the needs of the class and the overall aims and objectives of the group's learning, but it can also be valuably underlined how different kinds of literary discourse can create their own rules for their reading, or can set out deliberately to disorientate a reader and how all literary discourse – however unusual – requires reference to one or other set of norms

in order to create effects at all. Learning about the nature of literature involves learning about some of its operations as discourse.[2]
Learning about its operation as discourse is one essential
prerequisite for reading the sort of concrete poetry of which 'Off
Course' is a notable representative text.

7.3.4 Creative writing

One of the advantages of teaching concrete poetry is that it will
often contain uncomplicated syntactic structures of the kind
which can provide a real anchor for students' own writing. Much
creative writing is usually undertaken with the provision of a
stimulus drawn from a theme or 'experience'. A stylistic approach
to creative writing seeks the provision of models either based on
a whole text or on a particular linguistic structure(s). The
informing principle here is that students, especially those with
minimal experience of writing, should have to work within the
discipline imposed by a stylistic form. Asking students to write
a poem using only a **d m h** structure provides a starting point and
thus encourages confidence, teaches that all writing involves
linguistic discipline, provokes questioning of the relationship
between a stylistic form and the 'shape' of an experience or
subject for exploration and can provide incentives for innovation
which will always and necessarily be patterned in relation to
norms, whatever the degree of their 'imposition'. I am not
denying that content can be a most valuable starting point but am
suggesting that in the case of foreign students of English and
inexperienced native-speaking writers an anchoring of the activity
in style and form can be especially beneficial as a starting point
until confidence is built up. (For fuller analysis of these issues,
see Sinclair (1982) and, even more 'radically', Burton (1982).

One of the interesting features of poems written by my own
students to the structural pattern of 'Off Course' is the relationship between this **d m h** pattern and the number of poems about
death or suicide. The very fact that writers are not allowed to use
verbs establishes a connection between their absence and feelings
of unrelatedness, disorientation, no clear goal-directedness and
so on. Such work may therefore be usefully antecedent to the
process of interpretation of the text. Here is an example of such
writing produced by a Japanese student of English:

                                    The stone top
                                    The damp echo
                                    The cold wind
                                    The held breath
                                  The fading foothills
                                   The small trees
                                  The missed turning
                                  The hopeless face
                                 The chinks of light
                                   The life-line sky
                                  The greening moss
                                   The cold echo
                                  The stone steps
                                  The lost recourse
                                   The pelting rain
                                  The howling winds
            The stone tower   The stone body

For more examples of the use of creative writing in language and
literary study see Carter and Long (1987), unit 5.

7.3.5 Interpreting the text

For some people this is where we should arrive as well as the
whole object of arrival. I've taken a long time to get here in order
to try to demonstrate how much linguistic awareness can be
derived from an examination of the language of a text *as language*
and to challenge a prevailing view that literary texts cannot
'merely' be used for purposes of developing language competence.
For me a stylistic approach to textual or literary interpretation is
no more or less than another approach and is valuable only in
the sense that it is a valuable activity for some students (but not
necessarily for all). It would be wrong for our teaching of stylistics
to be dominated by interpretative strategies; otherwise stylistics
can become a restricted academic activity – both ideologically and
pedagogically.

Put in a crude way, stylistic interpretation involves a process
of making equations between, or inferences about, linguistic forms
and the meanings contracted by the function or operation of these
forms in a literary context. The whole issue of what is precisely
involved in this is very complex and stylisticians are as involved
as others in debates over what goes on in the process and over

how particular interpretative facts can be established in a verifiable way.[3] These issues cannot be addressed directly here
although one perspective is offered in the next section; the
following comments therefore carry the danger that they are
based on assumptions which have not been made particularly
explicit.

One of the 'equations' that can be made in relation to 'Off
Course' is between the omission of verbs and an impression of
weightlessness and suspension in which objects appear to be
located in a free-floating relationship with each other and with
the space surrounding them. The absence of verbal groups in the
poem equates with and produces a sensation of a weightless,
suspended condition of outer space where objects float about
according to laws different from those which normally pertain.

Another central point, and one confirmed by conclusions
reached in previous sections and through different approaches,
is the way in which the text shifts 'off-course', so to speak, at line
[15]. From about line [10] to the end of the text no new headwords or modifiers are introduced. The same features recur but
in different combinations resulting initially in something of a loss
of identity of the objects concerned. But from line [15] the collocations of modifier and headwords become increasingly random
or even incompatible (see section 7.3.2 above). So the connections in our 'inventory' between object and its attribute/classificatory
label seemingly get more and more arbitrary and void.

The typographical 'arrangement' of the text means that at the
end we are left in an unpunctuated, unending space of free-
floating connections where the mind perceiving these features in
this 'stream-of-consciousness-like' progression is apparently as
disconnected and 'off-course' as the objects themselves.[4] What
was previously an embodiment of a disorientation in gravity-free
conditions has now become a more profound dislocation. Where
for the most part the lines up to line [15] represent a clear and
definite, even if constantly changing, categorization of things, the
remaining lines succeed only in embodying the sense of a world
and/or mind shifting out of control.

7.3.6 Comparative textology

Texts are usually compared on the basis of related or contrasting themes; and there is little doubt that particular features of a text are placed in sharper relief through a process of comparison. A further dimension can be added by comparing texts which are constructionally and formalistically related. A stylistic examination of a text can provide a systematic and principled basis for grading texts for comparison or for further analysis. These texts can then be progressively introduced to students on the basis of their linguistic accessibility.

Literary stylistic work can be enhanced by such comparison as can be seen from a comparison of 'Off Course' with texts which have finite verbs deleted and/or exist as strings of nominal groups. Among the most interesting 'juxtapositions' are: Louis MacNeice, 'Morning Song'; George Herbert, 'Prayer'; Theodore Roethke, 'Child on Top of a Greenhouse',[5] Ezra Pound, 'In a Station of the Metro'. Prose passages organized in this way include the opening to Dickens's *Bleak House* and the opening to Isherwood's *Goodbye to Berlin*. We should explore here the similar and different effects produced in different literary contexts by the same linguistic procedures. Also, what other 'concrete' poems work in this way? What are the relations between verblessness, the unmediated presentation of objects and the literary movement of imagism – a useful network of connections when 'Off Course' is set against the above-mentioned 'imagist' poem by Ezra Pound:

In a Station of the Metro

The apparition of these faces in the crowd;
Petals on a wet, black bough.

Comparative textology moves the focus more centrally on to the essentially literary nature of the text (though the underpinning is consistently by linguistic means) and allows questions concerning differences between prose and poetry, between writers from the same period writing in similar ways, about literary movements, etc., and allows these questions to be generated at an appropriate level of abstractness. One seminal insight students should derive is that the same linguistic forms can function in different ways to produce different meanings according to context and according to the nature of the overlay of effects at other levels of language organization. As we shall see in the next section, interpreting such 'meanings' is no simple matter of one-for-one correlation between form and function.

7.3.7 Teaching the 'nature' of language through literature

There are several ways in which this can be done. One, which has already been touched on, involves an examination of differences and similarities in the way language is used in literary discourse compared with other discourses. The focus here is on the specifically literary nature of the object; but this can be reversed and questions generated about the nature of language itself with the literary context providing an impetus to those questions. To underline that each of the stylistic approaches described here exists in a relationship of mutual support to the other approaches I shall then proceed to examine some possible implications of a description of the 'nature' of language for an 'interpretation' of 'Off Course'. The ideological position assumed here is that literature can be used to advance the academic study of *language* as a human and cultural phenomenon. No direct connection is sought at this juncture between teaching *about* language and the development of language skills, although the whole area of such a potential connection is one in need of investigation by language teachers and researchers and is one to which stylisticians, in particular, could valuably contribute.

A recently published article relevant to such considerations is one by Michael Riffaterre (1973). It is entitled 'Interpretation and descriptive poetry' and is an analysis of the nature of language in poetry. Riffaterre's central point concerns what he terms the 'referential fallacy' – this is the view that the connection between a word and some object or referent is no more than arbitrary and that in poetry it is more often the case that words point to each other as much as they do to 'things'. The basic tenet is that of De Saussure and his view of the arbitrary nature of the sign. This is lucidly explained by Culler (1976: 19)

> There is no natural or inevitable link between the signifier and the signified. Since I speak English I may use the signifier represented by *dog* to talk about an animal of a particular species, but this sequence of sounds is no better suited to that purpose than another sequence. *Lod*, *tet* or *bloop* would serve equally well if they were

accepted by members of my speech community. There is no intrinsic reason why one of these signifiers rather than another should be linked with the concept 'dog'.

The interesting thing about 'Off Course' and poems like it is that it affords opportunities for making such insights available in a direct and accessible way. Linguistic awareness can be derived from the study of literary texts.

If the words in 'Off Course' such as *spacesuit, continents, debris, lifeline,* etc. are no more than arbitrary representations of their referents then what are the other relations within which they exist? If the words in their organization in this text do more than refer to some external reality of knowable 'things' then what are the internal relations? What *is* language doing in this poem? What does the poem help us understand about the nature of language? How might answers to the questions affect the nature of our 'interpretation' of the poem's meanings? (For a more theoretical argument along these lines with particular reference to concrete poetry, see Burton (1975).

'Off Course', like many concrete poems, draws attention to its own status as language artefact. In fact, the way in which objects acquire different attributes in a network of free-floating links and associations confirms its status as an artefact in which words contract patterns with other words. Not all the patterns are arbitrary but the way *words* change partners and positions works almost as if to underline their arbitrariness. In a sense, the poem becomes something of a metaphor for an aspect of the nature of language. The suspension of clear syntactic relations and subsequent loss of 'orientation' emphasizes the poem as *word* and allows us a conclusion that the poem is also 'about' its own language. (For an excellent and fuller discussion of the 'language' of concrete poetry, see Steiner 1981.)

In the interpretation of the poem in section 7.3.5 the text was interpreted in terms of a spaceship or at least a consciousness associated with the spaceship going 'off-course'. This meaning to the poem is conventional therefore in that it is predicated on an assumption that there is a neat, unquestioned and common-sense fit between a reflecting mind or consciousness and a knowable or imaginable world referred to in and by the vocabulary of that text. The analysis was made with reference to the confirmation of intuitions about the poem's 'meaning' by appeal to the linguistic facts of the text. An outcome of the kind of work at the interface of language and literature outlined in this section is to put into question taken-for-granted presuppositions about 'facts' and 'meanings'.

For example, as a result of this focus on the self-referential and arbitrary properties of words, it may now be possible to conclude that the discovery of such 'arbitrariness' on the part of the consciousness at the centre of the poem serves to free perception from the normal and conventional co-ordinates of one-for-one correspondences. This squares with the comments of some of the students with whom I have discussed this poem that, far from getting more desparate in tone, the text becomes more interesting and imaginative linguistically while the persona seems to be on the verge of quite new and original perceptions. So that we are 'off-course' in one sense, 'on-course' in another. Others point to the fact that if we read down rather than across the columns we enter a realm where things shift in and out of focus in a similarly liberating manner. Whatever our position, such exploration should lead us to conclude that the text offers no single position from which it is intelligible just as it is in the nature of the language we are investigating not to remain referentially static or fixed perpetually in one place. To quote again from Jonathan Culler's discussion of De Saussure's theories of language (1976: 113):

> One might say that Saussure's theory illustrates the 'otherness of meaning'. What my words mean is the meaning they can have in this interpersonal system from which they emerge. The system is already in place, as the ground or condition of meaning, and to interpret signs is to read them in terms of the system.

This kind of approach, when allied to a process of textual interpretation, cannot be viewed simply as a recipe for 'anything goes' but rather as an aid to recognition that meanings occur only by courtesy of the conditions or systems under which those meanings can be conferred. It leads to an 'opening out' or pluralization of interpretative possibilities.[6]

7.3.8 Studying the 'nature' of literariness

There is no space to deal adequately here with all the very

complex issues raised by this kind of study. (For further discussion see Fish 1973b.) But it is an approach which is part of a wider approach to the question: 'what is literature?' In turn, this issue is ignored all too often in the pursuit of further interpretations of established 'classics' by 'great writers' in the 'tradition' – and almost every question here begs a series of further questions. Since this seems to be a discourse of queries it may be appropriate to list some of the questions about *literariness* which can be explored within a framework of stylistics as a discipline and which may thus, in varying degrees, be effectively integrated with our other seven designs for a comprehensive stylistics.

Two basic question are: what is it in the organization of the language of a text which makes it a literary text? how and why does it differ from other discourse types? Comparative textological investigation is going to be primary here and in its relation to the poem 'Off Course' we should want to return here to such features of the text as the way punctuation is used, the nature and function of the repetitions and parallelisms, the role of the title and of typography, the way it displays its own language, the interpenetration or convergence of different linguistic levels in the creation or constitution of meanings. This may lead to further exploration of plurality of meaning in literary discourse (the hyperactivity of the signifier), of how different literary discourses and kinds of reading are socially constituted and of how different cultures can impose different kinds of 'reading'. Again the questions can be raised at various stages of a student's development in language and literary studies and are relevant to those various stages in the case of both native-speaking or foreign-language students. It has been the aim of this article to argue that the integration of language and literary study for mutual benefit and synthesis at a range of pedagogical levels *can* develop if the sort of policy for a comparative stylistics, initially outlined in sections 7.3.1–7.3.8, is given further consideration and exploration.

NOTES

1. (i) The title of this article is modelled on a far more radical and theoretically more substantial essay by Stanley Fish (1973a). By focusing primarily on pedagogical issues, the aim here has been to act only as a secondary stimulus to radical theoretical issues in stylistics. See also Burton (1982).

    (ii) I am grateful to Mick Short for detailed and perceptive comments on an earlier draft of this paper. I have made use of his advice, but the final responsibility, particularly for ignoring some of his comments, must be my own. I must also acknowledge help from Mike Stubbs and Bill Nash and the participants at a British Council seminar devoted to language and literature teaching in April 1982, at which this paper was read.

2. The point here is basic to the argument of H. G. Widdowson's *Stylistics and the Teaching of Literature* (1975). Widdowson's account is more detailed and contains (Ch. 6) some usefully practical teaching strategies; he also emphasizes, quite rightly in my view, the extent to which literary discourse fits into a model of a context of communication.

3. A radical account of the whole question is given in Culler (1981:Ch. 2, 'Beyond Interpretation').

4. (i) It would be interesting to check the relationship between stream-of-conciousness narratives and the predominance of nominal group (verbless) structures. The connection holds in the most 'famous' of such instances – Molly Bloom's soliloquy at the end of Joyce's *Ulysses*.

    (ii) For a useful EFL language syllabus of linguistic structures in literary texts, see Holst (1980).

5. See the discussion in Widdowson (1975:Ch. 6).

6. For an elaboration of the argument, with a fuller consideration of its relevance for the 'politics' of English literature, see Belsey (1980: especially Chs 1 & 2) and Coward and Ellis (1977). A key issue here is the question of the 'subject' or what I have loosely termed the 'central consciousness' of this discourse. Another point which should also be considered here is the extent to which a text which draws attention to the arbitrariness of its own language also refuses the possibility of a conventional 'I' behind or outside the text. Such a dissolution is a function of the dissolution of meanings which are found in classic 'realist' representations in which the referentiality of language to an ordered and intelligible world is paramount. If meaning is not pre-given and is neither anterior nor exterior to the text then it is created not through a 'central consciousness' but by the system of language in and by which the 'I' is constituted. If such a conclusion is used as a basis for interpreting 'Off Course', then the position of the human subject is even more tenuous.

EIGHT

Teaching study skills for English literature
Mick Short and Christopher Candlin

8.1 INTRODUCTION

This article constitutes a general description of a series of courses which have developed an approach to the teaching of English language and literature overseas that integrates the two areas of study. The first course (taught by University of Lancaster staff from the Department of Linguistics and Modern English Language and the Institute for English Language Education, Charles Alderson, Christopher Candlin and Mick Short) took place in Lancaster in the summer of 1980. The second (involving the same staff but also including some input from teachers of the Department of English Literature, University of Lancaster) took place in 1981. A similar approach was used during a two-month course taught in the University of Nanjing, China by Charles Alderson, David Carroll (Department of English Literature, University of Lancaster) and Mick Short in February/March 1981, under the auspices of the British Council and the Chinese University authorities in Nanjing.

The courses were all designed as in-service courses specifically for teachers of English who were involved in teaching both English language and English literature to non-native speakers of English.

8.2 PARTICIPANT NEEDS AND COURSE DESIGN

Our consideration of the specific needs of the teachers we were to work with led us to a set of conclusions which were then employed as input to course design:

8.2.1 The concentration should be on texts

Post-war English literature teaching in the overseas context has been marked by a fairly consistent 'flight from the text'. This is not surprising in the context of treating literary texts involving a sophisticated response to minute details of language, and culture-specific background knowledge and literary structure. Non-native teachers of English or specialist language teachers have felt uneasy when expected to provide guided responses based on these factors. They have frequently retreated into teaching *about* literature (for instance, giving students biographical facts about authors, descriptions of literary movements and critical schools, synopses of novels and plays) instead of teaching the literature *itself*. A similar impetus has led to courses on English culture and literary background. The theory underpinning such courses was that they provided the necessary information for a non-native speaker to understand a text. In practice, the background course tended to displace the texts, not surprisingly, as background is easier to teach. We can link this preoccupation with fact with a generally transmissive mode of teaching, characteristic of many language and literature classrooms throughout the world.

If literature is worth teaching *qua* literature, then it seems axiomatic that it is the response to literature itself which is important. There has been much critical debate in the twentieth century (cf. discussions of 'The Intentional Fallacy') about how much knowledge of the author, if any, one needs in order to understand a literary text. But whatever stand one takes on the minutiae of this debate, it is obvious that one can proceed a fair distance with no knowledge of the author at all. Indeed, some texts have no known authors, for example, ballads developed in the oral tradition, while others (for instance, the canon of George Eliot) are read by people who do not know the true identity of the writer. Of course, sometimes knowledge of the author is helpful. Often, however, it can be dispensed with. We would also wish to argue that the role of background cultural knowledge has often been overstressed and mistaught. Courses on cultural background of necessity lean towards statements of general, large-scale 'facts' about a culture. They are prone to trite judgement and sweeping remarks. But the background knowledge needed to interpret particular linguistic events (inside and outside literature) is often of a much more specific kind:

(i) Knowledge of the particular social situation and the particular participants involved: this is a part of what ethnographers of speaking subsume under the context of events and regard as essential to the understanding of linguistic messages. Teachers of literature implicitly draw upon this knowledge in their commentary upon texts.

(ii) Small-scale social facts: for example, in David Lodge's recent novel *How Far Can You Go?* the following sentence appears: 'It was necessarily a Registry Office Wedding.' In order to understand this sentence you have to know that divorced couples in England cannot (usually) be married again in church. It is difficult to imagine this fact, among a myriad of other conceivably relevant facts, turning up in a course on cultural background, very relevant though such information is in this particular case.

It was as a result of these considerations that we decided to teach texts and provide specific background as it was 'prompted' by the texts themselves.

8.2.2 Literature and language teaching should be linked and made mutually reinforcing

Early in this century the teaching of English literature to non-native students involved, in large measure, a concentration on the classics of English literature. The assumption was that if the students were continually exposed to the best uses of the English language, it would in some sense 'rub off' on their own performance in the language. The difficulty with this position was that many literary texts of a high calibre were difficult and inaccessible to these non-native English-speaking students. Much, after all, of what is best in English literature derives from ages linguistically very distinct from Modern English, and even modern writers present problems of comprehension, as they often break both writing conventions and the rules of English in the service of literary artifice. As a consequence, literature teaching began to disappear from the language classroom, to be replaced by a surrogate literature, commonly in the form of textbook dialogues and short tales, where learners were presented with the appearance of literature in the form of text devised to carry structure, but with none of its literary effect. The significant complementarity of patterning in both form and function, characteristic of genuine text, whether literary or non-literary, was replaced by a patterning of form only, free from any significance. This move is to us unfortunate for reasons other than that of the intrinsic interest in studying literature:

(i)   Contrary to much received opinion, it is difficult to make a *linguistic* distinction between literature and other kinds of language (see Werth 1976, Pratt 1977). If this is the case, there is no *a priori* reason for banishing literature from the language curriculum (although there may well be a need to grade literary texts in terms of difficulty and accessibility).

(ii) Although language and literature may appear to be distinct from the point of view of the teacher, they do not, necessarily, appear so to the learner, for whom, literature is also language.

(iii) Many students enjoy reading literature. As enjoyment plays an important factor in any learning process, literature is a potentially useful aid to the language teacher.

(iv) Literary texts often contain a number of different varieties of English. They can thus be extremely useful in sensitizing more advanced learners of English to linguistic variation and the values associated with different varieties (see Widdowson 1975).

(v)   If a student is taught language and literature by the same person, it is possible for the lessons to be mutually reinforcing. Literary texts, or extracts from them, can be used to break up language classes and used to identify difficulties that students experience in reading in general and in reading imaginative texts in particular. Similarly, there is no reason whatsoever why time should not be taken in a literature lesson to focus for a moment on a portion of text relevant to a previous language class.

8.2.3 The participants (and also, eventually, their students) should be made sensitive to the processes involved in reading

Reference to, and study of, the reading process is an area of common ground for literary criticism, linguistic approaches to literature (stylistics) and also for psycholinguistic studies in language learning. It was likely, then, that course participants would bring with them a wide range of expertise in the under-standing of the reading process (as, indeed, would the teachers on the course) and this could be drawn upon during the course itself.

8.2.4 The course should seek to relate the development of an integrated language and literature curriculum at the school level with that of the post-school tertiary institutions

The implications for the curriculum of much of the foregoing are that non-native school-leavers are rarely equipped for the demands made upon them by the literary departments of universities and colleges. They come with an impoverished command of the language, in many cases, and little exposure to the reading of complex, connected text, whether literary or non-literary. Yet, once within the tertiary institution, they frequently receive neither instruction in language nor participate in activities designed to improve their reading skill. They are doubly disad-vantaged. One way in which this situation might be improved, we felt, was to consider the planning of a connected and inte-grated curriculum covering both levels of instruction.

8.3 THE 1980 COURSE

The participants for this course were all teachers of English as a Foreign Language. Most of them were teachers at university or college level. A minority were secondary-school teachers. They came from a variety of countries, including European (Greece, Italy), African (Algeria, Senegal) and Latin American (Brazil, Mexico). As this was the first course of its kind at Lancaster, we saw it in terms of an approach which would not be so pre-planned that we could not react to needs which might emerge during the course itself. Questionnaires were sent to the participants before the course began in order to determine their felt needs. The initial plan for the course was devised partly from the results of these questionnaires and partly from the general background philosophy for the course described in section 8.3.4. The four-week course was planned, accordingly, one week at a time, in the light of comments and end-of-week questionnaires completed by the participants. This procedure enabled us, within the general design features of the course, to respond to comments, criticisms and requests from the participants as well as to accommodate developing ideas of the teaching staff. As all the participants were experienced teachers of literature, we made an early decision not to have a strand within the course concerned with traditional approaches to English literature and/or practical criticism. We felt that to do so would in large measure replicate the skills and approaches which the participants already possessed or were familiar with. Instead, we chose to give the students three course units operating in parallel throughout the four-week course.

8.3.1. Stylistic analysis (Mick Short)

Stylistics is a linguistic approach to the study of literary texts. It thus embodies one essential part of the general course philosophy; that of combining language and literary study. The first part of the unit dealt with introductory materials and techniques for the analysis of poetry (see Leech 1969); the second part with prose (see Leech and Short 1981); the third part with discourse analysis and drama (see Short 1981). At first sight, it might seem that such a technical approach to literature would not be appropriate to non-native teachers and learners of English. In some ways, however, such non-native learners have advantages over native speakers. The chief advantage is that, unlike English undergraduates, for example, foreign students have learnt how to analyse sentences grammatically and frequently have a considerable awareness of English phonological structure. They are thus often more consciously aware of linguistic structure and better equipped to analyse it and its relationship to meaning than, say, today's average native-speaking undergraduate student of English. They may, in addition, have a more consciously accessible awareness of larger-scale patterns of written and spoken discourse than native speakers.

One particular matter, relevant to the other course strands, but especially so for this unit, should be mentioned at this point. The course we had designed was specifically for teachers. It was stressed throughout that the techniques being taught ought to be useful for teachers in their understanding of language and litera-ture; it was also stressed that this does not necessarily mean that such methods of analysis should be automatically passed on unfiltered (or even at all!) to the pupils of the teachers concerned. Sometimes it would be appropriate to do so, and sometimes not, depending upon the level of linguistic and analytical skills of the students concerned. However, even if the level of a particular teacher's students was below that needed for a stylistic approach to be successful in class, the teacher would often be able to use his or her stylistic expertise to usefully inform more general and/or less technical discussion.

8.3.2. Reading in a foreign language (Charles Alderson)

This unit focused on three main areas: the product of reading, the process of reading, and difficulties experienced by foreign-language readers (see Alderson and Urquhart 1984). The first part of the unit examined the notion of levels of meaning that can be 'extracted' from texts, and related these levels to reading skills. The second part examined attempts to characterize the reading process and reading strategies, while the third part related what had been learnt from research into the teaching of reading (including the reading of literary texts) and the development of appropriate exercises and tasks for the EFL learner. The unit as a whole was concerned to make a point of using literary texts for discussion wherever possible, and related the processes involved in reading literature to those involved in reading non-literary texts. In addition to the link established between the stylistics and reading units through the joint use of the same texts (the reading unit followed the genre order established by the stylistics unit) it was also the case that the teachers of the two strands found themselves adopting similar language to describe the phenomena they were examining and a similar approach to the teaching of reading strategies and processes, especially when texts were examined in practical detail.

8.3.3. Curriculum development/discourse analysis (Christopher Candlin)

In this unit general procedures for curriculum development were applied to literary studies at both macro- and micro-levels. Stress was laid on the need to integrate the curriculum components of purpose, content/methodology and evaluation in an interdependent scheme (see Breen and Candlin 1981). In particular, emphasis was laid on relating course design to learners' needs both in terms of eventual target and in terms of the learning process, paying special attention to the level of overall linguistic competence and foreign-language reading skill of the learner. At this macro level there was, accordingly, greater focus on the learner as determiner of content choice than on the inclusion of a particular writer merely because he or she was a 'good' representative of the eighteenth century or who could not be reasonably excluded from any representative course on English literature. At the micro-level, the unit examined a variety of strategies for teaching literature in the EFL classroom, emphasizing in particular, variation across text-types and instructional mode (see Candlin and Edelhoff 1982). This aspect of the unit made a connection with the workshops (see section 8.6) and the stylistics unit's treatment of style variation in poetry.

This strand also examined new approaches to the analysis of spoken discourse and an explicit link was made with the stylistics unit in its analysis of drama and the presentation of character speech and thought in the novel. Some consideration was also given to a discussion of the expectations by tertiary level teachers of secondary level teachers and vice-versa. This was especially relevant to the issue of giving students adequate introduction to textual study skills and their development in the context of an overall national educational system.

Figure 8.1 is an attempt to capture the system of integrating the three course components, with the central focus on the description, interpretation and evaluation of texts. The diagram formed the basis of initial discussion wth the course participants on course content and organization.

Fig. 8.1   Course Components

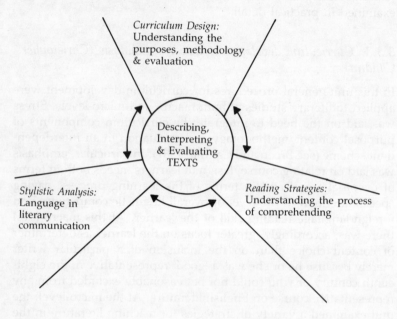

Curriculum Design:
Understanding the
purposes, methodology
& evaluation

Describing,
Interpreting
& Evaluating
TEXTS

Stylistic Analysis:
Language in
literary
communication

Reading Strategies:
Understanding the process
of comprehending

8.3.4. Workshops

The detail of the workshops is dealt with separately in section 8.6
below. It will, however, be helpful to know here that they were
conceived as being central to the course. They took place at the
end of each week, and a considerable amount of time was set
aside for the participants to work in small groups, developing
their own suggestions and materials. These teaching materials,
textual analyses and general comments were then offered to the
other course participants in workshop presentations. Each such
workshop was designed to link literature and language study by
comparing literary texts, or parts of texts, with their non-literary
equivalents, with the aim of encouraging participants to explore
similarities and differences in the texts in terms of form and function. We gave considerable attention to the implications for practical teaching; how particular texts might be taught to particular
students (or indeed, if it was appropriate to teach such texts at
all).

When the participants first arrived at Lancaster, it was clear that there was a considerable range of differing assumptions about the likely course content. Participants expressed interest in the selection of literary texts, techniques of teaching literature (generally and in relation to specific countries and audiences), current critical theory and its application to the teaching of literature, practical performance, the linguistic study of literary texts, the application of linguistic theory to the language of literature, especially in the bilingual context, creative writing and translation theory. No short course could hope to deal adequately with a minority, let alone all, of these topics. What it could do, and our description is intended to make this clear, is to provide a coherent approach to the teaching of literature, linked to the learning of language, within which at least some of these concerns could find a place. In the event feedback from the participants was very enthusiastic, although they suggested that they would have welcomed the addition of a fourth course strand concerned with more traditional literary criticism.

8.4 THE 1981 COURSE

The general philosophy of the course remained the same as that lying behind the previous year's programme. However, we took up the participants' suggestion from 1980 that we introduce a separate strand concerned with literary criticism. Unfortunately, however, the 1981 course could only be of three, rather than four, weeks' duration, thus raising the major problem of an expansion of course content coinciding with a reduction in available time. Once again, participants were drawn from a variety of countries (including Nigeria, Brazil, Argentina, Indonesia, Sudan, Finland, Turkey, Senegal, Algeria and Greece), with Nigeria and Brazil being particularly well represented. In addition, our feeling that the interests of a very small minority of secondary-school teachers had not been sufficiently well catered for in the 1980 course led us to restrict the 1981 course to teachers in tertiary education.

The inclusion of a new unit on literary criticism made for greater course cohesion in that it was scheduled to parallel the stylistics unit in its movement through the genres. The unit itself was appreciated during the course by the participants, yet in their end-of-course report an overwhelming majority suggested that it be dropped in any future year on the grounds that the techniques involved were sufficiently familiar to them. Moreover, its absence would allow them to spend more time in studying those new techniques and content areas which the course also provided. Ironically, then, the view of the second group of students directly opposed that of the first group and coincided with our original reasons in 1980 for not including it as a separate unit. Once again, feedback was extremely positive; indeed, one of the 1981 participants has since used the techniques developed in the drama section of the stylistics unit as the basis for an article in a Brazilian scholarly journal and one of the 1980 participants has introduced the general approach of the course to Greek teachers via conference presentation and publication.

8.5 THE NANJING COURSE

Within the same overall philosophy, this course differed from the others in a number of important respects. The participants were all Chinese teachers of English language and literature in Chinese universities and colleges with a strong interest in English literature. Accordingly, the course tutors (Charles Alderson, David Carroll and Mick Short) introduced a strand on post-war British Literature. This comprised a third of the available course time. The literature and the stylistics units were organized in parallel in terms of treatment of genre. Necessarily in this course, given that Christopher Candlin was not able to be a member of the teaching team, the aspect of curriculum development was only touched upon incidentally. The post-course feedback was good, especially from the more able participants. In its earlier stages, however, the course suffered for reasons unconnected with course content.

Firstly, there was a large disparity of expectations between teachers and taught in terms of teaching style. The participants expected to be informed of facts which could be committed to memory; the teachers, on the other hand, expected them to take a much more active role in analysis and interpretation. It took some time for an amicable accommodation to be reached. Those who have taught in China will recognize this lack of fit between students' expectations and Western teaching style.

Secondly, the participants were far from homogeneous in terms of ability and background. This did not, however, lead to any major alteration in the approach developed in the two previous Lancaster courses and seemed from participant feedback to offer an experience to the Chinese teachers which was relevant to their classroom needs.

8.6 THE WORKSHOPS

As we have indicated above, the workshops, although only one part of the overall course provision, did represent a significant opportunity for the participants to work in detail on a range of issues treated in outline in the other course strands. Accordingly, we list below the activities that took place during the half-day periods at the end of each week which were devoted to the workshops. It should also be pointed out that these sessions were preceded by up to a day's preparation by the students. The outcome of the small-group activities usually took the form of a group report examining the relationships between similar text-types chosen from literary and non-literary sources. The comparison typically involved the students in searching for both similarities and differences between the texts, initially in terms of formal linguistic differences. These formal characteristics had then to be explained in terms of particular functional relevance in both the texts in question. In addition, workshop participants were asked consistently to reflect on the pedagogic implications of the analyses they were engaged in, or the materials they were proposing for student use. In this way, analytical and descriptive discussion was firmly linked with practical teaching procedure. In summary, then, the workshops had three main aims:

(a) to encourage links between language and literature studies;
(b) to clarify the connection between linguistic form and prag-matic function;
(c) to design usable teaching materials for piloting in partici-pants' home situations.

For the purpose of illustration we list below a selection of work-shop titles and topics. The participants on each of the courses described above made their own selection from this 'bank' of possible activities:

  (i) the language of poetry and the language of advertizing;
 (ii) the language of instruction (e.g. on how to operate a tape-recorder) and poems making use of this particular variety (e.g. Ted Hughes, 'To Paint a Water Lily'; Henry Reed, 'Naming of Parts');
(iii) passport descriptions and character descriptions (e.g. Leonard Cohen, 'All There Is To Know About Adolph Eichmann'; Charles Dickens's initial description of Mr Bounderby in *Hard Times*);
 (iv) place descriptions (e.g. a travel guide to Chester and Charles Dickens's initial description of Coketown in *Hard Times*);
  (v) a nineteenth-century sermon and Mr Chadband's speech of thanks for the meal provided by Mrs Snagsby in *Bleak House* by Charles Dickens;
 (vi) dramatic texts and authentic, tape-recorded dialogue.

Occasionally, workshops were used to discuss more general matters of interest; for example, the interface between secondary and tertiary education, in order to examine what each sector expected from the other in terms of the teaching of language and literature; discussion of a set of proposals for a new style examination for literature within the set of Cambridge Proficiency Level examinations in English, focusing on the connections that can be made between literary and non-literary language.

  It should be emphasized that the workshops offered an opportunity for open-ended, flexible and free discussion. At times the participants found themselves stressing similarities between literary and non-literary texts, at times maintaining their distinctiveness. On occasion, as with Mr Chadband, the description of Coketown and 'To Paint a Water Lily', a writer could be seen to be using an established variety of English in special ways, thus using the variety concerned as a 'backboard' against which to create new meanings and effects. Whatever the outcome, the exercise was always found to be fruitful. Of course, these sessions and the activities of the main course strands were not intended to replace more traditional forms of literary discussion. Nonetheless, at the end of the courses, participants declared that they had on the one hand developed new and exciting ways to help non-native speakers of English appreciate English literature more fully, and, on the other, that they could now integrate more fully the teaching of language and the teaching of literature.

8.6.1 A workshop in detail

We have chosen item (iii) from the above list as an illustration of the kind of workshop task in which the course participants were engaged. In this particular case the group were asked to compare three texts, (a) a passport description from a British passport, (b) a poem by Leonard Cohen called 'All There Is To Know About Adolph Eichmann' and (c) the description of Mr Bounderby from Chapter 4 of *Hard Times*. Readers who are familiar with Chapter 6 of Widdowson (1975) will recognize some similarities between this workshop task and the discussion of literary and non-literary descriptions there. The generally comparative (literary *vs* non-literary) nature of the tasks which the course members were often set owes much to Widdowson's pioneering work, and we would like to acknowledge that fact here. We also pick a task maximally similar to that presented by Widdowson, however, in order to be able to use it to highlight some different assumptions between his approach and ours. This matter will be taken up in section 8.7 below.

The participants were asked to work together in small groups in order to:

(i)   examine the linguistic features which the texts had in common, if any;
(ii) examine the linguistic features which differentiated the texts from one another;
(iii) examine the similarities and differences in pragmatic function which could be said to give rise to the linguistic features noted;
(iv) consider how these passages might be used interestingly in their various teaching situations.

For ease of reference, the three texts are reproduced as Figs. 8.2, 8.3 and 8.4.

Fig. 8.2

Bearer Titulaire		Wife Femme	
Occupation	*University*	*Housewife*	
Profession	*Teacher*		
Place of birth	*Heathfield*	*Stockport*	
[5] Lieu de naissance			
Date of birth	*20.4.47*	*13.9.46*	
Date de naissance			
Residence	*England*		
Résidence			
[10] Height	*.5* ft. *5* in.	*5* ft. *2½* in.	
Taille			

Distinguishing marks *Scars on right-*
Signes particuliers *wrist and left knee*
                    mole on right-cheek

CHILDREN *ENFANTS*

[15] Name Nom	Date of birth Date de naissance	Sex Sexe
Hiroko E.	*16.4.72*	*F*
Benjamin W.	*16.1.74*	*M*

[20] Usual signature of bearer _____*M. H Shah.*_____
Signature du titulaire

Usual signature of wife _____*Mady Shah.*_____
Signature de sa femme

Fig. 8.2 – the passport text

The most obvious features associated with this text are its layout as a form, the use of two languages, English and French, and the fact that the text is composed entirely of noun phrases. In addition, the categories and features referred to by the noun phrases are either permanent or semi-permanent. All of these characteristics are a function of the fact that passports are used to identify individuals quickly and unambiguously. It is interesting to note that the printed noun phrases have a dual function, depending upon whether you are the individual filling in the form in the first place or an official reading the passport at a border post. In the first situation the phrases will be interpreted as questions (What is your profession? What was your place of birth? etc.); in the second they will be informatives. In other words, the text can be seen as having a basic question-plus-answer or topic-plus-comment form depending upon situational context. For the individual filling in the form, the dominant linguistic structure of the document to be completed and knowledge of its intended function constrain the linguistic form of the information supplied. Hence, in this particular case, the person filling in the form could have written, 'I have a scar on my right wrist and my left knee and I also have a mole on my right cheek.' He did not do so because he was aware, presumably, of both linguistic patterning in the document and its future function. The layout and the use of short noun phrases mean that the text can be read rapidly and easily. Features like height and distinguishing marks are permanent, and in addition to the inevitable photograph they aid identification. In a sense, the most interesting thing about this text is the absence of the sorts of features which we would normally associate with a text. The 'sentences' do not have intersentential links of any kind or any variety in the kinds of construction used. One consequence of all this is that it is more or less impossible to make inferential links of any real significance between one sentence and another. As a result, the text is straightforward, not just in layout but also by virtue of the fact that it is difficult to read underlying meaning into it. In other words, it could be deemed to count as an obvious example of what would traditionally be thought to be objective, non-literary language. And indeed, it is difficult to imagine a complete text with these features and these alone turning up in a book of poems. But of course such a form could turn up as part of a novel; and, with not many changes, at least the beginnings of literary interest can be achieved, as text (b) shows.

Fig. 8.3 the poem by Leonard Cohen

The first thing to notice about the Cohen poem is that it alludes to the notion of a passport, an identity card or some such thing. It does this most obviously by virtue of the fact that the first part

Fig. 8.3

ALL THERE IS TO KNOW ABOUT ADOLPH EICHMANN

	EYES:	....	Medium
	HAIR:	....	Medium
[5]	WEIGHT:	....	Medium
	HEIGHT:	....	Medium
	DISTINGUISHING FEATURES:	....	None
	NUMBER OF FINGERS:	....	Ten
	NUMBER OF TOES:	....	Ten
[10]	INTELLIGENCE:	....	Medium

What did you expect?

Talons?

Oversize incisors?

Green saliva?

Madness?

Leonard Cohen

of the poem, like the passport, is not normal running text but is
laid out as a form and consists of a series of pairs of noun phrases
which can be seen as questions and answers or minimal topics
plus minimal comments adding up to the description of an individual. Participants felt that they would be able to teach this
poem because it was not very difficult. It is worth noting that they
did not always feel that they would be able to teach the texts we
confronted them with for reasons like linguistic difficulty or lack
of background cultural understanding on the part of their
students. They also felt that by examining the passport text before
or along with the poem they would be able to sensitize their
students to the way in which the poem depended upon knowledge of the form and function of identity cards and the like for
its meaning and effect. It was suggested that students could be
asked to write passport descriptions of themselves. This would

produce effective language work as it would mean that the students would have to write in appropriate linguistic form, thus sensitizing them to the interrelation between form and function. The writing could also be used as the basis for interesting class discussion about this interrelation and about topics to do with personal identity, identity cards and so on. Language work of this kind would then help the students to see the allusive properties of the poem and the role that such allusion plays in understanding the text as a whole.

The reason that it is important to notice the 'identity card' form of the Cohen poem is precisely because the information given does not help us to identify the individual concerned. If we look at the right-hand column of the form we see that for all gradable characteristics Eichmann is described as *medium*. He does not, therefore stand out. The answers which do not use the word *medium* supply the most normal, and therefore the least distinguishing, comment. If we look at the left-hand column of topics, we find some features which one might reasonably expect to find on a passport, but some we would definitely not find. The number of fingers or toes would not appear because it is very unusual indeed to find people with more or less than ten of each. From the point of view of an official reading an identity card, then, information about the number of fingers would be so redundant as to waste his time. Any deviation from the norm would be so surprising that it would be bound to turn up under 'distinguishing features'. From all of this, it is plain to see that we as readers are meant to deduce that Adolph Eichmann, well known as an individual centrally involved in the Nazi massacre of Jews during World War II, despite his notoriety, was an ordinary man in all other respects. So much so, that we might well, in our minds, go on to think of other, parallel, possible characteristics – presumably he loved his family, for example. If the poem ended at this point we would have a text which consisted of an identity card format with not an enormous amount extra in straight linguistic terms. It would still be an interesting text, however, and to arrive at its meaning the reader would have to make inferences based upon textual pattern. The natural assumption is that someone who *looks* ordinary *is* ordinary and that someone who *is* evil should *appear* evil. Cohen demonstrates that this is not necessarily the case. Our course participants noted that a simple poem such as this could be used to help students become aware of the processes of inference which readers employ in order to understand texts. In terms of literary merit, what we have just outlined is not particularly complex or fine. But in pedagogic terms it was felt that what we had noticed so far was most certainly of use in getting students to understand how texts (and therefore literary texts) worked.

If we now move on to the second half of the poem, the first thing to note in terms of linguistic features is what stylisticians usually call 'internal deviation' (cf. Levin 1965). The identity-card format is broken by the line *What did you expect?* This line thus stands out. It is not a noun phrase, but a fully fledged sentence; it is typographically distinct from the previous items on the left-hand side of the page, and it is the first question. The question suggests that the reader, who in effect has been put in the same position as an official might be in examining Eichmann's passport, must have expected some other description of Eichmann than the one which he has just read. From this and the following questions we can infer that Cohen is suggesting that the reader (and therefore people in general) expect people who are labelled metaphorically as 'monsters' to exhibit all of the characteristics commonly associated with the class, an assumption which is obviously untrue. In other words, the contribution of the second half of the poem is to reinforce the message seen in the first half by approaching the issue from the opposite end. In the first half of the poem we are surprised that Eichmann appears so unexceptional because we expect (unreasonably, we soon realize) people who appear ordinary to be ordinary. Now what is being challenged is the unthinking assumption that people who act extraordinarily (in this case monstrously) should look extraordinary too.

Like the first half of the poem, this part turns out to be interesting in that it reveals processes of inference at work in the reader. Given the parallelism between *Talons?*, *Oversize incisors?* and *Green saliva?* we look for a way of connecting them together. They are all noun phrases functioning as questions, they successively occupy whole lines of the poem and they all refer to physical objects. Talons could belong to eagles as well as monsters; large dogs could have large incisors as well as dracula figures, and people who are ill could have green saliva as well as monsters from the late-night movies. But it is only the second kind of interpretation in each case which allows us to connect the items together into a satisfying pattern. The last item in the list, *Madness?* deviates from the rest in that madness is an abstract quality not a physical thing. This last item is thus foregrounded (as it is by being the last word of the poem). It is this question which brings with it the unthinking assumption (which, like the others, we now have to reject) that people who do abnormal things must be mad. A typical reaction to the mass murderer is to remove him from normal societal status by labelling him as insane. The eventual point, then, of the Cohen poem is to make us question this automatic assumption for Eichmann, and there-fore, by extrapolation, for others who might be deemed to be similar in some way.

By discussing linguistic form in considerable detail, the work-shop groups were able to come to a detailed understanding not just of the poem itself but also of how they as readers arrived *via* inferencing strategies at the interpretation that they discovered. One part of that process was a set of inferences based upon knowledge of the linguistic form of passports and identity cards and the typical functions which such documents served. An understanding of this fact itself then prompted pedagogical strat-egies designed to help their own students to understand both the poem and the procedures involved in arriving at that under-standing. Whether this was to be carried out at an explicit or an implicit level depended upon the students concerned. But in any such case, the belief was that in establishing solidly what was involved in understanding this relatively simple poem, students would be able to go on more confidently to tackle more complex pieces of writing.

Fig. 8.4 – Mr Bounderby

If we compare the description of Mr Bounderby with the other two descriptions, we can see that this one is very different in type both linguistically and functionally. There are some surface simi-larities, for example this text also has a series of noun phrases which constitute whole sentences. But this time the passage has an obviously rhetorical function. This is reflected in the structure of the noun phrases already alluded to by the repetition of *a man*

Fig. 8.4

Mr Bounderby

NOT being Mrs Grundy, who *was* Mr Bounderby?

Why, Mr Bounderby was as near being Mr Gradgrind's bosom friend, as a man perfectly devoid of sentiment can approach that spiritual relationship towards another man perfectly devoid of sentiment. So near was Mr Bounderby – or, if the reader should prefer it, so far off.

He was a rich man: banker, merchant, manufacturer, and what not. A big, loud man, with a stare and a metallic laugh. A man made out of a coarse material, which seemed to have been stretched to make so much of him. A man with a great puffed head and forehead, swelled veins in his temples, and such a strained skin to his face that it seemed to hold his eyes open and lift his eyebrows up. A man with a pervading appearance on him of being inflated like a balloon, and ready to start. A man who could never sufficiently vaunt himself a self-made man. A man who was always proclaiming, through that brassy speaking-trumpet of a voice of his, his old ignorance and his old poverty. A man who was the Bully of humility.

A year or two younger than his eminently practical friend, Mr Bounderby looked older; his seven or eight and forty might have had the seven or eight added to it again, without surprising anybody. He had not much hair. One might have fancied he had talked it off; and that what was left, all standing up in disorder, was in that condition from being constantly blown about by his windy boastfulness.

                                        Charles Dickens, *Hard Times*

who . . . and *a man with . . .* at the beginning of most of these NP-sentences, a repetition which helps to ensure that the reader notices the parallelism between the sentences. This rhetorical quality is also to be found in the presence of tropes like metaphor (e.g. *metallic laugh, brassy speaking-trumpet of a voice, windy boastfulness*) and paradox (*the Bully of humility*). Another obvious characteristic of the passage which marks it off from the passport description is the direct textual involvement of the reader by reference to him or her (*or, if the reader should prefer it, so far off*) and a question-and-answer sequence linked to discoursal features normally associated with conversation (*Not being Mrs Grundy, who was Mr Bounderby? Why, Mr Bounderby was . . .*). This involvement of the reader is one of the things which suggests that this description, unlike the passport, is not objective but subjective and value-laden. Dickens makes it appear as if the reader, like the writer, has a choice over wording, for example. He also uses a number of non-factive constructions, which thus reduce objectivity (*seemed to have been stretched, seemed to hold his eyes open, a pervading appearance on him of being inflated like a balloon, Mr Bounderby looked older, one might have fancied he had talked it off*). Mr Bounderby's description contains one or two features one would expect to find in a passport description (for example, we know his profession and his size), but there are also features of physical description which we would not expect to find, for example those which are impermanent (*he had not much hair*) or which are much too specific in type to count as general physical descriptive categories (*great puffed head and forehead, swelled veins in his temples*). The metaphors noted earlier assist this particular aspect of the description. They often refer to non-physical aspects of his character and, because they have to be interpreted non-literally, they give a much more specific descriptive impression than any passport.

These individual features are not merely present to give a detailed sense of the individual, however. From their presence we gain a series of insights into Mr Bounderby's character and his likely behaviour. The fact that he has a metallic laugh, for example, and that he is made out of a coarse material will help lead us to suppose that he is a rather vulgar man who may well not care overmuch for the feelings of others. The fact that he looks like an inflated balloon will lead us to think that he is rather pompous, and so on. Dickens thus makes use of the automatic connections between physical appearance and character that Leonard Cohen was at pains to point out are unreasonable. The participants in the workshop were able to see that the reason for the marked differences between this text and the other two lay in its very different function, that of giving an account of Mr Bounderby's general character, and ensuring that the reader disapproves of him and laughs at him. One obvious strategy to achieve such an end is to resort to exaggerated and comic description and to invite the reader to take on the stance of the writer. This strategy in turn leads to the employment of the linguistic features in the particular functional settings that were pointed out above.

When discussing how they might teach this text in class, the participants noted that the contrast between this text and the others would provide useful material for discussion. It was also suggested that an interesting task for students to do would be to write a passport description of Mr Bounderby and then compare it with Dickens's own description. The examination of literary text could thus be used to foster linguistic production on the part of the students. Discussion of the more simple texts examined in the first part of the workshop would help the students to cope with the more difficult description of Mr Bounderby.

This account of the results of a particular workshop cannot adequately describe the process of small-group discussion and debate which we have referred to earlier and which are essential to this particular teaching methodology. Our description also does not focus, except in general terms, on classroom applications. We hope, nonetheless, that it offers some insight into the nature of workshop activity and that from it readers can themselves construct similar tasks and recognize how the study of literary and non-literary texts can be mutually reinforcing and of reciprocal benefit for the teaching of language and literature at different levels.

8.7 CONCLUDING REMARKS – LITERARY AND NON-LITERARY LANGUAGE?

In section 8.2.2 we stated that it is difficult to make a *linguistic* distinction between literature and the rest of language. By this we mean that, despite a widespread assumption to the contrary, we know of no particular linguistic feature or set of linguistic features which are found in literature but not in other kinds of text. This became particularly clear to the course participants and ourselves when, in another workshop, we compared the language of poetry with the language of advertizing. We quickly discovered that the sorts of features which we traditionally associate with poetry (e.g. rhyme, metre, ambiguity, metaphor, parallelism, linguistic deviation) and which certainly turn up in literary texts also appeared in abundance in advertizing language. So much so, that in this particular workshop the course participants began to analyse the advertisements in the kind of way that we would traditionally reserve for literature, talking, for example, of the effectiveness, strikingness and freshness of the language involved. In a sense, we were discovering nothing new here. Leech (1966a) devotes a whole chapter (Ch. 20) to the presence of literary tropes, etc. in television advertizing. Once we examine the functions of advertizing and poetry we discover that the two 'genres' have much in common. It is a common factor in both kinds of text, for example, that they are designed to be memorable and have an emotional effect on the reader or hearer. Given functional similarity it is surely unsurprising that we find similarity in terms of linguistic features.

One possible objection to this attack on the notion of a special literary language is that advertizing is marginally a linguistic art form in any case. But such linguistic features also turn up in text-types which traditional critics would be less happy to accept as aesthetic objects. Gläser (1975) examined scientific texts for the presence of what she called 'emotive features' and concluded that 'Even in scientific and technical English, emotive elements do occur. In the given context they have a communicative function. Emotive features are justified whenever they help in conveying information and in facilitating the communicative effect on the part of the recipient of the message.' Short (1986) demonstrates that a particular deviant structure, the polysyndetic list construction, occurs regularly in a corpus of non-literary texts as well as a series of literary ones.

It is as a result of accumulating evidence of this kind that we wish to agree with linguists like Fowler (1971a) and reject the traditional notion that there is a separate literary language. If there is a distinct corpus of texts which can be called 'literature' it would appear that the corpus will have to be defined at least partly in socio-cultural rather than in linguistic terms. In turn, it is for these reasons that although we wish to endorse Widdowson's (1975) advocacy of a comparative approach to literature teaching involving extracts from literature and extracts from other texts, we would not want to encourage the use of the comparative approach, as he explicitly does, to develop in the learner 'an awareness of the nature of literary writing as a type of discourse'. It may be that there is a quantitative difference between the occurrence of certain linguistic features in literary as opposed to other kinds of text, and this could be determined by empirical research. But even if such a quantitative difference were found, it would only be a quantitative and not a qualitative one. Another possibility, and to our minds a much more likely one, is that if we assume a particular text to be literature we, as readers, may well attempt to process it in ways partially different from texts we assume not to be literature. Evidence of this kind of procedure can be found in our earlier examination of the character descriptions. For example, our attempt to make sense of *Talons?/Oversize incisors?/Green saliva?/Madness?* in the Cohen poem involved not only the search for a meaning for each of the lines which connected them together in a sensible way (a strategy based on relating parallel and contiguous items together so that they are related semantically to one another, which, it should be noted is used in the processing of all kinds of English texts), but also an assumption that the meaning we arrived at should fit in with the rest of the text so that it formed an organic and patterned interpretative whole. The more we are successful in interpretative strategies of this kind, the more likely it is that we will perceive the text not so much as a literary one in the non-honorific sense (good or bad) but as an *interesting* (and therefore to at least some extent good) text. This is particularly so if the text is seen to have other interesting features like density of meaning and a high degree of inferrability.

What is being suggested here, then, is that if readers feel some need to process a text as a literary artefact (perhaps because they have been told that it is literature on the jacket of the book or by a friend, perhaps because it contains a high degree of linguistic features traditionally associated with poetry or some other literary genre, and so on) they will attempt to apply a set of special interpretative conventions. The more they succeed in doing this while at the same time arriving at a consistent interpretation, the more likely they are to see the text as valuable in some way. In other words, the strategy set may be applied to literally any text, but the more successful the application of that set is, the more valuable the text will be perceived to be. This suggestion is only a tentative one, but it has the merits of both taking into account the available evidence about the linguistic structure of literary and other texts and also providing the outline of an account of the relationship between the honorific and non-honorific definitions of literature. It may be, of course, that similar interpretative strategies are employed by readers when processing texts which they do not perceive as being literature, but it is not obvious that they do, and so the processing approach looks like a fruitful one to pursue in academic terms. This is also why our course in general, and the workshop sessions in particular, were used to examine not just similarities and differences between the structure of the different texts concerned but also involved the examination of how we as readers built up meaning in our interaction with the text. Like the assumption that literature is linguistically distinct from the rest of language, the suggestion that readers process texts which they perceive as literary in different ways from other texts is verifiable, and we would welcome attempts to demonstrate or refute our suggestions. In so doing, others will contribute to the debate over the nature of literature and language and also, in the long run, help to discover more effective ways of teaching them in the classroom.

NINE

With double tongue: Diglossia, stylistics and the teaching of English

Sylvia Adamson

One of the most striking features of the English language is its possession of what Bradley called an 'unequalled profusion' of synonyms. It amounts almost to a double lexicon, in which items from the original Germanic word-stock are paired with items derived from Romance languages. And among the Romance languages, the prime source is Latin itself. Greenhough and Kittredge (1901: 106) calculated that 'a full quarter' of the vocabulary of Latin had found its way into English by 1900; and Bradley suggested that, apart from grammatical operators, Latinized English could provide a complete alternative language: 'The Latin element in Modern English is so great that there would be no difficulty in writing hundreds of consecutive pages in which the proportion of words of native English and French etymology . . . would not exceed five per cent of the whole' (Bradley 1904: 63).

The stylistic and semantic effects of this language within a language have been hotly disputed. If Dryden, for example, regarded Latinization as a necessary means of giving 'ornament' to 'our old Teuton monosyllables', Thomas Huxley rejected it as 'debased'; if Elyot argued that the native English lexicon was semantically inadequate, Orwell claimed that its Latinate supplement was semantically opaque: 'A mass of Latin words falls upon the facts like soft snow, blurring the outlines and covering up all the details' (Orwell 1946: 348). Sir Ernest Gowers, perhaps the last great Arbiter of English usage, attempted to hold the ring between these positions, and followed Bradley in recommending that in any given context 'the word fittest for our purpose' should be chosen, without regard for its origins (Gowers 1948: 34). But the recommendation of eclecticism, while it settles controversy, opens up questions. What is the appropriate 'purpose' for each half of the double lexicon? In what contexts and on what terms can Germanic and Latinate coexist?

My excuse for revisiting this ancient battle-site in the English lexicon is that I believe we are now in a position if not to answer such questions, at least to address them more cogently. I shall argue that an understanding of the phenomenon of *diglossia* gives a new insight into the historical genesis of the double lexicon and into the nature of the relationship between synonymic pairs in the contemporary language, an insight which has important consequences both for the analysis of literature and for the teaching of English as a foreign language.

9.1 THE NATURE OF DIGLOSSIA

Diglossia is the term introduced into English by Charles Ferguson (1959) to describe a particular kind of sociolinguistic situation, which he defined from the instances of Greece, Haiti, German-speaking Switzerland and the Arab countries. In speech communities such as these, there exists alongside the normal range of regional and social dialects, a superposed variety of the same language which is formally distinct and functionally specialized. For convenience of reference, I shall follow Ferguson's practice in calling this variety the High style (or H) and the other varieties collectively the Low style (or L). These terms are not, however, altogether satisfactory, since they evoke, without precisely co-inciding with, the traditional categories of *altus*, *medius* and *humilis* distinguished in post-Ciceronian manuals of rhetoric. More illuminating are the terms which Ferguson himself seems initially to have favoured – the Classical and the Colloquial – or the terms common in German discussions of this phenomenon, *Schrifts-prache* and *Volksprache*. What these alternatives point to is the fact that in all the cases of diglossia that Ferguson examined, H is both in form and in function pre-eminently a *literary* language. For a major precondition for the development of diglossia seems to be the existence of a body of literature whose language provides the model for the forms of H (Ferguson 1959: 247), and the basis of the specialization of function is that H is the variety normally associated with the written language (in the defining languages, this commonly includes journalism and even personal letters) and with those forms of spoken language which could be regarded as an extension of reading: official 'compositions' such as church sermons, university lectures, parliamentary speeches and poetry recitations. L, by contrast, supplies the medium of ordinary conversation, and any attempt to use H in this context is felt to be 'pedantic and artificial' (Ferguson 1959: 245). As a natural corollary, L is the form of the language initially acquired by children, whereas mastery of H is 'chiefly accomplished by means of formal education' (Ferguson 1959: 239).

In diglossic communities, then, the occurrence of H canonically marks a discourse as the product of a public occasion, an official or learned speaker, and the written medium. The nature of its relationship with the L varieties is most graphically illustrated by a particular form of code-switching that is highly characteristic of diglossic communities: 'In all the defining languages it is typical behaviour to have someone read aloud from a newspaper written in H and then proceed to discuss the contents in L. In all the defining languages it is typical behaviour to listen to a formal speech in H and then discuss it, often with the speaker himself, in L' (Ferguson 1959: 236).

Ferguson's paper has become something of a classic in its field, inspiring a considerable body of subsequent research. The work has, however, developed in two quite distinct directions. In one line of enquiry, represented by Fasold (1984), sociolinguists have taken 'functional distribution' to be the 'heart and soul of the diglossia concept' (Fasold 1984: 53), and, largely under the influence of Fishman (1967), have extended the range of the term *diglossia* beyond Ferguson's original narrow definition to cover a variety of other situations in bilingual and monolingual communities where a prestige variety for use in formal settings coexists with one or more informal varieties.

The alternative, and more conservative, reading of Ferguson, which is the one I shall adopt here, is found, for example, in Haas *et al.* (1982). This line of enquiry has, by contrast, concentrated on those features that *distinguish* diglossia from other forms of bilingualism. As a result, its affinities are less with studies of language variation than with research into the linguistic and sociolinguistic effects of writing, literacy and literature. For in Ferguson's account of diglossia, diglossic H differs from other prestige varieties in that it does not derive from any *spoken* Standard current in the community. Instead, what characterizes diglossia is the presence of a dual Standard, of written and spoken norms. Canonically, the two coexist in a relationship of complementary distribution; in most societies, however, they are found in a state of competition for each other's domain and for the allegiance of their users. Alexiou (1982) and Mirambel (1964) have argued, for instance, that the history of Greek since the nineteenth century shows the simple opposition between written and spoken forms evolving into 'a series of complex and constantly changing oppositions which affect writing and speech in different but interrelated ways' (Alexiou 1982: 173–4). I want to suggest that a similar historical process began in English in the seventeenth century, when literary and colloquial norms were set apart by the conscious creation of a literary Standard.

9.2 THE 'INKHORN' CONTROVERSY

> Some seeke so far for outlandish English, that they forget altogether their mothers language. And I dare swear this, if some of their mothers were alive, thei were not able to tell what they say.
>
> (Thomas Wilson, *Arte of Rhetorique*, 1553)

English became the language of official functions in England by successive stages of promotion, replacing French in the later Middle Ages as the language of government, law, fashionable literature and correspondence, and replacing Latin as the language of scholarship and scholarly literature during the Renaissance. But there was no simple act of substitution. Rather, in each case, the form of English that inherited these official functions was one that had been heavily influenced by the forms of the language it superseded. The Renaissance case is particularly well-documented, largely because of the bitter controversies that attended both the transference of functions from Latin to English and the Latinization of English forms (Jones 1953; Baugh 1959: 243–50, 257–82). The source of the dissension was the paradoxical conjunction in the period of a desire to enshrine the classics as a repository of cultural values and literary models with a desire to promote the cause of the national vernacular. The logical compromise between these positions appeared in the movement to make the vernacular an adequate medium for translation from the classics by augmenting it from the linguistic and rhetorical resources of the classical languages; but this in turn became the target for attack by the more extreme linguistic nationalists, such as Thomas Wilson.

The terms in which the debate was cast are revealing. For the Latinizers, the key terms are Elyot's 'augmentation', Chapman's 'inricht', Dryden's 'magnificence and splendour' (Jones 1953: 209; Baugh 1959: 260, 264); the goal of both translators and educators was a language fit for elevated topics and public occasions. By the objectors, this was constantly seen as an abandonment of 'natural' language or 'common speech' in favour of an artificial language created from 'books' and the 'inkhorn' (Jones 1953: 94–141; Baugh 1959: 260–4). The elevated register, that is, was recognized – and rejected – precisely as a *Schriftsprache*.

The effect of the 'inkhorn' movement on the syntax and style of the emerging literary Standard has yet to be systematically studied and assessed, although Latin influence on particular constructions seems fairly clear (Sørensen 1957). But in the lexicon, the effects were spectacular: the importation of Latin words reached, in Jespersen's words, 'gigantic dimensions' (Jespersen 1958: 106 ff). Other scholars have attempted more precise calculations. Baugh, for example, suggests that 10,000–12,000 new words were introduced into English between 1500 and 1650, the great majority coming from Latin (Baugh 1959: 280); Barber, working from a 2 per cent sample of the *OED*, attributes 393 Latin loans to this period, which, if representative of the whole vocabulary, would give a total closer to 20,000 (Barber 1976: 166–7). Whatever the exact figure, the lexical upheaval in the Renaissance was clearly remarkable – and remarkable not only for its scale, but also for the fact that, unlike most linguistic changes, it had its epicentre in the written language.

It is the combination of these factors that explains the appearance in the early seventeenth century of a crop of dictionaries of 'hard words'. These are the first monolingual English dictionaries; and the restriction of their domain is significant. They do not arise from the perception that one group of speakers is cut off from the vocabulary of another by regional or social divisions: few of the seventeenth-century dictionaries include, for example, dialectal variants, or terms drawn from trades or manual crafts. Instead, the advent of dictionaries marks the existence of a large slice of English vocabulary which English speakers are unlikely to encounter *in speech*, but which must be mastered by anyone wishing to be fully *literate*. Hence Blount advertises his *Glossographia* as 'very useful for all such as desire to understand what they read'; Bullokar commends his *Expositor* to the 'greatest Ladies and studious Gentlewomen, to whose reading (I am made believe) it will not proove altogether ungratefull'; and the expressed aim of Cawdrey's dictionary is to teach 'the true writing and understanding' of borrowed words

> . . . with the interpretation thereof by plain English words gathered for the benefit and help of Ladies, Gentlewomen or any other unskilful persons, whereby they may the more easily and better understand many hard English words which they shall hear or read in Scriptures, sermons or elsewhere, and also be made able to use the same aptly themselves.

In this context, it is instructive to compare the prefaces and design of these early dictionaries with those of the late eighteenth century. The latter are predominantly 'pronouncing dictionaries', offering the social aspirant, the foreigner, or the 'native of Aberdeen' instruction in prestige forms of speech, or, in the words of Kenrick's title-page, 'the present Practice of polished Speakers in the Metropolis' (Hayashi 1978: 118 ff). By contrast, the seventeenth-century lexicographers envisage their customers as deficient in education, rather than rank or 'polish' (Bullokar and Cawdrey are typical in dedicating or addressing their work to 'ladies' and 'gentlewomen'); the language skills they inculcate are those of 'reading' and 'writing' rather than speaking; and the language they offer access to is the new Latinized English. Primarily, it is the language of a literature translated or imitated from the classics: hence the practice, initiated by Cockeram and Bullokar, of providing the 'unlatined' with a guide to classical allusion in the form of what Bullokar called 'a brief nomenclator, containing the names of the most renowned persons among the ancients'.

One other feature of dictionary design is crucial to our understanding of the role of the Latin element in English, because it provides evidence that many of the new words were introduced not so much to fill gaps in the referential range of English as to provide a parallel lexicon in an alternative style: both Cockeram and later editions of Bullokar offer their reader separate sections of synonyms to enable him to translate 'vulgar' or 'ordinary' words into their 'scholastick' or 'refined and elegant' equivalents. And in many cases the lexicographers were themselves instrumental in increasing the available stock of synonyms, by their practice of generously plagiarizing earlier bilingual dictionaries, taking the 'vulgar' words from the English column and supplying their 'refined' counterparts by a discreet Anglicization of the entries in the Latin column (Starnes & Noyes 1946: 22, 32–3, 40–3). The mood that gave rise to this practice is explained by Dryden when he describes his difficulties in translating the *Aeneid*. It is not that English lacks a semantic equivalent of, say, Virgil's *'mollis amaracus'*, but that 'if I should translate it *sweet marjoram*, as the word signifies, the reader would think I had mistaken Virgil: for those village words, as I may call them, give us a mean idea of the thing' (Preface to the *Aeneid*).

As a result of this process of 'enrichment', then, there emerges during the course of the seventeenth century a variety of English which displays many of the characteristics of a diglossic H register. It is formally distinctive – and notably so in its lexicon; it is prestigious through its association with the language of a literary heritage (originally the classics, later the neo-classical styles of those whom the lexicographers styled the 'Best Authors'); it is acquired by education and precept; and, most importantly, it is felt to be divorced from the language of ordinary speech.

9.3 THE HARDENING OF LEXICAL OPPOSITIONS

> Talking of the Comedy of *The Rehearsal*, he said, 'It has not wit enough to keep it sweet.' This was easy; he therefore caught himself and pronounced a more rounded sentence; 'It has not vitality enough to preserve it from putrefaction.'
>
> (Boswell, *Life of Johnson*, 1791)

During the eighteenth century, England developed many of the political and social conditions which commonly lead diglossic communities to look for a single unified and unifying national Standard (Ferguson 1959: 247; Barrell 1983: 17–50, 110–75). As happened in Greece later in the century, it was to the H variety that prescriptive grammarians and lexicographers turned for their models of correct usage. There was a widespread belief that the propagation of Latinized forms would 'fix' the diversity and changeability of speech forms, and place English on the rational foundations of universal grammar. Johnson, for example, is quoted as saying: 'every language must be servilely formed after the model of some one of the ancient if we wish to give durability to our works' (Baugh 1959: 339).

Boswell's anecdote provides us with a glimpse of Johnson carrying his principles into practice, consciously cultivating Latinized English as a marker of civilized conversation. But the anecdote is no less important for what it implies about the attitudes and practices of ordinary eighteenth-century speakers. It shows that even Johnson, fine Latinist though he was, did not speak spontaneously in Johnsonese; the Latinate synonyms came to him as the product of reflection rather than instinct. And the terms in which Boswell casts his narrative are equally suggestive: he evidently perceives Johnson's self-translation as a shift not only from informal to formal styles (*easy* to *rounded*), but also from a form of expression that is naturally uttered (*he said*) to one that is, as it were, read from a script (*pronounced a . . . sentence*).

These attitudes are, of course, to be expected at the beginning of the normative movement. Many of the Latinate words for which Johnson is famous were at that time still relatively neologistic, and some of them have, as Webster anticipated, since disappeared from the language. It might be expected that those which did survive would, 200 years later, have become naturalized and have lost their distinctive 'inkhorn' character. To test this possibility, I asked groups of native speaker informants to rate thirty words on a five-point scale of formality, the experiment being arranged so that each word was encountered in isolation, to prevent informants making direct comparisons in the case of synonyms. I shall return to the full table of results later[1]; here I give the averaged scores for a representative selection of Latinate and Germanic forms, including the pairs from Boswell's anecdote:

Table 9.1 Average scores

Latinate		Germanic	
parsimonious	5.0	mean	1.5
putrefaction	4.8	rot	1.3
apprehensive	4.0	frightened	1.9
preserve	3.6	keep	2.3
vitality	3.5	sweet	2.0

What this table reveals is not just a divergence, but a marked polarization: the widest gap in numerically adjacent scores is that which separates the lowest-rated Latinate word (*vitality*) from the highest-rated Germanic (*keep*), and the rating difference between synonyms ranges from 1.3, in the case of *preserve – keep*, to 3.5, in the case of *parsimonious – mean*. When, in an additional questionnaire on the same material, informants were asked to supply appropriate contexts of use for each word, the top-scoring items were regularly singled out for special comment. Between 80 per cent and 90 per cent of those questioned, for instance, expressed the view that *putrefaction* and *parsimonious* were words they would *never* use themselves and would expect to meet only in some form of written discourse. What this suggests is that modern speakers have much the same intuitions about vocabulary as Boswell and Johnson: that is, they experience Latinate and Germanic items as distinct and qualitatively different.

The persistence of such a marked stratification in the English lexicon is very much in line with Ferguson's observations in diglossic communities, where the functional distribution of H and L varieties often remains stable for centuries (Ferguson 1959: 240–1). It also supports his hypothesis that prescriptive attempts to resolve the opposition in favour of H will be unsuccessful unless H serves also as the colloquial Standard for some other community to which members of the diglossic community feel an allegiance (Ferguson 1959: 248). It is arguable that the vitality of Latinized English in the seventeenth and early eighteenth centuries is attributable to the continued use of Latin as a scholarly *lingua franca* and to the widespread admiration for the cultural institutions of ancient Rome. The subsequent decline of Latin – paradoxically the result, at least in part, of the success of H – left H in a state well described by Joos's term for the most formal styles of discourse: it has been 'frozen' as the language of

education and books (Joos 1961). Its creative use is now confined
to a diminishing elite whose classical education gives them a
working knowledge of Latin roots and derivational morphology.
The degree to which these are alien to the productive processes
of word-formation in normal spoken English is indicated by the
high incidence of malapropism among native speakers. Jespersen
has noted that the incapacity to manage long words is a distinc-
tively English source of humour (Jespersen 1958: 134); and the
range of its victims – Dogberry, Mrs Malaprop, Tony Weller,
Bertie Wooster – is one more piece of evidence of a lexical
diglossia that has remained constant through time and across
class boundaries.

The failure of the H vocabulary to become integrated into the
colloquial Standard has had important consequences for the
semantic structure of English. There are, that is, systematic differences in meaning between L and H forms which are directly
attributable to the dichotomous learning conditions of diglossia.
L forms are learned early, learned through speech, and learned
in the context of actual experience; hence, they are interpreted by
reference to the ranges of past experiences with which they are
associated. By contrast, the H forms are learned in an academic
context and interpreted by reference to a prescribed definition.
One consequence of this is that 'hard words' are, paradoxically,
semantically less complex. As a rough index of the difference, we
can compare the *OED* entries for the *parsimonious – mean* pair. What
we find is that whereas a single sense heading is sufficient to
define *parsimonious*, seven sense headings are required to account
for the semantic range of *mean* (and this, of course, excludes its
homophones). It is for this reason – the fluidity or indeterminacy
of meaning in the L vocabulary – that the reader of Boswell's
anecdote is much more likely to have misconstrued Johnson's
meaning in its L version, equating *sweet* perhaps with *pleasant*
rather than *fresh*; in the H version, by contrast, to the reader for
whom *putrefaction* is meaningful at all, its meaning will be relatively precise.

The H forms are not only less polysemic than the L forms, they
are also associated with a different *kind* of meaning. This appears
most strikingly in the case of H–L synonyms. It is not surprising
that synonyms should in time diverge in meaning, since it has
often been observed in sociolinguistic studies that 'speakers do

not readily accept the fact that two different expressions actually "mean the same" and there is a strong tendency to attribute different meanings to them' (Labov 1970: 297; cf. Bolinger 1977). In the case of the H–L pairs the process of semantic divergence is remarkably systematic, and the kind of meaning associated with each member of a pair again results directly from the difference in learning conditions outlined above. The H forms have connotations of conceptual clarity and emotional neutrality, while the L forms are associated with physical reality and subjective response. The nature of the opposition is well illustrated in the results of another informal experiment, in which pairs of sentences constructed around H–L synonyms were presented to native speakers, who were asked to comment on the difference, if any, in their meanings. Some of the pairs are given below, with a selection of typical comments:

1. (a) He was always showy. (b) He was always ostentatious.
   A.H.: In (a) I think of his clothes, in (b) it's more his behaviour.
   T.D.: They mean the same, except that (a) is more disapproving.

2. (a) His sister is a whore. (b) His sister is a prostitute.
   C.B.: (b)'s a description, (a)'s just an insult.
   J.F.: (b) means she does it professionally.

3. (a) I mean to finish this book. (b) I intend to finish this book.
   N.H.: (a) sounds more determined, but I think the speaker of (b) is more likely to succeed.
   J.F.: The speaker of (a) probably didn't finish the last book.

In each case, the informants seem to assume that the (a) sentences are being used for evaluation or self-expression; by contrast, the (b) versions are more likely to be interpreted as making statements or conveying information. Where both versions are construed purely descriptively, then (a) is typically interpreted as referring to a percept, (b) to an extrapolated concept (as in A.H.'s response to the *showy – ostentatious* pair). In the most general terms, the L vocabulary is associated with an experiential mode of reference, the H vocabulary with a noetic mode.

These judgements are matched by usage. The degree to which the two layers of the lexicon are associated with systematic differences in significance is again most clearly seen where the H–L synonyms occur together. This extract from a contemporary letter is typical: 'Maurice is the same, only more so; parsimonious, if not mean.' Here *mean*, although cited by dictionaries as a synonym of *parsimonious*, is used, rather, as an intensifier, paralleling the *same, only more so* of the previous clause, and adding an emotional colour to the statement of fact. Similarly, in the motto of a U.S. motel chain, which advertises itself as:

Inexpensive but not Cheap

it is clear that here too the H term refers to the neutral financial facts, whereas the L term *cheap* adds a strong pejorative colour and is therefore negated. A variation on the pattern appears in this extract from an examiner's report:

I showed that our decisions had not been equitable, and, might, therefore, have been unfair.

Here – although, again, *unfair* and *not equitable* are offered as equivalent alternatives by the *OED* – *unfair* is again presented as something *more* than not equitable, in this case, a consequence (*therefore*). Native speakers whom I have asked to interpret the sentence have tended to construe *not equitable* as describing some practice or process, *unfair* as expressing moral disapproval of its consequences.

In all these cases the synonyms appear in the same order: H followed by L. This is the most common sequence in figures of this type, and it gains its effects from the main semantic oppositions of the dual lexicon: it operates, that is, by moving from the monosemic to the polysemic, from the noetic to the experiential. The relatively monosemic nature of the H item allows it to stand as an abstract statement of the semantic content that constitutes the common ground between the synonyms, leaving the more polysemic L item open to scrutiny for alternative meanings. The kind of meaning it then yields is typically experiential:

often it points up the practical consequences of an abstract concept. So, in these particular examples, *cheap* hints at the reduction in quality that goes with low price, *mean* at the failure to give that can be one way of reducing expenditure.

One important result of this process of glossing is that by force of retrospective comparison, the H term may be reinterpreted: its abstractness may appear as an *evasion* of concrete reality, or a means of disguising painful facts. It is this capacity of the noetic mode to 'name things without calling up mental pictures of them', as much as the stylistic elevation of its Latinate forms, that caused Orwell to claim that 'the inflated style is itself a kind of euphemism' (Orwell 1946: 347–8). The power of H-to-L glossing to suggest the presence of euphemism in the H term means that it readily becomes an instrument of satire, used to deflate pretension or expose insincerity. There is a strong satiric undercurrent in the *parsimonious–mean* example, and this comes to the surface in many literary uses of the form, as, for instance, in the self-debunking idiolect that Dickens creates for Mr Micawber in *David Copperfield*: 'The twins no longer derive their sustenance from Nature's founts – in short, they are weaned'; 'It is not an avocation of a remunerative description – in other words, it does *not* pay'.

Examples of the alternative ordering of synonyms, that is, L followed by H, are much rarer in ordinary speech. Where it does occur the sequence is generally used to convey not so much a change of meaning as an enlargement in scale or an intensification in degree. It is as if the chief connotative value carried by the H words in this sequence is that of the grand style with which they are canonically associated. So, commonly occurring examples are: 'it's very big; in fact, it's enormous'; 'he's not just bright, he's brilliant'. In rhetorical terminology, if the H–L sequence is a natural instrument of bathos, the L–H sequence is an instrument of hyperbole.

What I have tried to show in this review of the attitudes and practices of native speakers, is that the lexical split, which originated in a functional distribution of styles between written and spoken mediums, public and private occasions, and authoritative and intimate discourses, has become psychologized so that it is now associated with two ways of knowing (noetic and experiential) and two ways of valuing (idealist and realist).

9.4 THE DIVIDED LEXICON IN THE LITERARY TEXT

9.4.1 Dramatic voices

> Claribel, you're incredible! Do you know what that means? It means you're a *very* naughty dolly.
>
> (Elizabeth W., aged 6)
>
> Remuneration! O that's the Latin word for three farthings.
>
> (*Love's Labours Lost* 3.i, 136–7)

Self-glossing was a practice adopted by many writers of the early sixteenth century, in a conscious effort to make their meaning clear. These examples from Elyot's *The boke named the Governour* are typical:

> metamorphosis, which is as moche to saye as, chaungynge of men in to other figure . . .
> the education or fourme of bringing up of the child . . .
> begynnyng at the most inferiour or base . . .
> made his exile to be to him more facile and easy . . .

The order in which I have arranged the examples is intended to suggest the process by which explication turned into variation and the alternation of synonyms established itself as a feature of later Renaissance styles (Lewis 1969: 74–87). The dual function of variation is acknowledged by Puttenham when he includes *sinonimia* among the 'figures rhetoricall', whose purpose is both to 'beautifie' and to 'give sense'. He notes that this figure has been called the 'interpreter' because one synonym expounds the other, but adds: 'I for my part had rather call him the figure of Store . . . which store doth much beautifie and inlarge the matter' (*The Arte of English Poesie*, Ch. XIX).

The use of self-glossing as a rhetorical device has been reported in a number of diglossic or bilingual communities. What is clear from studies such as Salisbury's account of redundant translation in Papua New Guinea, or Sankoff's description of oratorical code-switching, is that these practices serve a variety of expressive and conative functions and that they draw on the connotational rather than the denotational differences between the codes (Salisbury 1972; Sankoff 1971: 45–9). All this is implicit in Shakespeare's play on the word *remuneration*. The joke only works if a translation, strictly speaking, is unnecessary. It is an expressive rather than an explicatory gloss, and it hinges on an opposition between some of the associated values of the dual lexicon discussed in the last section: specifically, H as the language of euphemism is debunked by L as the language of plain facts.

In Shakespeare's drama, however, and more generally in drama of the Elizabethan/Jacobean period, the dual lexicon becomes as much the source of dramatic tension as of jokes, and it does so because the investing of its two halves with specific values – public *vs* private; power *vs* solidarity; idealism *vs* realism – means that H and L forms can be used as indices of different perspectives on life. Conflict between such perspectives can then be sharply focused in moments of dialogic glossing, in which one character, in effect, subverts or criticises the stance or value-system of another.

In *Troilus and Cressida*, for example, the staple of Thersites' contribution to the play is to put in question the heroic vision of love and war entertained by other characters. His method is linguistic: he constantly transposes what he hears from H terms into L. So, when Cressida ends her soliloquy on the problems of sexual fidelity with a Latinate couplet:

> . . . O then *conclude*
> Minds sway'd by eyes are full of *turpitude*
>   (5.ii, 111–2) [author's emphasis]

Thersites, overhearing, provides an equivalent expression in L, which uncovers the personal application and the practical consequences hidden beneath her abstract generalization:

> . . . she could not publish more
> Unless she said, '*My mind is now turned whore*.'
>   (113–4) [author's emphasis]

Similar translations from abstract into practical terms appear in *Othello*, for example, when Cassio and Iago engage in a kind of antiphonal description of Desdemona:

> Cassio: She's a most *exquisite* lady
> Iago: And, I'll warrant her, full of game . . .
>   (2.iii, 18–19) [author's emphasis]

> Cassio: She is indeed *perfection*
> Iago: Well, happiness to their sheets!
>   (28–9) [author's emphasis]

This exchange is placed at the beginning of the scene in which Iago engineers Cassio's downfall and it provides a speaking demonstration of the nature of the contrast between the 'bookish theoric' Cassio and the pragmatic 'honest' Iago, or more generally, between the romantic and ribald perspectives which they represent. The victory of ribald over romantic in the scene is dramatized linguistically when Cassio is induced to apply his H term of approbation, 'exquisite', to one of Iago's drinking songs. Significantly, Iago's first move in his later campaign to corrupt Othello also involves linguistic subversion: in exchange for Othello's Romance verb, he offers a Germanic alternative, which provides a suggestive new interpretation of the action that is described:

Othello: Was not that Cassio *parted* from my wife?
Iago: Cassio, my lord? No, sure, I cannot think it,
          That he would *steal* [Q1 *sneak*] *away* . . .
          (3.iii, 37–9) [author's emphasis]

Where *part* is neutral, *sneak* is markedly colloquial: the OED finds no examples of its use in literary language before this period, and on the evidence of eighteenth century lexicographers, it may even have been associated with rogues' cant. Certainly criminal connotations come to the surface in other Shakespearean uses of the verb, e.g. 'a poor unminded outlaw sneaking home' (*I Henry IV*, 4.iii,58). In the Folio revision, vulgarism is avoided, but criminality persists, this time in the second meaning of the verb *steal*. In either case, the opposition with *part* strikingly exemplifies the affective imbalance between H and L (see 9.3 above): *sneak* derives its force from an associated context of use, *steal* from its plurality of senses; both, in dialogic contrast with the polite and abstract *part*, achieve affective priority, the first as (seeming) more brutally 'honest', the second as more semantically charged.

However, the very ease with which the dual lexicon lends itself to dialogic glossing and antithetical characterization points to an incipient problem arising from the semantic bifurcation of synonyms. The parallel lexicon, that is, could be said to introduce a rigid and artificial dualism into descriptive language, making the choice between noetic and experiential less optional than compulsory, and so driving a wedge between, say, idealist and realist terms of reference. The opposition may be re-valued – the idealist term may be perceived as euphemistic or the realist as cynical – but it is not so easily resolved, and without a resolution or synthesis we receive an over-simplified analysis of experience and of human character.

It is partly as a response to this problem of finding a comprehensive descriptive language that we should see Shakespeare's practice of *monologic* glossing. Here a provisional synthesis of noetic and experiential is achieved by coupling H and L in sequence, as though the speaker were looking at the referent from two perspectives in succession:

> . . . this my hand will rather
> The multitudinous seas incarnadine,
> *Making the green one red.*
> (*Macbeth* 2.ii, 58–60) [author's emphasis]

> Absent thee from felicity awhile,
> *And in this harsh world draw thy breath in pain*
> (*Hamlet* 5.ii, 347–8) [author's emphasis]

In both these examples the shift from H to L involves not so much a change of referent, as a re-analysis of it. In the first, Macbeth describes the bloodiness of his crime twice over; but whereas his initial formulation in H describes the magnitude of the act, the second, translating the same image into simple perceptual terms drawn from L, seems rather to emphasize its unnaturalness. In the second case – Hamlet's injunction to Horatio not to commit suicide – the two co-ordinated imperatives focus on complementary aspects of what it means to forego the comforts of death, and they do so by drawing on the complementary strengths of the two lexical strata. In the first line, the key words *absent* and *felicity* are from the H register and are used to convey an intellectual apprehension of a state which they simultaneously dignify by their own stylistic formality. By contrast, the second line turns to the physical consequences of living on, and expresses these in monosyllabic and predominantly Germanic vocabulary.

What is noticeable, comparing these monologic glosses with the dialogic examples, is the way that the doubling of perspective serves not only a referential function but an indexical function, the compounded viewpoint reflecting back a greater roundedness on the character able to encompass both halves of the gloss. Monoglossic characters appear by contrast monochrome, caricatured, either less or more than fully human. Agamemnon is a notable example. He is pretty much a monolingual H speaker and the effect is of a character who has been entirely subsumed into his role as 'noble general'. An extract from his opening speech to the Greek princes establishes his style:

> As knots, by the *conflux* of meeting sap,
> *Infect* the sound pine and *divert* his grain
> *Tortive* and *errant* from his course of growth.
> (*Troilus and Cressida* 1.iii, 7–9) [author's emphasis]

Compared with Orwell's samples of political oratory in the twentieth century, Agamemnon's allowance of five Latinate words per three lines might appear moderate; but they are placed in key positions for the sense, and the effect on a contemporary audience may be judged from the fact that of the five (italicized), *divert* and *errant* (in the sense intended here) were relatively recent coinages – (both are given glosses in Bullokar's *Expositor* of 'hard words') – while, according to the *OED*, *tortive* and *conflux* may even have made their first appearance in English in this very passage. But what is particularly striking is that where Agamemnon does use the figure of *sinonimia*, it is only in order to gloss one 'hard word' with another: the sequence *tortive and errant* seems designed deliberately to elevate his discourse beyond that of his audience both on and off the stage.

But the result is that the speech strikes us as a caricature rather than an image of a language of power. In Forster's terms, Agamemnon is perceived as a 'flat character'. Hamlet and Macbeth, conversely, appear as 'round characters', by virtue of their use of H-to-L code-switching, which lends itself to interpretation as the expression of a sudden movement of mind or surge of feeling. The crucial importance of code-switching in creating the impression of three-dimensional personality is most strikingly illustrated when Agamemnon is set alongside another 'noble general', Othello. For Othello's opening speeches are also highly Latinate, sufficiently elevated from the colloquial to bear out Iago's descriptions of them as 'bombast circumstance' and 'fantastical lies'. And yet we perceive Othello as a rounded character, a real human being, rather than a target of satire. This perception is linguistically rooted in his capacity to shift from H to L. Even his first speech, which asserts – by statement and diction – his 'royal' status, concludes:

> But that I love the gentle Desdemona,
> I would not my unhoused free *condition*
> Put into *circumscription* and *confine*
> For the seas' worth.
>   (1.ii, 24–7) [author's emphasis]

Like Agamemnon, he enhances his projected self-image with a cluster of Latinisms, including an H-to-H gloss. The sequence *circumscription and confine* is remarkably similar to *tortive and errant*: in both cases we have what looks like an explicatory gloss, in the raised form of a movement from a neologistic Latinism to a more familiar H term, but the explicatory process is baffled by the fact that the second term is being used in what to a seventeenth-century audience would be an unfamiliar sense – 'erring' rather than 'itinerant', 'confinement' rather than 'border' – and is there-fore as neologistic as the first. In Puttenham's terms, *sinonimia* is here a device to 'inlarge the matter'. What distinguishes Othello's speech from Agamemnon's, however, is the presence of striking contrasts in diction: the boasting assertion in H is preceded by a completely unadorned statement of feeling in L – *I love* – and followed by an assessment of the extent of that feeling – *for the seas' worth* – which breaks the frame of Latinity, blank verse and iambic metre simultaneously, to give the image and rhythm of colloquial speech. The effect is curiously moving, as though we have been given a glimpse of a private man behind the public hero, of a sincere feeling behind the rhetorical splendour.

9.4.2 Poetic voices

> The artifices of inversion by which the established order of words is changed, or of innovation, by which new words, or meanings of words, are introduced, is practised, not by those who talk to be understood, but by those who write to be admired.
>   (Dr Johnson, *Life of Cowley*, 1781)

The problem of characterization we have been looking at in the drama, becomes, in non-dramatic forms – poetry and the novel

– the problem of finding an appropriate language for the poet or narrator. And here we are concerned less with the accreted connotations of H and L than with their initial functions as markers of a split between written and spoken, literary and colloquial.

H, as we have seen, is the code canonically used for writing and characteristically associated with literary discourse. Ferguson notes that in most diglossic communities, although some literature is produced in L, there is a pervasive belief that 'real' literature should be written in H (Ferguson 1959: 236–8). It was precisely the belief that Latin was the only language prestigious and dignified enough for literary purposes that led to the evolution of English H in the seventeenth century, and the persistence of this view at the level of popular sentiment is responsible for the extremes of Johnsonese that are still to be found in the correspondence columns of newspapers.

Within the poetic tradition, Milton firmly established H as the language of epic, traditionally the 'highest', most prestigious literary genre. In the invocation of his Muse, the Holy Spirit, in Book I of *Paradise Lost*, he asks for – and institutes – a style equal to the 'highth of this great argument':

> . . . what in me is dark
>   Illumine, what is low raise and support;
> *(Paradise Lost*, 1, 22–3)

The vocabulary here works on both semantic and stylistic levels to realize his ambition. The qualities rejected are expressed in and associated with L (*dark* and *low*), those desired are in H (*illumine, support*): the spatial metaphor (he desires to be *raised* from a *low* position) corresponds precisely to the associations of its polarized vocabulary. In effect, the play of antonyms here works to reject the language of ordinary speech in favour of the kind of H-based 'grand style' which Shakespeare prophetically prefigured in the language of 'godlike' Agamemnon. And so powerful was the influence of Milton's formula that a century or more later, Wordsworth drew on the same style to characterize the aims of his own 'high argument' in the Prospectus to *The Recluse*:

> . . . to win the vacant and the vain
>   To noble raptures.

Of the five content words here, only *win* is Germanic, and in the first line, the conjunction of *vacant* and *vain* – both in their etymological rather than their colloquial senses – provides an example of that H-to-H *sinonimia* which Shakespeare used to mark the relentless grandeur of Agamemnon and Othello.

What is striking about this example is that it was Wordsworth who, in the Preface and Appendix to the *Lyrical Ballads*, made the first major attempt in English, not merely to displace H as the expected language of poetry, but to provide a theoretical ground for its dismissal. Poetic Diction, by which Wordsworth means the neo-classical style of Milton and his poetic descendants, is repudiated on the grounds that it is a 'distorted' language in 'differing materially from the real language of men in any situation' – on the grounds, that is, precisely that it is a *Schriftsprache*. The alternative model of poetic discourse that he proposes is one in which the poet descends from the 'supposed height' he adopts by writing in H, and becomes a 'man speaking to men' – thus abolishing the distinction between literary and colloquial, and making his text a representation of voice. Wordsworth's polemic is informed by a democratic humanism which demands that literature must leave the territory of the literate elite and occupy the common ground shared by poet and audience.

The problem is that the democratic ideal cannot be realized by writing in L, even though L is the register canonically associated with speaking and spontaneous self-expression. The reason for this is the sociology of diglossia, which means that an exclusive use of L is likely to evoke, for most readers, the social identity of a child or illiterate. The very ability to read, that is, cuts readers off from being monolingual speakers of L and causes them to interpret its persistent use as an image of naive speech rather than speech *per se*. Thus when Wordsworth, in 'The Sailor's Mother', attempted a near-literal transcription of ordinary speech, producing, for example:

> When last he sailed he left the bird behind
> As it might be, perhaps, from bodings of his mind

Coleridge found the result was a disastrous incongruity between the 'exclusively colloquial' level of idiom and the presence of poetic markers such as rhyme and metre (*Biographia Literaria*, Ch. XVIII).

The solution to the problem is in fact the same technique as, in dramatic forms, creates the illusion of rounded personality. A voice that is both naturalistic and poetic is generated by code-switching between H and L, where one style is persisted in long enough to establish itself, before being interrupted by an unmistakable marker of the other style. It is the occurrence of H that establishes the literary status of the text. It is the rupturing of H that creates the sense of the spoken breaking through the written. And it is the alternation of the two styles that constantly revivifies the reader's sense of the spokenness of L. This is the compromise adopted by Wordsworth himself:

> There was a time when meadow, grove, and stream,
> The earth, and every common sight,
> To me did seem
> *Apparelled* in *celestial* light,
> [5] The glory and the freshness of a dream.
> It is not now as it hath been of yore; –
> Turn wheresoe'er I may,
> By night or day,
> The things which I have seen I now can see no more.
> ('Ode on Intimations of Immortality from Recollections of Early Childhood,' 1–9) [author's emphasis]

Here the H–L patterning maps the pattern of the sense: the transfiguring visionary experience is described in the most markedly H terms of the stanza, foregrounded and given force by the contrast with the predominantly L context, in particular the short simple words of line 3. The return to ordinary sight and ordinary speech is a modulation, however, rather than a descent, the threat of bathos averted by alternative forms of heightening such as the use of the intermediary Romance term *glory* as a stepping stone from *celestial* to *freshness*; the appearance of archaisms such as *hath* and *yore*, and most notably in the last line the introduction of a characteristically Miltonic 'distortion' of syntax – object-fronting – to dignify the long sequence of L monosyllables.

> I heard among the solitary hills
> Low breathings coming after me, and sounds
> Of *undistinguishable motion*, steps
> Almost as silent as the turf they trod.
> (*The Prelude*, 1, 329–32) [author's emphasis]

> . . . Once again
> Do I behold these steep and lofty cliffs,
> Which on a wild *secluded scene impress*
> Thoughts of more deep *seclusion*; and *connect*
> The landscape with the quiet of the sky.
>
> ('Lines written a few miles above Tintern Abbey', 4–8) [author's emphasis]

The most striking feature of these passages is the way their overall design repeats that of the *Ode* stanza. In each there is a clustering of H terms at what is both positionally and thematically the centre of the sentence. The first example is one of the epiphanies of fear recorded in *The Prelude*, a moment when the child becomes aware of Nature as a living and chastening force: and it is to refer to that sense of mysterious life that Wordsworth turns to an H–H pairing – *undistinguishable motion* – of which the first element, daringly, occupies a full half of the measure of the line, causing the voice and mind to linger on the mystery it describes. The second passage, by contrast, describes the typical experience of the adult Wordsworth, the interaction of perceived and perceiver; here again it is expressed by a cluster of Latinate terms (italicized), and more particularly by a play on the most markedly H word in the passage, as the *secluded* scene is subjectively mirrored in the thoughts of *seclusion*. In both cases, the H groupings occur within a predominantly L frame: the first, indeed, provides a classic case of H–L glossing when the H pairing is immediately paraphrased in L.

From the viewpoint of general literary implications, there are two important results of these examples of code-switching. The first is the creation and authentication of two voices in the text, which we might call the bardic and the human. By sheer force of contrast with the opposing code, the Wordsworthian L, though never a transcription of the language of ordinary speech, creates the illusion of it; the Wordsworthian H, conversely, appears not as Poetic Diction but rather as vatic utterance, a voice modulating into heightened language in spontaneous response to heightened experience.

The second effect is just as important. This concerns the interplay of L and H as markers of experiental and noetic modes of description. It is notable that in all of these three examples, the shift from one stratum of vocabulary to the other is matched on the level of 'plot' by a shift between perception and conception, or between a moment of new insight and the physical elements of a scene that provided the context or impulsion for it. It is equally notable that, in each case, it is the central moment of intuition or communion that is described in the noetic mode. An explanation for this distribution is to be found, I think, in Wordsworth's theory of memory:

> . . . the soul,
> Remembering how she felt, but what she felt
> Remembering not, retains an obscure sense
> Of possible sublimity. . .
>
> (*The Prelude*, 2, 334–7)

What this suggests is that the experience of feeling can be narrated but not re-entered. Wordsworth therefore narrates it in words which can make it conceptually available and, by their own elevation, hint at its *possible sublimity*, but which preserve its experiential mystery by failing or refusing to give it concrete realization. Each reader, if he is to feel the shock of *seclusion*, *celestial* vision, or *undistinguishable motion* must reconstruct it for himself from the raw materials of a landscape that is given to him in the experiential mode.

9.4.3 Narrative voices

> . . . so wide appears
> The vacancy between me and those days,
> Which yet have such self-presence in my mind
> That, sometimes, when I think of them, I seem
> Two consciousnesses, conscious of myself
> And of some other Being.
>
> (*The Prelude*, 2, 28–33)

Wordsworth frequently described himself as possessing *two consciousness* or *two natures/The one that feels, the other that observes*. His theories of observation and of memory, that is, involve a self-division which corresponds to that which in his style is represented by his exploitation of the H–L opposition. Dualisms of this kind are central to all forms of narration where the act of narrating is separated in space and time from the act narrated. Recent work in the novel, for instance, encourages us to see it as a blend of what Benveniste (1966) called *histoire* (impersonal narration where 'no-one speaks') and *discours*, the language of ordinary conversation (in Wordsworth's terms 'a man speaking to men' in a 'real situation'). In the novel these two modes frequently appear as the division between narrative and dialogue, when the characters' 'speech' emerges from a surrounding 'written' text. But other and subtler interactions are possible. One which has attracted considerable attention is that involved in what Bally (1912) called *style indirect libre*, where the reader is given the impression of a seamless narrative composed of a character's 'discours' and the author's 'histoire'. Descriptions of this style have concentrated on its syntactical bases (Banfield 1982, Hamburger 1973, Adamson forthcoming); but in English the divided lexicon provides by itself such a powerful marker of the written-spoken experiential-noetic distinctions that its contribution ought to be examined too.

Dickens provides a particularly interesting test-ground. Compared with contemporaries such as George Eliot or Trollope, he is sparing in his use of *style indirect libre*. Nevertheless, many of his narratives invoke the distinction between narrator and narrated: in Wordsworth's terms, this may be a difference between past and present states of consciousness or between observing and feeling selves. In such cases, he often resorts to H-L code-switching to register a shift in perspective, as in the following examples from *David Copperfield*:

> He asked me if it would suit my convenience to have the light *put out*; and on my answering 'yes', instantly *extinguished* it.

> I . . . *went upstairs* with my candle directly. It appeared to my childish fancy, as I *ascended* to the bedroom . . .

These examples of *sinonimia*, dismissed as redundant variation by Jespersen (1958: 126–7), are in fact a special case of expressive glossing, in which the distribution of H and L forms corresponds to the structural layering of the narrative. In the first example, the opposition between *put out* and *extinguished* reflects quite straightforwardly the distinction between the colloquial and literary status of the L and H lexis: the L form occurs in the reported speech of the character, its H synonym in the section that represents the writer's encasing summary of events. In the second example, this opposition between the spoken and the written extends to a more general opposition between character and narrator which draws on the major connotative values of the divided lexicon. The L form in the first sentences (*went upstairs*) encodes the point of view of a child protagonist for whom it would be the appropriate register of speech and focuses on an event reported in terms of its physical details (*with my candle*). The use of the H synonym in the second sentence correlates with an explicit distancing and dissecting of the experience recorded in the first. By the introduction of *childish* (which seems to carry its senses both of 'young' and 'foolish'), the narrator, the adult David Copperfield, expresses his temporal and mental separation from his earlier self, and his greater maturity and rationality are reflected in the more elaborate syntax of this second sentence, as well as in its focus on the epistemic rather than the physical aspects of the action it describes (*appeared to my . . . fancy*).

If we replace this example in its context we can see how code-switching relates to larger movements of the narrative and other elements of the style:

> [1] That evening, as the last of its race, and destined evermore to close that volume of my life, will never pass out of my memory.
> [2] It was almost ten o'clock before we heard the sound of wheels.
> [3] We all got up then; and my mother said hurriedly that, as it was so late, and Mr and Miss Murdstone approved of early hours for young people, perhaps I had better go to bed. [4] I kissed her, and went upstairs with my candle directly, before they came in. [5] It appeared to my childish fancy, as I ascended to the bedroom where I had been imprisoned, that they brought a cold blast of air into the house which blew away the old familiar feeling like a feather.
>
> (*David Copperfield*, Ch. VIII)

The passage has the structure of a flashback sequence. The first and last sentences explicitly assert the distance between narrating adult and narrated child (*to close that volume of my life; my childish fancy*), and linguistically too they illustrate that distance with their more complex syntactic structure and their higher proportion of H vocabulary (*destined, volume, memory; ascended, imprisoned, familiar*). Within that frame, the past comes alive again in a narrative vignette of the moment which concluded *that evening*. For many writers, such revivifications of memory provoke the use of *style indirect libre*, and Dickens here is no exception: at the centre of the remembered moment David ventriloquises rather than reports or quotes his mother's speech. What Dickens does not do, however, is use this style as a means of representing the narrator's empathy with the position and perceptions of his former self (as, for example: 'By this time, it was almost ten o'clock. Was that the sound of wheels? We all got up now . . .'). Instead, he renders the child's point of view primarily by shifting into a consistent L to describe the sequence of events: *we heard the sound of wheels, we all got up, I kissed her, went upstairs, they came in.*

In this context, the L–H gloss with which we started – *went upstairs – ascended –* functions very much like a boundary marker, foregrounding the point of transition from child voice to adult voice, past self to present (a transition marked at the opening of the vignette· by the paragraph boundary dividing [1] from [2]). That what happens here, at a more abstract level, involves an opposition between character-focus and narrator-focus is suggested by the different handling of time on each side of these boundaries: in sentences [2] and [4] events are recounted – as they might be experienced – as a simple linear progression, in which one occurs *before* another. In the framing sentences, [1] and [5], the particular moment narrated is placed in a much larger time-scale and related to other events that become visible from a more distant and omniscient point of view: (*last of its race, destined to close, will . . . pass; had been imprisoned, old familiar feeling*).

The same patterning of H and L can be found in Dickens' third-person narratives, and here too there is a characteristic correlation of L with character-focus and H with narrator-focus.

> When no one in the house was stirring, and the lights were all extinguished, she would softly leave her own room, and with noiseless feet descend the staircase, and approach her father's door . . . and in her one absorbing wish to be allowed to show him some affection, to be a consolation to him, to win him over to the endurance of some tenderness from her, his solitary child, she would have knelt down at his feet, if she had dared, in humble supplication.
>
> No one knew it. No one thought of it. The door was ever closed, and he shut up within. He went out once or twice, and it was said

in the house that he was very soon going on his country journey;
but he lived in those rooms, and lived alone, and never saw her,
or inquired for her. Perhaps he did not even know that she was in
the house.

(Dombey and Son, Ch. XVIII)

Where in the last example, it was by glossing that the contrast
between H and L was foregrounded, here it strikes our attention
by sheer weight of numbers. There is a heavy concentration of
H items in the first paragraph (e.g. *extinguished, descend, approach,
absorbing affection, consolation, endurance, solitary, supplication*),
while L is so predominant in the second that even the relatively
mild *inquired* stands out as an exception.

Both paragraphs represent the situation of the neglected Florence, but they do so in very different ways, going beyond the
obvious shift in topic from mental to physical description. In the
first paragraph, we are initially invited to perceive Florence from
the outside in a sequence of visual and auditory impressions
(*lights . . . extinguished, softly, noiseless*) and when we turn to her
emotional life it is to find it described in a heavily conceptualized
H vocabulary that reinforces the sense of an omniscient analysis.
In the second paragraph, by contrast, the camera moves as it
were behind Florence's eyes. We focus on what she focuses on.
Hence her actions are not among those described and her
emotional states are represented in terms of the situation that
evokes them. She has moved, in short, from the position of
perceived to that of perceiver, and correspondingly, the paragraph as a whole consists of a series of translations into the
experiential mode of elements presented noetically in the
preceding paragraph. Thus her *absorbing* concentration on her
father reappears here in his dominance as syntactic and thematic
subject; her *solitary* state is translated into the concrete particulars
of neglect and exclusion that make it up (*no one knew, no one
thought, door . . . closed, he shut up*, etc.); the temporal duration,
expressed in the first paragraph only through the iterative aspect
of the verb (*would . . . leave*), is here translated into the *ever/never*
appropriate to a subjective experience of duration, where present
time seems all time; and finally, the epistemic omniscience of the
first paragraph, where possible or future actions (Florence
kneeling to her father) are as confidently reported as the actions

that are actually performed, is replaced by the epistemic uncertainties appropriate to a partial perspective (*once* OR *twice*, IT WAS SAID . . . *he was* . . . *going*, PERHAPS *he did not even know*).

In classic *style indirect libre*, this kind of empathetic attempt to render experience from within the viewpoint of a character is commonly expressed by introducing markers of the character's NOW into the generalised past tense of narration (Flaubert's development of the *imparfait* is perhaps the most famous instance). And there is, in fact, one sentence of this type in the passage, where NOW is represented by the progressive aspect and a proximal deictic adverb (*he was very soon going on his country journey*). The fact that this sentence occurs in the second paragraph supports the diagnosis of the subjective status of this paragraph; but the sentence is almost equally interesting in being the *only* token of this type and in being confined to the representation of *speech*. There are no examples in the main body of the narrative, where other novelists might have written, for instance: 'No one was thinking of it. The door was ever closed now'. Instead, as in the passage from *David Copperfield*, Dickens relies on the power of the L lexis to render the experiential immediacy of his character's situation and on the shift from H to L to mark the modulation from omniscient to empathetic narration.

9.4.4 Conclusion

In this section (9.4.1–3), I have tried to review and exemplify, necessarily briefly, the literary functions performed by the dual lexicon across a range of genres. What the examples show is that from the moment of its literary appearance, the dual lexicon has significantly shaped the literary representation of subjectivity. The tendency for the two halves of the lexicon to take on distinct values has meant that they can be used individually to represent well-defined perspectives or value-systems, but that in order to convey the sense of a total apprehension, writers have had to employ both halves in counterpoint. The effect of this antiphonal interplay varies from genre to genre, but always it produces the image of a *voice*, whether of author, character, or narrator, speaking to us from within the text.

9.5 THE DIVIDED LEXICON IN THE EFL CURRICULUM

> ... if the present prevalence of our language should invite
> foreigners to this dictionary, many will be assisted by those words
> which now seem only to increase or produce obscurity. For this
> reason I have endeavoured frequently to join a Teutonic and Roman
> interpretation – as to CHEER, to gladden, or exhilarate – that every
> learner of English may be assisted by his own tongue.
>
> (Dr Johnson, Preface to *A Dictionary of the English Language*, 1755)

Twenty years ago the question 'What is the role of literature
in foreign language teaching?' would have caused surprise, and
the form of the question might even have seemed perverse. For
at that time, the teaching practices of most schools and universities in Britain were based on the firm assumption that learning
a foreign language was the necessary but slightly regrettable
preliminary to reading a foreign literature. Since the early 1970s,
however, the shift to *communicative competence* as the generally
accepted pedagogical goal of language courses, and the consequent emphasis on the spoken language as the medium of
instruction, have meant that literature has been relegated to an
increasingly peripheral role in the modern-languages curriculum
– with the result that some of our most sophisticated and highly
regarded university courses are now producing graduates whom
one external examiner describes, in mingled admiration and
dismay, as 'bilingual illiterates'.

The same trend can be observed in most European countries
and at all levels of education. It is notable that the Recommendation on the teaching of Modern Languages, adopted by the
Committee of Ministers for the Council of Europe in 1982 (Rec.
No. R (82) 18), makes no mention of a role for literature in its list
of 'measures to be implemented' for the promotion of language-
learning in member states; and this omission is repeated in most
of the syllabuses developed within the framework of the two
Modern Languages Projects through which the Council has tried
to disseminate its 'learner-centred' approach (for an overview, see
European Modern Language News vol. 1, no. 1, 1985). The A-
level syllabus in French proposed by the Joint Matriculation Board
in 1984 for introduction in 1988 is typical, both in its concentration
on language-in-use and in its marginalization of literature.

Throughout the Working Party's report, literary language is mentioned only as one variety among others, with no particular advantages or privileges, and it is proposed that an adequate reading programme to support the syllabus 'need not necessarily be wholly or even partly' literary (p. 3). As though to underline the point, no literary texts were included in the specimen questions sent out with the report.

As far as the teaching of English as a foreign language is concerned, this kind of syllabus has been popular for a number of years, and there are even signs that the swing of the pendulum away from literature-based courses is reaching the end of its arc. The current position is well reflected in the *British Council Activity Review: English language and literature* (Rutter *et al.* 1985), which both traces the steady 'downward drift in the priority accorded to the promotion of English literature' since the introduction of new modes of ELT activity and argues for a change in direction to remedy what is now seen as a 'generation of neglect' (pp. 52–60).

As yet, however, there have been few practical proposals for ways of re-integrating literature into the language-teaching programme. Paradoxically, if the language-teachers' distrust of literature was caused originally by literary scholars' neglect of language issues in favour of literary history (Rutter *et al.* 1985 speaks caustically of 'erudite surveys of English literature for students who lacked the basic English needed to read it'), it has been sanctioned by the recent boom in the various linguistic approaches to literature that go under the title of stylistics. This is because most of these approaches – whether taking their inspiration from the Prague School or from MIT – have consistently defined and discussed literary language as a 'deviation' from, or 'defamiliarization' of, ordinary spoken language. Hence literature must appear as a special case of language use, which may deserve the respect and interest of the theorist, but which can never supply or exemplify a norm for the language-learner and can never, therefore, serve as a pedagogical instrument.

Even those who have attempted to rehabilitate literature in the language curriculum have accepted the premise of deviance and have produced, as a result, some rather strained and specious defences. Alex Rodger (1982), for example, makes the claim that by teaching the foreign learner the aberrant forms provided by literature you will inevitably highlight for him what is communicatively normal and grammatically orthodox by a process of inversion. I find this is a curious claim, uncomfortably close to the classic *lucus a non lucendo* argument. At the very least it proposes an unnecessarily tortuous method of proceeding, for the linguistic norms and practices to which the learner most imperatively needs to be introduced are those in which his target language deviates from his native language, and in these cases his native language itself provides the most accessible, relevant and illuminating source of contrasts. Widdowson (1979b) tries the opposite tack to Rodger, arguing that if literature deviates from grammatical norms, so does the spoken language and there is therefore no reason to exclude literature from language courses. But this is at best a weak claim: the argument *against ex*clusion can only be converted into an argument *for in*clusion if it is supported by evidence that the kinds of deviance which are held to characterize literary language are the same as those which the learner is likely to encounter in his everyday linguistic interactions. Widdowson provides no evidence of this kind, and all the research on literacy that has accumulated in the last ten years should warn us of the dangers of making any *a priori* assumption of straightforward correspondences between the deviations – and even the norms – of spoken and written discourse (e.g. Goody 1977; Tannen *et al.* 1982; Olson *et al.* 1985).

My own view is that we may best enhance the role of literature in the language curriculum by abandoning the premise that its language is inevitably more complex and contorted than the language of speech. In fact, I want to suggest that in certain crucial areas literature provides a *simplification* of features or systems which appear in the spoken language with a complexity that makes them virtually unteachable. In these cases, literary texts provide a practice-ground for the language-learner, in which he has the unusual privilege of working with linguistic data that is simultaneously idealized and natural.

Register is one such area. Interest in teaching register has developed as a direct consequence of the communicative approach to first- and second-language learning, as teachers have increasingly accepted that 'a language' is not a unitary system of signs, but a collection of registers, or varieties, each with its distinctive forms and appropriate social functions. The mastery of a range of registers is no less than essential if the learner is to achieve creative self-expression in a foreign language or social assimilation in a foreign culture.

But while the need to teach the learner when to say what to whom is now fully recognized, it is not so obvious how such a skill is to be taught. It is suggestive, for instance, that while the theoretical volumes of the *Edinburgh Course in Applied Linguistics* have sections on varieties of language and on the relevance of sociolinguistics to language-teaching, Volume 3, which is the volume concerned with the practical techniques of pedagogy, leaves these subjects out (Allen and Pit Corder 1973). And many of the text-books that do attempt to teach register seem to rely on their students learning, as it were, by osmosis, through simple exposure to a range of examples. It is easy to see why. Any attempt to describe the distinctive features of particular registers reveals that 'a register' is as much of an idealization as 'a language'. In particular, the implied assumption that registers are homogeneous and discrete is challenged by a wide variety of evidence: the distinctive formal features of a particular register may correlate only sporadically with the relevant social context; there may be formal inconsistencies within the code itself; and, almost invariably, the categories of any taxonomy of register overlap, as when the regional dialect of one group of speakers is adopted as the formal style of another group. Most confusingly of all, few or no utterances are encoded in a single register. In fact, as Hudson emphasizes, speakers inhabit a multidimensional social space in which the individual items of any utterance may relate to different dimensions. As an extreme example, Hudson offers:

> John'll be extremely narked

and comments:

> each word except *be* relates to a different dimension in this social space: *John* (rather than, say, *Mr Brown*) locates the speaker relative to John, *'ll* (rather than *will*) locates the occasion on the casual–formal dimension, *extremely* locates the speaker . . . on the educated–uneducated dimension, and *narked* . . . locates him region-ally (Hudson 1980: 140–1).

Hudson's example points to two conflicting conclusions. First, that what the learner crucially needs to acquire is not an anthology of codes, but a mastery of code-switching. Second, that code-switching in the form practised by native speakers may be a skill too subtle and intricate – or just too idiosyncratic and haphazard – to be coherently taught or learnt.

It is here that literature can help. What we find in literary diglossia is a simplified model of code-switching, where the multiplicity of registers is reduced to two, H and L, and those two are formally well-defined by the Romance–Germanic split in the lexicon. But simplification does not here mean distortion or trivialization. For literary diglossia models the fundamental contrasts which the student must learn how to manage – such as the contrast between formal and intimate levels, ideational and expressive functions – and literary examples can be found to provide the learner with a process of gradual approximation to the complexities of actual discourse.

Such a programme is very much in accord with recent thinking on second-language acquisition which points to its analogies with the processes at work in the development of pidgins and creoles (Klein 1985: 30–2; Schumann 1975). In this view, the initial phase of language learning corresponds to the phase of pidginization, in that the learner accepts a simplification and impoverishment of the language event in the interests of securing some minimal communication. But there comes a time – as in the phase of creolization – when the learner needs to enrich his seccnd language so that it provides him with the resources to 'mark his social identity within the target culture or to express subtle psychological states or needs to native speakers of the target language'. It is at this point that speakers spontaneously expand their vocabulary 'to include synonyms with different connotata' (Schumann 1975: 149).

The analysing of literary diglossia provides particularly useful exercises for learners who have reached this phase of development. What the dual lexicon offers them is a simple system of formal oppositions, which has the advantage, as Dr Johnson noted of a parallel feature in his own practice as a lexicographer, of being perceptually salient to speakers of both Romance and Germanic languages. The lexicon is not, of course, the only marker of a language's different styles, but it is in English the most obvious marker, and therefore provides a ready and secure diagnosis of stylistic level for less advanced students, and for more advanced students this may become the basis of an investigation into the more elusive components of style, such as syntax. For the less advanced learner the advantage of the dual lexicon as a stylistic marker lies in the fact that in many syntactic constructions, a change of style can be manifested through simple lexical substitution, as in Trudgill's example of formal and informal variants: 'Father was fatigued after his journey' *vs* 'Dad was tired after his trip' (Trudgill 1974a: 110). This last factor is particularly important in helping the student to make the shift from analytic to productive skills. The dual lexicon, which forms the basis of much of the characteristic word-play of native speakers of English, lends itself very readily to the kind of language games and creative writing assignments which are playing an increasing part in the curriculum of foreign learners (e.g. Mummert 1985; Maley and Grellet 1981; Morgan and Rinvolucri 1983).

Finally, in case what I have been suggesting should seem to reduce literature to a purely instrumental role in the pursuit of linguistic competence, I want to suggest that the study of the dual lexicon forms a vital part in the understanding of literature itself. The student who has reached an understanding of lexical diglossia has simultaneously been learning about an important phenomenon in the English literary tradition, a phenomenon which may even be its uniquely defining characteristic, or at least the leading contributor to its peculiar distinction among European literatures. The 'unequalled profusion' of synonyms in English, when installed as a structural duality in the lexicon, produces that richness of texture and intricacy of movement which, however deplorable in the eyes of classicists such as Matthew Arnold, have been the hallmark of English literary style since the Renaissance[2].

NOTES

1. *A Note on the French Connection*
   The Latinized vocabulary introduced into English as a result of Renaissance 'enrichment' joined a word stock that was already divided between words of

Germanic origin and words imported from French. The specific role of the French element in English requires a separate consideration in itself. But the way it affects the stylistic judgements I have described in this chapter can be adequately gauged by looking at the full table of results from the experiment reported in 9.3 (the prefixed letters offer a slightly simplified account of the sources from which the words entered the language: L = Latin, F = French, G = Germanic)

Table 9.2 Results

(L) parsimonious	5.0	(F) distress	3.2	(F) chair	2.0
(L) putrefaction	4.8	(F) beautiful	3.0	(G) sweet	2.0
(L) ostentatious	4.8	(F) invalid (n.)	2.8	(G) frightened	1.9
(L) apprehensive	4.0	(F) familiar	2.6	(G) ill	1.7
(F) elegant	4.0	(F?) coarse	2.4	(G) pretty	1.5
(L) vitality	3.5	(F) shocked	2.3	(G) mean	1.5
(L) agitated	3.3	(G) keep	2.3	(G) rot	1.3
(F) grieve	3.2	(G) book	2.2		

What is revealed here is an interesting combination of stratification and gradience. There is still a clear demarcation line half way up the scale of formality: no Germanic word scores above 2.3 (*keep*) and only one French-derived item – significantly, a monosyllable – appears below that point (*chair*). Furthermore, even relatively low-scoring French-Romance words rate as H by comparison with synonyms or near synonyms from the Germanic stock (note the relative scores of *invalid* vs. *ill*, *beautiful* vs. *pretty*, *coarse* vs. *mean*, *shocked* vs. *frightened*). Similarly, the very highest ratings are reserved for the learned Latin polysyllables.

However, in contrast to the table presented in 9.3., there is no gap in the middle, rather a smooth gradience in which the French-derived lexicon links and partially interpenetrates the Latin and Germanic strata (the exact position of each item depending on an interplay of such factors as frequency of occurrence, number of syllables, date of borrowing, semantic field). The picture presented by this table suggests the possibility that the French element in English might provide a stylistic median not subject to analysis in terms of the H–L dichotomy, and indeed resolving the various oppositions it encodes. This is precisely the claim made, in effect, for Addison's language by Dr Johnson when he calls it 'the model of the middle style'. This valuation of Addison is echoed by Arnold, who finds in Addison a unique example of classical stylistic purity in English prose. But significantly, Arnold regards Addison as an aberration from the norm, and the structure of Johnson's encomium points to the more usual way in which English writers have exploited the French-Romance layer in English vocabulary:

> Whoever wishes to attain an English style familiar but not coarse, and elegant but not ostentatious, must give his days and nights to the volumes of Addison. (*Life of Addison*, 1781)

Just as Milton associated a 'high' style with Latin lexis and a 'low' style with Germanic, so Johnson, in negotiating the case for a *middle style*, does indeed envisage it in terms of French vocabulary: Addison's style is *familiar* and *elegant*. But the 'middle' status of these items is not represented as intrinsic to them; rather, it emerges from a double opposition by which *familiar* is perceived as H when juxtaposed with the monosyllabic *coarse*, and *elegant* appears L by comparison to the Latinate *ostentatious*. In other words, Johnson does not himself use a monoglossic middle style, but puts the French lexicon which might be thought to constitute such a style into a series of H–L oppositions. The relatively unmarked status of French-derived words means that they may occupy either the H or the L slot in any given context, depending on the words with which they are juxtaposed. But in most contexts and for most writers, they are forcibly annexed to the dualistic patterns of *diglossia*, rather than providing the means to avoid or resolve its dualisms.

2. The kernel of this chapter was a paper presented at the Triangular Colloquium on 'The Role of Literature in Language Teaching and Learning' held in Paris in September 1984, under the joint auspices of the British Council, the Goethe-Institut and AUPELF (see Adamson 1985). I would like to express my thanks to the British Council for inviting me to take part in the colloquium, and to the other participants for the fruitful discussions that took place on that occasion. In revising and expanding the original paper, I have benefited very much from the comments and advice of Edith Harding, Terry Moore, Mick Short and, particularly, John Woolford. In preparing my experimental results, I was greatly helped by the numeracy of James Adamson. Finally, my most important debt is to the late Hugh Sykes Davies, who first drew my attention to the importance of the dual lexicon in English.

TEN

The language of poetry: The application of literary stylistic theory in university teaching*

Peter Verdonk

This Chapter gives an account of a project in literary stylistics which I recently carried out with fairly advanced students in the English Department of the University of Amsterdam. The objective of the project was to scrutinize a number of theories and techniques that are to be found within the 'New Stylistics', and to exemplify these approaches by analysing some twentieth-century poems.

10.1 NARROWING DOWN THE FIELD

As far as I know, it was Roger Fowler (1975: 4) who coined the term the 'New Stylistics', which, as he pointed out, should not be taken as a common denominator of a particular school of stylistics, but as a pragmatic designation of the output of writings produced over the last twenty-five years or so by scholars mainly in Great Britain and the United States, who have been trying to come to grips with the language of literature.

Fowler also provides a brief survey of the characteristics of the New Stylistics and he concludes that 'theoretical catholicity' is one of them. Indeed, a mere glance at a bibliography on the subject will suffice to appreciate that since the publication of Sebeok's *Style in Language* in 1960, which is usually taken as a convenient starting-point for this flood of activity, stylistics has received much impetus from the multifarious developments in linguistics during the same period.

It is therefore obvious that to make a short-range project with students workable, one has to select a limited number of approaches, which should preferably show some kind of inter-relation and unity of thought. In narrowing down the field, I developed a predilection for the stylistics originating from the body of research carried out in Britain (also starting in the 1960s) in the neo-Firthian or Hallidayan school of linguistics. Taking my students' linguistic expertise into account, I set out on essentially text-oriented approaches and compiled for them a select bibliography of writings produced mainly in the earlier stage of this British tradition, which has recently been designated as 'classic' stylistics (D'haen 1986: 3). The items featuring in this reading list are included in the bibliography at the end of this book. As in some respects British stylistics has been influenced by the Russian formalists, the Prague aestheticians, and international structuralism, the working bibliography also included Jakobson (1960), Mukarovsky (1964) and Culler (1975).

After preliminary talks about this theoretical framework, we focused our attention on some of the writings of Leech (1965), Fowler (1971a: 219–37), Widdowson (1974), and Cluysenaar (1976 & 1982) (in fact, we dealt with them in this order) for the actual application of some stylistic models.

10.2 MOTIVATION OF THE PROJECT

Having set these bibliographical bounds to the project, I shall now discuss its chief motivation. Though I have no wish to get involved in the old controversy about the relevance of linguistic stylistics to literary criticism, this project has been set up with students of both disciplines on the assumption that a sensitive and effective linguistic perception that leads to subtle stylistic distinctions does provide a secure basis for an aesthetic appreciation of literature. Another motive is the desire to counteract the falling off of a formal knowledge of language due to the present-day educational spirit, at least in The Netherlands. It must be admitted that the average student has learnt to talk quickly and very easily, which is in itself a joyful phenomenon, but I am afraid that this success has often been attained with the sacrifice of the ability to reflect on language with patience and sensitivity.

This is not the place to rehearse the fundamentals of linguistics and stylistics that are needed to evolve such an aptitude for the workings of language. Suffice it to say that with the help of illustrative material I have tried to show my students that literary stylistics is primarily concerned with the relation between linguistic form and literary function. Furthermore, I have emphasized time and again that stylistics should never be reduced to some mechanical ticking off of the linguistic features of a text, but that, on the contrary, intuition and personal judgement (based on observable textual features) are of paramount importance.

10.3 PLACE IN THE CURRICULUM, DURATION AND TEACHING FORMAT

Before discussing the internal design of the project, I wish to give some factual details about its place in the curriculum, its duration and its teaching format. After completing an eighteen-month uniform introductory programme, our students split up into three main streams: modern linguistics, historical linguistics (both applied to English) and English and American literature. Each main-stream programme consists of a certain proportion of compulsory and optional courses varying in content, intensity, teaching format and length. Literary stylistics comes under the optional courses and as it is considered to be an interdisciplinary subject, it can be chosen by literature as well as linguistics students.

The course lasts one semester (which is thirteen weeks of our academic year) and usually there are two seminar groups involved with about fifteen students each for two hours per week, which means that I have twenty-six hours of actual teaching time for each group.

The classroom model for a project like this is very important and I fully agree with Roger Fowler (1986: 178) that the seminar format ensures maximal involvement of the students while the teacher's role is less dominant. As a result the students feel more inclined to share their views and ideas and to cooperate on oral and written assignments.

10.4 INTERNAL DESIGN OF THE PROJECT

As to the internal design of the project, I wish to emphasize that I have found it to be of crucial importance to bring about a firm link between what Leech (1977) called the three levels of exegesis: the *linguistic level* of non-aesthetic discussion, the *literary critical level* of aesthetic discussion, and an intermediate level which he called the *stylistic level*. It is on the stylistic level that linguistic statements are selected for their relevance to the aesthetic discussion on the literary critical level. For this selection of relevant linguistic features, I encouraged the students to apply some stylistic theories (for example, the theory of *foregrounding*, which will be discussed in section 10.5) and, at the same time, to keep an open mind on aesthetic considerations. As a matter of fact, both my students and I have found this interplay between the non-aesthetic and the aesthetic to be quite revealing and fruitful.

With this objective in mind and after several try-outs in the preceding academic year, when the students came up with a lot of valuable suggestions, I finally decided on the following physical organization of the project.

The first three weeks were spent on introductory talks about the theoretical basis of the project, though I took care that these talks were interspersed with practical applications of the various stylistic models. As a result of this approach the students became highly motivated to have a go themselves.

After these preliminaries, I handed out a working-schedule (covering the remaining ten weeks) on which the students were asked to enter themselves for the following assignments (at the end of the project, all students were supposed to have done assignment B, while they had a choice between assignment A or C):

Every *even* week – *Assignment A:*

Two or three students were to present an article to the seminar to be chosen from: Leech (1965), Fowler (1971a: 219–37), Widdowson (1974), Cluysenaar (1976: 50–75) and Cluysenaar (1982). These writings were to be discussed in this order. (In order to facilitate discussion, all members of the seminar were supposed to have studied the articles beforehand.)

Every *odd* week – *Assignment B:*

Two or three students had to hand out on paper a stylistic analysis of a twentieth-century poem based on the model suggested in the article discussed in the preceding week.

Assignment C:
> Two or three students had to make sure that they had a preview of the stylistic analysis referred to in assignment B so that they could make evaluative comments and lead the discussion when the analysis was presented to the seminar.

It was my role to chair these proceedings, to come up with suggestions whenever the discussion got stuck, to intervene when the discussion was sidetracked, to make notes, and so forth.

10.5 ANALYSIS OF PHILIP LARKIN'S 'GOING' BASED ON THE MODEL PROPOSED BY LEECH (1965)

At this point I would like to turn to the presentation of some of the stylistic analyses resulting from the seminar discussions described above. As I have said, there were some thirty participants in the project so that they must of necessity remain nameless, but all the same I wish to make a point of giving them the share of the credit that is due to them.

The first poem for which we suggest an interpretation based on a literary stylistic analysis is Philip Larkin's 'Going' (1955). We have proceeded on the model of analysis proposed by Geoffrey Leech (1965). In his analysis of Dylan Thomas's 'This Bread I Break', Leech proceeds from linguistic description to literary interpretation. Pointing out that 'a work of literature contains dimensions of meaning additional to those operating in other types of discourse', he expresses the view that linguistic description cannot be applied to literary texts without proper adjustments and he incorporates three stylistic concepts: *cohesion*, *foregrounding* and *cohesion of foregrounding*.

Endorsing the view that it is the linguist's aim to make 'statements of meaning', Leech refers to the work of J. R Firth (1957: 32–3 and 190–215), the founder of the neo-Firthian or British school of linguistics. Leech points out that 'meaning' in the above quotation must be given a wider sense than usual, sometimes including every aspect of linguistic choice: semantics, vocabulary, grammar, or phonology, and though Leech mentions it later in his paper, it is convenient to anticipate and to add here another aspect conducive to meaning, *viz.* context of situation. In Firthian linguistic theory, meaning is looked upon as a complex phenomenon, its various aspects being relatable to features of the external world as well as to the several levels of linguistic analysis. Context of situation refers to the whole set of external world features considered to be relevant in the analysis of an utterance at these levels (Firth 1957: 192). Leech adds to this that in literature we have to construct such a context from the text itself.

We shall now suggest an interpretation of Larkin's poem in the light of a linguistic analysis extended with the above-mentioned stylistic categories of description: cohesion, foregrounding and cohesion of foregrounding.

Going

There is an evening coming in
Across the fields, one never seen before,
That lights no lamps.

Silken it seems at a distance, yet
[5] When it is drawn up over the knees and breast
It brings no comfort.

Where has the tree gone, that locked
Earth to the sky? What is under my hands,
That I cannot feel?

[10] What loads my hands down?

10.5.1 Cohesion

Leech defines *cohesion* as 'the way in which independent choices in different points of a text correspond with or presuppose one another, forming a network of sequential relations'. So what is of interest is the way in which these linguistic choices form patterns of intra-textual relations on any of the levels of linguistic description: phonology, grammar, semantics and pragmatics.

The cross-references to the postponed subject[1] *an evening* in line 1 are only made by grammatical means, *viz.* by the pronominal *one* in line 2, the pronoun *that* in line 3, and by a high concentration of the pronoun *it* in three consecutive lines: 4, 5 and 6. It is noticeable that there is no attempt at repetition of the noun *evening* by means of lexical items so as to reinforce its contextual meaning. In part, this meaning is conveyed grammatically. The article *an* modifying *evening* (1) as well as its pronominal cross-references carry a suggestion of indefiniteness. This notion is reinforced by the cohesive grammatical structure of the poem: two long declarative sentences, which, evidently, do not contain enough information about *an evening* to prevent the following three relatively short WH-questions.

Furthermore, there is the repetition of three negative elements: *never* in the clause *never seen before* (2) expresses *unfamiliarity* with *an evening*, while *no* in the descriptive clauses *That lights no lamps* (3) and *It brings no comfort* (6) conveys its negative aspects.

The most obvious grammatical pattern in this poem is the selection of the present tense in lines 3, 4, 6, 8, 9 and 10. As a matter of fact, the passive *is drawn up* (5) and the aspectual verbal forms *is coming in* (1), *seen* (2) (here we assume the underlying structure 'one that has never been seen before'), and *has gone* (7), also have a present tense form in their explicit or implicit auxiliaries. In fact, there is only one past tense: *locked* in line 7. This predominance of the present tense seems to suggest an inescapable immediacy.

10.5.2 Foregrounding

Referring to the theory of aesthetics and language from the Czech School (see Garvin 1964), Leech interprets *foregrounding* as 'a motivated deviation from linguistic, or other socially accepted norms'. Elsewhere (in Fowler 1973: 75), he defines foregrounding as 'the violation of rules and conventions, by which a poet transcends the normal communicative resources of the language, and awakens the reader, by freeing him from the grooves of cliché expression, to a new perceptivity'.

In our poem there are many foregrounded groupings of lexical items as a result of the following deviant choices from the language code:

(i)   'an evening is coming in' (1)
(ii)   '(an evening) That lights no lamps' (3)
(iii) 'Silken it (an evening) seems at a distance' (4)
(iv) 'it (an evening) is drawn up over knees and breast' (5)

(v)   'It (an evening) brings no comfort' (6)
(vi) '(the tree) that locked earth to the sky' (7–8)

In (i), (ii) and (v) the noun *evening* which normally has the feature of inanimacy is given a human feature. In (iii) and (iv) the same noun is also used in highly unpredictable collocations. If we set up the frames *Silken . . . seems at a distance*, and, *When . . . is drawn up over the knees and breast*, the noun *evening* is not available for selection in these positions. A normal choice, particularly in the second frame, would be, for example, the nouns *sheet* or *blanket*.

If we take the verb *lock* in (vi) to mean 'to fix or to join firmly together', the choice of the noun *tree* is abnormal, not to mention the semantic oddity of the collocation *locked earth to the sky*.

The above instances of lexical foregrounding are clear illustrations of metaphorical language in which linguistic forms should be given something other than their normal (literal) interpretation.

There is grammatical deviation in the pattern *Silken it seems at a distance* (4) in which the subject complement *silken* is preposed.

Furthermore, the syntactic ambiguity of *What is under my hands, / That I cannot feel?* (8–9) could be regarded as a way of foregrounding this WH-question. The clause *That I cannot feel* can be seen as an adverbial (of result): 'so that I cannot feel', though it also seems possible to regard the constituents *what* and *that I cannot feel* as being in an attributive relationship.

There is also an example of internal deviation in this poem, *viz.* in the stanzaic structure. The poet deviates from his own pattern and thereby from our expectations created by the poem, when he concludes with a one-line stanza after three stanzas consisting of three lines each. As a result, the last stanza is foregrounded and placed in focus.

10.5.3 *Cohesion of foregrounding*

The third stylistic descriptive statement with which Leech extends the linguistic categories of description is *cohesion of foregrounding*. By this is meant the manner in which 'the foregrounded features identified in isolation are related to one another, and to the text in its entirety'. So this feature may occur when certain foregrounded elements, though deviant from normal language use, form a cohesive intra-textual pattern and thus become normal in the context of the poem as a whole.

With regard to this stylistic category, it may be observed that in our poem there is such a predominance of deviant lexical collocations which are foregrounded against normal usage (particularly with the noun *evening*) that they take on a normality in the context of the poem as a whole and can be regarded as a form of cohesion.

Further extended foregrounding is observed in the phonology of the first six lines of the poem in which there is a striking predominance of sibilants: there are fourteen /s/ or /z/ phonemes.

10.5.4 Linguistic stylistic description 'locked to' literary interpretation

Now that we have pointed out several linguistic and stylistic features of the poem, we must ask the question 'To what extent are these features artistically significant?' It will be clear that a satisfactory answer to this question will narrow (or perhaps even close) the gap between linguistic stylistic description and literary interpretation.

For a possible interpretation of the poem, we still need a *context of situation*, which we must infer from the text itself. The situation that suggests itself to us is that of the hour of death of the I-person in the poem. We shall take this situation as a starting-point and examine to what extent the cohesive and foregrounded features fit in with this particular level of interpretation.

The association of *an evening* with imminent Death is conveyed by the grammatically cohesive patterns that suggest 'indefinite-ness', 'unfamiliarity', 'negative aspects', and 'inescapable im-mediacy', as well as by the foregrounded lexical patterns in which this noun occurs: *an evening* is given animate features; it is coming in and it has never been seen before. So it is not just any evening. It seems to have come unexpectedly (cf. 'death's dateless night', Shakespeare, *Sonnet 30*), because people have not lit their lamps. However, the ensuing darkness will persist because this 'evening' *lights no lamps*. It seems useless to try and keep away the darkness of this evening of Death as one would keep away the darkness of an ordinary evening: with lamps. The predominance of sibilants in the first six lines describing the coming of the evening can be seen as reinforcing the stealthy way in which Death is approaching.

In the second stanza *evening* seems *silken . . . at a distance* but *when it is drawn up over knees and breast, it brings no comfort*. The idea of a (silken) sheet or blanket suggests itself. The image of being covered may be associated with dying. However, the I-person is not dead yet, because then the sheet would also have covered his head. The 'sheet of Death' is only seemingly silken and *brings no comfort*.

The third stanza differs very much from the previous ones, which consist of two long sentences. Here we are confronted with two relatively short questions following each other without stopping for an answer. This indicates the persona's growing anxiety at his approaching death. The questions concern his decreasing consciousness of his surroundings. He can no longer see the tree *that locked earth to the sky*. Is it the 'tree of life' (*Genesis* 2: 9)? His diminishing sensibility is also apparent from the fact that he can no longer feel what is under his hands, or, alternatively, that because something (Death?) is under his hands, he cannot feel at all any more (see our discussion of the syntactic ambiguity of *What is under my hands, / That I cannot feel?* in 10.5.2). This becoming numb may be seen as a symptom of dying.

We have already observed that the last one-line stanza is foregrounded and therefore gets the maximum of attention. One is inclined to interpret this as the last moment before actual death. Death has now enveloped the I-person entirely and he feels its terrible weight: *What loads my hands down?* This last question also remains unanswered, only silence remains. It is the silence of Death: the I-person is no longer 'going' (we now fully understand the title of the poem!); he is 'gone'.

10.6 A BRIEF EXPOSÉ OF A STYLISTIC MODEL PROPOSED BY WIDDOWSON (1974)

The most important feature of Widdowson's stylistic model (1974: 202–31) seems to be the idea that a literary text can be construed as a 'secondary language system', a micro-language, formed by the relations which the writer has set up between the language items within his text. For the interpretation of any text, Widdowson continues, we must recognize not only these intra-textual relations but also the extra-textual relations that exist between the language items occurring in a text and the code from which they derive. The intra-textual relations set up between linguistic items within a literary text create contextual meaning, while the extra-textual relations yield the significance which the items have according to the code, i.e. their referential meaning.

In Widdowson's view it is typical of literature that these two sets of relations do not join to produce one new unit of meaning. On the contrary, 'they overlap to create a unit of meaning which belongs to neither one nor the other: a hybrid unit which derives from both code and context and yet is a unit of neither of them' (1974: 206).

Elsewhere Widdowson has written that if stylistics is to make any valuable contribution to criticism, literature must be studied as a mode of communication, and in such a study, means and ends must be given equal attention and shown to be interdependent (1980: 235–41). For an appreciation of what a writer tries to convey, we must study the means he is using in relation to the linguistic resources he can draw on. Since such an examination does not yield enough information about the communicative effect of the writer's linguistic means, we must also know what ends are achieved on that score. According to our understanding, this concept of style emphasizes the contributions of 'form' to 'content', in brief, style is looked upon as 'meaning'.

10.7 ANALYSIS OF JON SILKIN'S 'DEATH OF A SON' BASED ON THE MODEL PROPOSED BY WIDDOWSON (1974)

After this very brief exposé of Widdowson's stylistic approach, I wish to examine its applicability to the interpretation of poetry and we present here an analysis of Jon Silkin's poem 'Death of a Son' (from Allott 1950: 383–5).

Death of a Son
(who died in a mental hospital aged one)

Something has ceased to come along with me.
Something like a person: something very like one.
    And there was no nobility in it
        Or anything like that.

[5]   Something was there like a one year
Old house, dumb as stone. While the near buildings
    Sang like birds and laughed
        Understanding the pact

They were to have with silence. But he
[10]   Neither sang nor laughed. He did not bless silence
    Like bread, with words.
        He did not forsake silence.

But rather, like a house in mourning
Kept the eye turned in to watch the silence while
[15]   The other houses like birds
        Sang around him.

And the breathing silence neither
Moved nor was still.

I have seen stones: I have seen brick
[20]   But this house was made up of neither bricks nor stone
    But a house of flesh and blood
        With flesh of stone

And bricks for blood. A house
Of stones and blood in breathing silence with the other
[25]   Birds singing crazy on its chimneys.
        But this was silence,

This was something else, this was
Hearing and speaking though he was a house drawn
    Into silence, this was
[30]   Something religious in his silence,

Something shining in his quiet,
This was different this was altogether something else:
    Though he never spoke, this
        Was something to do with death.

]35]   And then slowly the eye stopped looking
Inward. The silence rose and became still.
The look turned to the outer place and stopped,
    With the birds still shrilling around him.
        And as if he could speak

[40] He turned over on his side with his one year
Red as a wound
He turned over as if he could be sorry for this
And out of his eyes two great tears rolled, like stones,
                                        and he died.

In our analysis we shall proceed in agreement with
Widdowson's proposal 'to pick on features in the text which
appeal to first impression as unusual or striking in some way and
then explore their ramifications'.

One of the striking features in this poem is the use of the pronominal *something* in the first two stanzas. *Something* usually refers
to an inanimate object, but here it is used with reference to the
son, a human being. In the subsequent stanzas, however, the
child is referred to by means of the personal pronouns *he, him* and
the possessive *his*, which is in agreement with the rules of the
code. As a result of this overlap of intra-textual and extra-textual
reference of *something*, it acquires a hybrid meaning, giving the
son both inanimate and human attributes.

A similar process is found in lines 19–24: 'I have seen stones:
I have seen brick / But this house was made up of neither bricks
nor stone / But a house of flesh and blood / With flesh of
stone / And bricks for blood. A house / Of stones and blood in
breathing silence . . .' After the son has been compared to a
house in the preceding stanzas: *a one-year- / Old house, dumb as
stone* (5–6) and *a house in mourning* (13), the persona tells us
explicitly that *this house was made up of neither bricks nor stone* (20).
In this way he breaks the rules of the code, taking away some
of the features of the referent *house*, and then makes up for the
deficiency by placing the deviant items *flesh* and *blood* in a pattern
with *house: a house of flesh and blood / With flesh of stone / And bricks
for blood* (21–3). In the very next line, however, the feature *stone*
returns in the phrase *A house / Of stones and blood* (23–4). As a
result, the noun *house* also gains a hybrid meaning conveying
both animate and inanimate qualities.

The above observations show that the poet does not only sever
the extra-textual relations by referring to a person as *something*
and by presenting a house *of neither bricks nor stone* (20), but he
also breaks the intra-textual relations he has set up within his

poem. First he constructs the phrase *a house of flesh and blood* (21), which requires us to give the noun *house* a significance beyond that which it carries in the language code, and then he diminishes this contextual meaning again by referring to the extra-textual features of the referent *house*, reintroducing the feature *stones*, though preserving the deviant item *blood*, which yields *a house of stones and blood* (23–4).

The poet also breaks up intra-textual relations within the context of the poem without recurrence to extra-textual relations with the code. In the second stanza, the boy is compared to a house and consistent with this deviant intra-textual pattern, the other children (if we assume that they are also mental patients in the same hospital) are referred to as *the near buildings* (6). Apparently, these children are lively and cheerful, as we can gather from the highly deviant clause *the near buildings / Sang like birds and laughed* (6–7). This deviation holds for the lexical collocations only, because the syntax is entirely regular: subject – predicator – adverbial (of manner). However, in the fourth stanza we find: *The other houses like birds / Sang around him* (15–16). It will be observed that the prepositional phrase *like birds* has been given a different place, *viz.* following the subject and preceding the predicator. In this position, the phrase still functions as an adverbial, but it is now not only related to the process denoted by the verb (as in lines 6–7), but also to the subject. *The other houses* (15) can thus be construed as bird-like in other ways besides their singing. Many of the adverbials in this position show their relationship with the subject by allowing a paraphrase like 'They were like birds when they sang around him', showing a complement relationship between the subject *they* and the prepositional phrase *like birds*. This syntactic shift prepares us for the poet's severance of the intra-textual relations set up by him between *the near buildings* (6), *the other houses* (15) and the other children, because in the seventh stanza, he no longer compares these children to buildings or houses but only to birds, which are *singing crazy* on the chimneys of the one remaining 'house': the dying boy. The boy and the other children are no longer of a kind: 'A house / Of stones and blood in breathing silence with the other / Birds singing crazy on its chimneys' (23–5).

Another stylistic feature that arrests our attention is the frequent repetition of one and the same lexical item, *viz.* the noun *silence*. Widdowson remarks that literature, and indeed all art, creates 'patterns out of deviations from normality and these patterns then represent a different reality from that represented by the conventional code'. What are the patterns involving the word *silence* in this poem and what different realities are created by them?

The first occurrence of *silence* in line 9 is not entirely unexpected, because we have already been told that there was *something . . . like a one-year- / Old house, dumb as stone* (5–6). However, the collocational pattern in which the word *silence* is used deviates from the conventions of the code: 'While the near buildings / Sang like birds and laughed / Understanding the pact / They were to have with silence' (6–9). So we have here another instance of overlapping of extra-textual relations which link the word *silence* with the code ('condition of not speaking') and intra-textual relations which link it with the contextual situation in which it seems that the cheerful children felt free to sing like birds and to laugh, because they understood *the pact they were to have with silence*. At one level of meaning, *silence* may be taken to refer to the dying boy, as in lines 17–18. *And the breathing silence neither / Moved nor was still*, and, being mental patients themselves, the other children would of necessity have some mysterious bond with the dumb little boy ('the pact they *were to* have with silence').

The other contextual patterns in which the word *silence* is placed also accrete to it a wealth of meanings over and above that which can be recovered from the code.

Thus the lexical patterning in the third stanza creates obvious biblical echoes: *He did not bless silence / Like bread, with words. / He did not forsake silence* (10–12).

In line 14, *Kept the eye turned in to watch the silence*, there is a collocational clash with the verb *watch* expressing visual perception and its abstract object. Here *silence* is within the boy; in lines 23–4 and 29 the boy is within *silence*: *A house/Of stones and blood in breathing silence* (23–4), and *he was a house drawn / Into silence* (28–9), while the boy ɪs *silence* in lines 17–18, and probably also in line 26: *And the breathing silence neither/Moved nor was still* (17–18), and *But this was silence* (26).

In lines 29–30 *silence* is again related to religion: *this was/Something religious in his silence*, and we notice that after *He did not bless silence / Like bread, with words* (10–11), *something* (the dying boy) acquires a religious attribute. The structurally identical lines 30–1: *Something religious in his silence, / Something shining in his quiet* emphasize the link between *something religious* and its parallel *something shining*: the religious feature seems to be shining through now, the persona can see it. The son has become quite different from the *something* of the first line.

In line 36 *The silence rose and became still*, the word *silence* is again used in a highly deviant lexical environment. We feel inclined to relate this line to lines 13–14: *like a house in mourning / Kept the eye turned in to watch the silence*. Of a house in mourning the curtains are lowered, its inhabitants cannot look out ('they keep their eyes turned in'), and inside reigns the silence of grief. In line 36 we find *the silence rose and became still*. Does this mark the end of mourning? Did the curtains rise (*the silence* [of mourning] *rose*) because the house is no longer in mourning and is there an end to the acute pains of grief (*and became still*)?

We are perfectly aware of the fact that we have touched upon only very few of the manifold contextual problems and their resultant meanings in this moving poem and that this brief discussion has raised more questions than it has answered. Nevertheless, we think we have shown that, at any rate in this poem, 'form' and 'content' are interdependent, in other words, that style is 'meaning' (for more on this very complex issue see Leech and Short 1981: 12–73). The poem's style reflects the disorderly thoughts, the confrontation with different realities and unrealities, caused by the untold grief of the persona for the death of his small son.

10.8 ANALYSIS OF SYLVIA PLATH'S 'ARIEL' BASED ON THE MODEL PROPOSED BY CLUYSENAAR (1982)

We now turn to Anne Cluysenaar (1982), who has expressed the view that a consideration of fairly obvious lexical and syntactic features of a literary text can be made to yield semantic information that may be found relevant to its literary description and evaluation. Since Cluysenaar's paper was primarily intended for those engaged in teaching English literature to non-native speakers, she recommended a simple approach to observe these formal properties. Hence there is no need to discuss this approach separately.

We propose to analyse Sylvia Plath's 'Ariel' (1965) along the lines suggested by Cluysenaar, though we will also make use of some extra-textual information, such as the fact that Ariel[2] was the name of Sylvia Plath's horse. We will also take into account the poet's symbolic use of colours, which can be found in her other poems as well.

Ariel

> Stasis in darkness.
> Then the substanceless blue
> Pour of tor and distances.
>
> God's lioness,
> [5] How one we grow,
> Pivot of heels and knees! – The furrow
>
> Splits and passes, sister to
> The brown arc
> Of the neck I cannot catch,
>
> [10] Nigger-eye
> Berries cast dark
> Hooks ———
>
> Black sweet blood mouthfuls,
> Shadows.
> [15] Something else
>
> Hauls me through air ———
> Thighs, hair;
> Flakes from my heels.
>
> White
> [20] Godiva, I unpeel ———
> Dead hands, dead stringencies.
>
> And now I
> Foam to wheat, a glitter of seas.
> The child's cry
>
> [25] Melts in the wall.
> And I
> Am the arrow,
>
> The dew that flies
> Suicidal, at one with the drive
> [30] Into the red
>
> Eye, the cauldron of morning.

At the lexical level of the poem we find that the largest set of lexical items refers to parts of the body:

> *heels* (6), *knees* (6), *neck* (9), *thighs* (17),
> *hair* (17), *heels* (18), *hands* (21), *eye* (31).

That *neck* (9) refers to the horse is clear. With the exception of *eye* in the last line, the other items seem to refer either to the rider or to the horse, and in line 6 perhaps to both. This lexical string denotes the physical aspect of the ride. However, the ambiguity as to the possessor of the *eye* in line 31 illustrates that the action described is more than just physical. For *eye* contains a whole range of possible references, of which that to a part of the body is only the most obvious one. One might conclude that the predominantly physical process ends in line 21, where the persona is liberated from all that captivates her, here symbolized by the shedding of her physical being.

The next conspicuous set of lexical items is formed by words referring to colours:

> *blue* (2), *brown* (8), *black* (13), *white* (19), *red* (30)

of which *black* is reinforced in *darkness* (1), *nigger-eye* (10), *dark* (11) and *shadows* (14), and *red* in *blood* (13). *Blue* and *brown* are fairly neutral and undramatic colours and do not have the strong symbolic implications which black, white and red have in Sylvia Plath's poetry. (Cf. *black* in 'Daddy', and *red* and *white* in 'Tulips'.) All colours mentioned – with the possible exception of *white* (19) – have reference to the real landscape or the physical setting of the poem. *Blue* (2) and *brown* (8) are merely part of this setting, whereas *black* (13), *white* (19) and *red* (30) point to the symbolic dimension of the ride. So here, as in the previous lexical string, we find a transition from the physical, the natural to the symbolic level.

The third lexical string is formed by items referring to nature:

> *tor* (3), *furrow* (6), *berries* (11), *air* (16), *wheat* (23), *seas* (23), *dew* (28).

It is significant that with the first four items, the persona seems to experience nature as something external. The last three items, however, apart from possibly functioning at a literal level, are used as images to express the rider's sensation of personal disintegration and unification with nature:

> White
> Godiva, I unpeel
> Dead hands, dead stringencies.
>
> And now I
> Foam to wheat, a glitter of seas. (19–23)
>
> And I
> Am the arrow,
>
> The dew that flies
> Suicidal, . . . (26–9)

Pondering over this sense of disintegration and the rider's complete identification with nature, we are tempted to regroup the above lexical set as below and to add *red/Eye* (30–1) and *cauldron* (31) assuming that they refer to the rising sun. The result is that such a lexical framework comprises the four elements: earth, air, water and fire, of which, according to pre-scientific ideas of physiology, all matter is composed.

tor, furrow (*berries'* and *wheat* can be associated with the earth)	— EARTH
air	— AIR
seas, dew	— WATER
red/Eye, cauldron	— FIRE

Continuing this line of thought, we notice that the string of lexical items referring to water can be extended further: *foam* (23), *melts* (25) and perhaps also *the . . . blue / Pour* (2–3).

Though we are anticipating one of the possible readings of the poem, we wish to point out here the irony in *The dew that flies / Suicidal* (28–9), if we bear in mind that water is universally thought of as a life-giving force.

Even a brief look at the syntax suffices to say that the poem's grammar is extremely complex and in some lines highly ambiguous. The appendix shows an attempt at a syntactic analysis, which reveals a number of striking characteristics that are conducive to the overall meaning of the poem.

The marking of the syntactic constituents shows the boundaries of the sentences, clauses and phrases, and also where they do not coincide with a line-end. It will be noted that there is a very large number of run-on lines, in many of which the syntactic pull is particularly strong because the run-on occurs within a phrase. This feature has a marked effect on the verse-movement, because after the opening line *Stasis in darkness*, which true to its wording is actually the only still point in the whole poem, the reader is hurried forward and thus seems to join in the rider's rush throughout the poem to *red/Eye, the cauldron of morning* (30–1).

There are probably a number of causes that can be assigned to the poem's overall impression of syntactic complexity and ambiguity. We notice some verbless clauses, e.g. in lines 1 and 2–3. Furthermore, there are a number of obscure syntactic relationships, e.g. the phrases *sister to / The brown arc / Of the neck I cannot catch* (7–9) and *Black sweet blood mouthfuls* (13). Assuming that our analysis makes sense, we observe that at several places a given syntactic constituent is delayed, e.g. *Shadows* (14), *Thighs, hair* (17) and *Flakes from my heels* (18). It is also difficult to know whether *Flakes* is a verb or a noun and whether it is related to *Something else* (15). Another such disturbing question concerns *unpeel* (20). Is it really a transitive verb or is it intransitive? Whatever it may be, the syntax of the poem seems to be well-adapted to its subject, since these complexities and ambiguities are a clear reflection of the fleeting impressions of the surrounding landscape that rushes past as well as of the whirling thoughts caused by the rider's ecstasy and impetuous urgency.

The first and most literal reading of the poem offers a description of a horse ride, with horse and rider setting out in the dark of an early morning galloping in ecstasy towards the rising sun. Interwoven with this first reading and never entirely separate from it, is a more symbolic one in which the ride takes on a spiritual dimension. In the literal reading the *Stasis in darkness* is that of horse and rider poised for action. *Stasis*, however, which also carries the meaning of 'stoppage' or 'stagnation', can be seen as applying to the inner state of the persona: totally passive, withdrawn from life. The ride becomes a way of escaping from this stagnation and of finding release in the fiery sunrise, the beginning of a new day.

It is important to realize that this process of liberation is not initiated by the persona, but that it is brought on by a force outside. In the beginning it is the horse, in line 15 it is *Something else* and although towards the end the rider has completely merged with the movement (*I am the arrow*), the source of the motion is still outside the persona.

When *Something else* (15) propels the rider through the air, all inessentialities and restrictions are shed. There is purification (*white* in line 19), the rider having become as naked as the mythical heroine Godiva, there is disintegration (*Thighs, hair; / Flakes from my heels*) and a complete merging with nature. At last the rider reaches unity, which until then had not been total (cf. *The brown arc / Of the neck I cannot catch*, lines 8–9).

The lines *The child's cry / Melts in the wall* (24–5) stand out rather oddly. They are obscure, but they seem to convey impotence and inability to communicate. In spite of this the persona regains self-confidence: *And I / Am the arrow* (26–7), speeds on and finds ultimate release in the *red / Eye, the cauldron of morning*.

That this is the key-phrase in the poem is made perceptible by the fact that, whereas the rest of the poem is neatly divided into three-line stanzas, this last line stands apart. It is the culmination of the ride and it is rich in ambiguity. Though the word *eye* fits into the first lexical string of parts of the body, its immediate context suggests a number of different readings. For example, the word *arrow* (27) leads us to associate the *red / Eye* (30–1) with the 'bull's eye': the persona has reached the ultimate goal of the ride. When we interpret *eye* as something that is central or is felt to be central, i.e. the 'core' of something, another reading suggests itself: *Eye* as *I*. This reading is supported by the process of 'unpeeling', the shedding of inessentialities as described in the central stanzas of the poem. The *Eye/I* then is the persona's pure, raw, red essence, the core of being.

It gradually becomes clear that the ecstatic ride, the gallop for liberation may also be a ride towards destruction:

> And I
> Am the arrow,
>
> The dew that flies
> Suicidal, at one with the drive
> Into the red
>
> Eye, the cauldron of morning.

>   (26–31)

The rider has escaped from the *hooks* (12) and *dead stringencies* (21) have been shaken off. *Stasis* has been turned into motion, darkness has become light. Yet this light is fiery, aggressive, and the rider could be consumed by it. The rider has become *wheat, dew,* both symbols of fertility, but the dew will evaporate in the heat of the sun. *Stasis,* though negative in its meaning of 'stagnation', etc., is positive when it implies 'a state of balance or equilibrium', whereas *morning,* which has positive connotations when it is seen as an image of the birth of a new day, of new hope and energy perhaps, acquires a negative shade of meaning as a result of its being equated with *cauldron* (i.e. in its sense of 'a state of unrest or upheaval'). Thus the poem ends on a superbly ambiguous note.

In her book *Introduction to Literary Stylistics* (1976: 32) Anne Cluysenaar postulates that 'each [literary] work sets up, by the way in which its particular elements interact, a balance of forces which must be understood as a unique structure'. Such 'dominant structures' are linguistic patterns which may reveal meaningful events at any level of linguistic form. These events must be related at all levels with each other and with formal poetic (and other) structures, and to wider aspects of meaning.

Following these precepts, we have based our reading of this poem mainly on its 'dominant' lexical and syntactic structures and have also related the latter to the verse-movement. In other words, what we have attempted is to bring out the poem's unique balance of formal – semantic interactions.

10.9 EPILOGUE

Obviously, the above three stylistic analyses form only a small part of the total output of the project (actually fifteen poems were submitted to an analysis), in which about thirty students took part (and, I may say, they all carried out the assignments described in section 10.4 with a great deal of enthusiasm and a strong motivation to make the thing a success). Yet these three analyses are fairly representative of the students' level of achievement.

During the evaluation of the project, the general feeling of the students was that they had learnt to look at poetry with different eyes: they had learnt to ask questions about the language of a poem that they might otherwise have ignored.

In section 10.1 I said that having to make allowances for my students' knowledge of linguistics at the time of the project, I had to work with essentially text-oriented approaches. I am well aware of the limitations of these models and that the recently developed functionally, i.e. socially and communicatively, oriented dimensions of analysis will add to the literary critical potential of stylistics. On the other hand, an account of textual structure and its semantic implications will keep its *raison d'être* in literary stylistics. Besides, I think that the stylistic analyses presented in this chapter are by no means too formalist and that they consistently show what Short (1986: 161) refers to as 'the inferential approach to language'. In other words, the meanings attached to the foregrounded, cohesive and parallel structures in these three poems are based mainly on the reader's intuition, and his or her social and cultural experience.

Anyway, what I have been striving to bring about in my students has never been, and probably will never be, better expressed than in the memorable words that Peter Porter wrote in 1978:

> It is the duty of art [poetry in this case] to make palatable somehow the real tragedy of the world. It must tell the truth about the facts of that tragedy at the same time. This is a tall order but one which poets have to face up to. One way of doing so, I believe, is to question the machinery of language, to try to test the worth of the words we use to describe our feelings, I don't mean games with words, but a constant awareness of the shapes language makes of itself. Such questioning means that poetry can never hope to be very popular. Yet its feelings should be universal.

APPENDIX

'Ariel', Sylvia Plath   *Notes*

1. Stasis in darkness.   1   We assume: 'There
    ‾S‾‾‾‾‾‾‾A‾‾‾‾   is (a) stasis in
                                                    darkness.'

2   Then the substanceless   2–3   We assume: 'Then
         A   ‾‾‾‾‾S‾‾‾‾‾‾   follows the
    blue →→   substanceless blue
                                                    pour of tor and
3   Pour of tor and distances.   distances.'
    ‾‾‾‾‾‾‾‾‾S‾‾(contnd)‾‾‾‾‾‾

4   God's lioness,   4   Ariel is also a
    ‾‾‾‾‾Vocative‾‾   Hebrew name
                                                    signifying 'lion of
                                                    God'.

5   How one we grow,   5–6   We assume: 'How
    ‾A‾ ‾SC‾ ‾S‾ ‾V‾   we grow one, (how
                                                    we become) a pivot
6   Pivot of heels and knees! –   of heels and knees!'
    ‾‾‾‾‾‾SC‾‾‾‾‾‾‾‾‾
    The furrow →
    ‾‾‾‾S‾‾‾‾

7   Splits and passes, sister to →→   7–9   We assume: 'I
    ‾‾V‾‾(coord.)‾‾   ‾‾‾SC‾‾   feel/am (like) a
                                                    sister to the brown
8   The brown arc →→   arc of the neck I
    ‾‾‾‾SC‾(contnd)‾‾   cannot catch.'

9   Of the neck I cannot catch,
    ‾‾‾SC‾(contnd)‾‾‾‾‾‾‾‾

10 Nigger-eye →→   10–12 & 14 We assume:
    ‾‾‾S‾‾‾‾   'Nigger-eye berries
                                                    cast dark hooks –
11 Berries   cast dark→→   (dark) shadows.'
    ‾‾S‾(contd)‾ ‾V‾ ‾DO‾

12 Hooks ——
    ‾DO‾(contnd)

13 Black sweet blood mouthfuls,   13   We   assume: 'I
    ‾‾‾‾‾‾‾‾DO‾‾‾‾‾‾‾‾‾   remember/I still taste
                                                    these mouthfuls of
14 Shadows.   black sweet blood
    ‾DO‾(contnd from 12)   when eating the
                                                    nigger-eye berries.'

'Ariel', Sylvia Plath		Notes	
15	$\underset{S}{\underline{\text{Something else}}} \rightarrow$	15–17	We assume: 'Something else hauls me, thighs, hair, through air.'
16	$\underset{V}{\underline{\text{Hauls}}} \; \underset{DO}{\underline{\text{me}}} \; \underset{A}{\underline{\text{through air}}} \text{ ——}$		
17	$\underset{DO \text{ (contnd)}}{\underline{\text{Thighs, hair;}}}$		
18	$\underset{V}{\underline{\text{Flakes}}} \; \underset{A}{\underline{\text{from my heels.}}}$	18	We assume: 'Something else (15) flakes from my heels.'
19	$\underset{\text{Vocative}}{\underline{\text{White}}} \rightarrow\rightarrow$		
20	$\underset{\substack{\text{Vocative} \\ \text{(contnd)}}}{\underline{\text{Godiva,}}} \; \underset{S}{\underline{\text{I}}} \; \underset{V}{\underline{\text{unpeel}}} \rightarrow$	19–20	Alternatively: 'Like White Godiva I unpeel – ' in which case 'White Godiva' functions as an adverbial.
21	$\underset{DO}{\underline{\text{Dead hands, dead stringencies.}}}$	20–1	We assume: 'I unpeel (shed) (my) dead hands, dead stringencies.'
22	$\underset{cc}{\underline{\text{And}}} \; \underset{A}{\underline{\text{now}}} \; \underset{S}{\underline{\text{I}}} \rightarrow$		
23	$\underset{V}{\underline{\text{Foam}}} \; \underset{SC}{\underline{\text{to wheat, a glitter of}}}$ $\underline{\text{seas.}}$	23	We look upon 'to foam' as an intensive verb here; hence 'to wheat, a glitter of seas' is marked as a subject complement.
24	$\underset{S}{\underline{\text{The child's cry}}} \rightarrow$		
25	$\underset{V}{\underline{\text{Melts}}} \; \underset{A}{\underline{\text{in the wall.}}}$		

'Ariel', Sylvia Plath   *Notes*

---

26   And I →
     ‾‾ ‾
     cc S

27   Am the arrow,   27–29   We assume: 'I am
     ‾‾ ‾‾‾‾‾‾‾   the arrow, (and)
     V   SC   the dew that flies
                                                         suicidal.' (One
28   The dew that flies →   would expect
     ‾‾‾‾‾‾‾‾‾‾‾‾‾‾‾‾   'suicidally'. Cf.
     SC (contnd)   *Webster's Third New*
                                                         International
29   Suicidal,   at one with the   *Dictionary (1976)*:
     ‾‾‾‾‾‾‾   ‾‾‾‾‾‾‾‾‾‾‾‾‾‾   'The ouzel . . . flies
     SC (contnd)   A   suicidally through a
     drive →   waterfall.')
     ‾‾‾‾‾

30   Into the red →→   30–1   We assume an
     ‾‾‾‾‾‾‾‾‾‾   appositive
        A   relationship
                                                         between 'the red
31   Eye, the cauldron of morning.   eye' and 'the
     ‾‾‾‾‾‾‾‾‾‾‾‾‾‾‾‾‾‾‾‾‾‾‾‾‾‾‾‾   cauldron of
        A (contnd)   morning'.

[NOTE: '→' marks run-on lines
        '→→' marks a 'stronger' run-on line because the run-on occurs
        within a phrase.]
For this analysis we have chiefly made use of the terminology and
general view of grammar presented in Quirk *et al.*, *A Grammar of Contemporary English* (1972). The following abbreviations are used: S = subject;
A = adverbial; SC = subject complement; V = verb; DO = direct object;
cc = coordinating conjunction.

NOTES

* I would like to thank Mick Short for his valuable comments on an earlier version
  of this paper and Katie Wales for her stimulating response. As usual, the
  responsibility for whatever flaws that still exist is entirely mine.

1. For our syntactic analyses of the poems we have made use of the terminology
   and general view of grammar presented in Quirk, R. *et al.* (1972).
2. The name of Ariel is full of allusions such as:
   (a) a Hebrew name signifying 'lion of God';
   (b) in *Isaiah* xxix, 1–7, it is applied to Jerusalem;
   (c) in astronomy it refers to a satellite of Uranus;
   (d) in demonology and literature, it is the name of a spirit. Thus Ariel is one
       of the rebel angels in Milton's *Paradise Lost*; a sylph, the guardian of
       Belinda, in Pope's 'Rape of the Lock'; but best known as an 'ayrie spirit'
       in Shakespeare's *The Tempest*. (See *Brewer's Dictionary of Phrase & Fable*
       (1963). Cassell & Co Ltd.)

ELEVEN

How to do things with texts: Towards a pragmatic foundation for the teaching of texts

Willie Van Peer

11.1 WORDS, WORDS, WORDS. . .

There are various ways in which to read the famous quotation from *Hamlet*. Steven Birkhoff, in one of his performances of the play, pronounced *words* while holding an imaginary book in front of himself, uttered the second *words* while upholding it with the cover between thumb and forefinger and the pages dangling down. The last *words* came as he shook the cover slightly and watched the imaginary words falling down from between the pages. To me, this was a strikingly new way of performing this phrase, highlighting its meaning in a fresh and unforeseen way. It could be argued that such is the general function of the theatre and of actors: to bring to life the meaning potential of texts. To be able to do so, an actor must gain insight into the text, its structure and its function. The present article argues that very much the same may be said of texts in education. In order to succeed in their educational task, teachers should be equipped with insight into the forms and functions of texts.

The importance of such insight may be deduced from several factors. First of all, nearly all subjects at school and university make frequent use of text(book)s of some kind in order to convey their content. Moreover, we witness at present a growing social importance of texts. The number and kinds of newspapers, articles, journals, administrative forms, magazines, leaflets, etc. both produced and read, increases constantly in our society. It is almost impossible to live an ordinary everyday life without sufficient reading skills. Hence the importance of *literacy* in education, which I should like to define as the differentiated and integrated ability to use and produce texts in a socially adequate way. But this requires teachers to be aware of what it means to be able to read and use texts adequately. The present article is a reflection on the position texts hold within the educational system. It aims to show that the actual use of texts may be characterized by a poverty of the methods of teaching, and that this state of affairs is due to the somewhat barren theoretical notions of 'text' which are held by educators in general. I will therefore argue in favour of a new and more resourceful concept of 'text' and of a more appropriate set of teaching techniques.

11.2 TEXTS, TEXTS, TEXTS. . .

Any effort to improve on the use of texts in education should be based on a theoretically well-founded concept of what texts are. At present, however, few elements that may constitute such a foundation are to be found. Rather it is the case that the term 'text' is used in a variety of ways. These, I should like to suggest, reflect everyday notions of the term, lacking analytic insight and explanatory power. Five such common notions of text will be briefly illustrated.

The first sense in which the term 'text' is often used is that of 'record'. In this meaning texts are *written witnesses* to some kind of event in reality. They may be of different types, e.g. a contract, a political manifesto, or a bus ticket, but they crucially may all be used as 'evidence' of some kind or other, for instance of an alibi, the truth of ones words, the authenticity of ones intentions, the occurrence of a historical event, or the existence of a particular state of affairs within a culture. As such the notion 'text' is used by the historian when he studies historical documents, which he treats as sources to be investigated. It is similarly used by the anthropologist, the philologist, the judge or the student of law. A newspaper report or the minutes of a meeting are 'texts' in this sense too, because they may be taken as 'records' of some kind.

A different tradition uses the term 'text' with the (mostly tacitly) assumed epithet *literary*. Texts, in this view, are the products of literary authors, known or anonymous, and preserved by society because of their literary merit, their moral value, or for some other reason. 'Texts' are, in this view, the object of literary studies. As such this view has a long and venerable tradition, still unbroken, as witnessed by Iser (1978), giving one of his books the title *The Act of Reading* although it only deals with the reading of (narrative) literary texts. In the teaching of both mother-tongue and foreign language this notion is often implicitly held by teachers when they almost exclusively select literary texts as the object of their reading lessons. Both this sense and the previous one are too narrow definitions of 'text'. It is intuitively clear that there exist many other kinds of texts besides literary texts and 'records'.

A third meaning of the term 'text' is that of *composition*, written according to particular principles of argumentation. This notion has its roots in ancient rhetoric, i.e. in the orator's preparation of the language he will use to persuade his audience, and finds its present-day exponent in the profession of the speech writer, who purportedly writes texts according to certain professional techniques, so that they might have a beneficial effect (from the addresser's point of view). Scholastically this text-notion is often realized *via* essay writing. Having students to write 'texts' mostly implies having them write essay-like texts, in which argumentation and principles of organization are highly valued. It will be clear that this notion, like the preceding ones, over-constrains the definition of 'text'.

This is not the case for the two remaining text-concepts. One of these considers as a text any well-formed and interpretable linguistic *utterance within a communicative context*. Accordingly, texts may consist of just one word, or of lots of words. The crucial aspect of the definition is met if the linguistic sign is found in actual communicative usage. In general this idea of considering texts as 'meaning-in-action' is mostly associated with German text-theorists, such as Hartmann (1968), Schmidt (1973), or Weinrich (1976). While this approach has succeeded in drawing attention to the communicative function of texts, it faces the difficulty of not being able to distinguish texts from other kinds of linguistic utterances, e.g. a conversation, an interview, or an exclamatory utterance.

A similar shortcoming may be observed in the fifth definition of 'text'. This takes a text to be any meaningful combination of two or more sentences. This definition evolved as a spin-off from the development of generative grammar. Text, in this paradigm, is any *suprasentential* linguistic structure. The work of European text-linguists such as Van Dijk (1972), or Petöfi and Rieser (1973) are mostly associated with this definition. Its problem is that the undefined notion of 'sentence' is smuggled in and consequently multiplied. Moreover, it seems to imply that there are no texts consisting of just one sentence. And this is contrary to fact. Consider, for instance, the following poem by Ezra Pound:

Alba

As cool as the pale wet leaves
of lily-of-the-valley
She lay beside me in the dawn.

Similarly one encounters a multitude of 'texts' in daily life consisting of (sometimes even half-) sentences, e.g. *No smoking* or *Personnel only*. For ease of reference, each of the five definitions outlined above is summarized briefly here. A text, in each of these accounts, is:

(i)   a record;
(ii) a literary work of art;
(iii) a composition;
(iv) a (set of) meaningful utterance(s);
(v)   a linguistic structure of two (or more) sentences.

Various objections may be raised against each of these notions. First of all, definitions (i), (iv) and (v) are unable to distinguish texts from other kinds of language use, while (ii) has nothing to say about non-literary texts. Only (iii) may be used to distinguish between texts and other things, but then only on a normative, not a descriptive basis. Moreover, (i) and (iii) suggest that texts must necessarily be written, and (ii) also implies this. (Although literary studies in general do acknowledge the existence of oral literature, rather little work is done concerning oral texts. What *is* done, is more often carried out in other fields of study, such as anthropology, or the study of folklore.) Definitions (iv) and (v) do allow for oral texts, but this concession evaporates at once, since, in this view, any kind of language use is 'text'.

A final, and much more important question is whether the definitions offer any *explanation* for the existence and functions of texts. (i), (ii) and (v) can hardly be said to provide any kind of explanation at all. (iv) does yield some kind of perspective on text-functions, but as we have seen, without any focus. In (iii) one may perceive some kind of educational goal: texts seem to exist because people learn by them. Although this is in itself a fruitful idea, as shall be pointed out later, definition (iii) cannot explain why texts came into being in the first place, nor *why* they happen to be interesting learning instruments. Nor does it have much to say about the functions of texts outside educational settings.

This conclusion may seem disappointing: none of the text-concepts discussed so far is without serious problems. It is therefore perhaps not surprising to see that more recent approaches to the problem, such as De Beaugrande and Dressler (1981) have tried to find a solution by combining several elements from different text-notions. Hence a text is defined as a linguistic structure possessing a cluster of seven characteristics, i.e. cohesion, coherence, acceptability, intentionality, informativity, contextuality, and intertextuality. The lack of one of these seven characteristics will reveal a 'non-text'. Apart from the vagueness of some of these criteria, and the fact that some of them do not differ from notions used to define linguistic structures at other levels of description, e.g. acceptability and intentionality, it is quite possible to find 'texts' which do not match the criteria but nevertheless are unproblematic texts in an intuitive sense. Consider, for instance, the following.[1]

Sagittarius

Romance and friendships may not be all you wish them to be, but at least conditions at home will be more relaxed and you'll get a lot of pleasure out of what you're doing there this week. Be prepared for unexpected visitors on Saturday. For parents, the most enjoyable features of the holiday will be those you share with children.

Even a superficial glance at the text reveals it to lack any overt suprasentential cohesion in De Beaugrande and Dressler's (1981: 3) sense. Nevertheless, it would be counter-intuitive to call this a 'non-text'. Moreover, the notion of cohesion has been shown as non-constitutive of textuality by Van Peer (forthcoming a).

The conclusion must be that it seems hard to pin the notion of 'text' down in any adequate way. The question then becomes: why is it that different text-concepts are so poor in analytic and explanatory power? The reason for this is, I should like to suggest, because they do not take into account *pragmatic* aspects of language. Is such an approach to texts possible? That is the subject of the next section.

11.3 A PRAGMATIC APPROACH TO TEXTS

A new contribution to the development of a pragmatic notion of texts which both contains and transcends the previously developed concepts has been made by Ehlich (1984). Some attention to this development is therefore warranted. The approach takes man in his quality of social being, acting together with other human individuals. During this interaction, knowledge of the world (and of others) is acquired and accumulated: not everything has to be re-invented again and again. One of the major instruments to conserve knowledge once it has been acquired, is human language. Through language, experiences may be objectified, and hence communicated. There is, however, a serious problem involved, i.e. the *transient* nature of the linguistic medium. The sounds of speech vanish the very moment they are uttered.

How then can knowledge be transmitted through language, if its very nature is one of evanescence? One attempt at solving this fundamental problem has been the development of particular forms of speech acts, which, as will be demonstrated later, form the basis of what we call texts.

The analysis of speech acts is the task of *pragmatics*, which aims at providing a description of language use in terms of participants carrying out (series of) linguistic actions in a particular situation. As basic ingredients of nearly all human communication, a speaker (S) and a hearer (H) are required. Normally, the situation (N) in which S and H communicate is one of physical co-presence.[2] Hence S and H normally share the same time and space configuration, indicated by the subscripts, e.g. N_i or N_j. Furthermore, participants perform speech acts (A). By performing A, S simultaneously utters sounds (u), performs a propositional act (p) and an illocutionary act (i).[3] Everyday discourses may thus be represented formally as in Figure 11.1.

Notice how the speech acts A_i and A_j differ in each of the two situations depicted.

Fig. 11.1 Representation of everyday discourse

$$S_i \text{----} \rightarrow A_i \text{----} \rightarrow H_i \qquad S_j \text{----} \rightarrow A_j \text{----} \rightarrow H_j$$

$$N_i \qquad\qquad\qquad N_j$$

$$\text{Whereby } A_i = \left\{ \begin{array}{c} u_i \\ p_i \\ i_i \end{array} \right\} \qquad \text{Whereby } A_j = \left\{ \begin{array}{c} u_j \\ p_j \\ i_j \end{array} \right\}$$

The problem of how the transcience of human language may be superseded through the use of 'texts' is well illustrated through a social institution existing since at least early history, i.e. that of the *messenger*. Thereby role-switching is essential: S_i communicates something to the messenger, who is then H_i, but who becomes S_j at a later point in time and in a different place, in order to communicate the message to H_j. Using the same system of analysis, Ehlich is able to represent the pragmatics of the messenger-situation as in Figure 11.2.

What may be seen in Figure 11.2 is that the speech act (A_i) remains the same in both situations (N_i and N_j): it has been carried through time and space, thereby transcending the normal limitations of human speech. In other words, A_i has been *detached* from its original situation N_i, and has been re-introduced into a new situation N_j. In this way the original speech act has been

Fig. 11.2 Representation of the messenger-institution

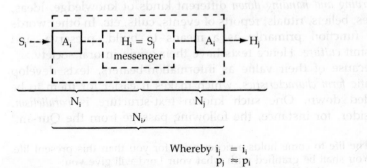

$$\text{Whereby } \begin{array}{l} i_j = i_i \\ p_j \approx p_i \\ u_j \approx u_i \end{array}$$

expanded; it has become 'transportable' into other situations. It is *this* characteristic of linguistic use that Ehlich sees as forming the basis for what we call 'text'. Texts, in other words, are speech acts which are detached from their original time-and-space situation, and have been or may be re-introduced into another time-and-space configuration, thereby superseding the fundamental limits of one single eye-to-eye communication. Texts in this way become information-carriers, able to transmit knowledge through time and space. For instance, a text may be used to pass on knowledge or values from one generation to another. The formal representation of this process may be rendered as shown in Figure 11.3.

Fig. 11.3   Representation of textual communication

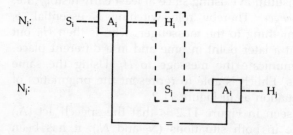

The process resembles that of the messenger, but the quality of H_i is different here, in that H_i is considered, not only as a medium to carry A_i from S_i to H_j, but as a real participator in the information-conveying process. As such we may at this stage perceive one crucial fact about texts in general: they serve the purpose of *preserving and handing down* different kinds of knowledge, ideas, values, beliefs, rituals, reports of events, cults, etc. In other words they function primarily as a means to build, preserve, and transmit *culture*. Hence texts have their origin in oral society.

Because of their value as information-bearers, texts develop specific *form characteristics*, which makes it easier for them to be handed down. One such known text-structure is *parallelism*. Consider, for instance, the following passage from the Qur-ān:[4]

> The life to come holds a richer prize for you than this present life.
> You shall be gratified with what your Lord will give you.
>   Did He not find you an orphan and give you shelter?

Did He not find you in error and guide you?
Did He not find you poor and enrich you?
Therefore do not wrong the orphan, nor chide away the
beggar. But proclaim the goodness of your Lord.

As may be observed, the language used in the example is highly
symmetrical, making it easier to remember, and hence less prone
to alteration in the process of its being handed down orally. Once
writing has been invented (or acquired) other ways of text-
production and reception come into being. Writing makes it possible to fully detach the speech act from the situation of production
and reception. So writing brings about texts which stand on their
own: the essential characteristics of the speech act are incorporated into the *medium* of transmittal. As a consequence of this
materializing of texts, various *procedures for handling texts* come
into being: providing commentaries on a text, procedures for
interpreting it, asking questions about it, discussing it, etc. Such
interpretative activities associated with texts are a spin-off of the
change to written texts (which form the bulk of texts produced
and read nowadays), and, as we shall see instantly, are reflected
in educational practice.

The theoretical approach to texts advanced by Ehlich still
contains the essential notions of the concepts discussed earlier in
this article. It explains the fact that texts are a particular kind of
record, i.e. one of human knowledge (in its widest sense). It also
allows texts to be of a *literary* nature, in so far as they may be in
the form of stories, poems or plays. The observation that texts
possess specific form characteristics reflects the *composition*-view-
point. Moreover, that texts are *meaningful utterances* is self-evident
in the pragmatic approach. Finally, the information-bearing
character of texts accounts for the fact that they have a certain
length, usually more than one sentence. At the same time, the
pragmatic definition allows for the existence of *oral* texts, while
it is still able to distinguish texts from other kinds of spoken
discourse. The most important gain coming from this approach,
however, lies in its explanatory power: texts are elaborated
speech events aimed at knowledge conservation and delivery in
human society. This reveals one of their most fundamental
characteristics, and explains their position in (formal) education,
and indeed their crucial importance for any kind of *socialization*.

11.4 THE USE OF TEXTS IN EDUCATION

As a logical conclusion to the foregoing, one would expect texts to be used as *sources of knowledge and values* in education. This consideration would imply that teachers exploit texts in such a way that pupils may learn how to *use* such information-sources. Remembering what has been pointed out before concerning the variety of procedures available for handling texts once they are written, one would expect teachers to employ a considerable variation in methods to study texts in the classroom. However, this is not the case. One particular text-processing activity frequently used is that of *questioning*: after having read a text, pupils answer questions on it. The problem then becomes whether, and how questioning contributes to the general aim of learning to use texts adequately. One way to investigate this problem lies in the analysis of questions as they appear in text-books. One could, for instance, make use of the classification of questions developed by Davis (1968), distinguishing between questions aimed at:

(a)   recalling word meanings;
(b)   drawing inferences about word meanings from context;
(c)   finding answers to questions answered explicitly in the text;
(d)   weaving together ideas in the text;
(e)   drawing inferences from the context;
(f)   recognizing a writer's purpose, attitude, tone, mood;
(g)   following the structure of a passage.

Although one might criticize some of the categories used, an interesting aspect of this classification lies in the fact that it shows an increase in cognitive complexity needed to answer the question as the list unfolds[5] while at the same time it displays a similar increase in relevance concerning the basic characteristics of texts that have been outlined before.[6] Using Davis's categories as a framework for analysis, the following double hypothesis may be formulated:

(1)   The majority of questions asked are of a kind involving the lowest degree of mental complexity, or in the terminology of Bloom (1956), are to be situated at the lower levels of the taxonomy of cognitive objectives.
(2)   The kinds of questions showing the weakest links with the

pragmatic function of texts will be the most frequently asked, while questions which are intimately linked to this function will be relatively rare.

If this hypothesis holds, then one must conclude that the prevailing mode of working with texts in classrooms goes against the grain of one of the most fundamental characteristics of texts as linguistic events. The causes for this situation are to be found in the institutional character of education. Learning experiences are shaped according to structural modes of interaction developed within the context of the educational institution. This peculiarity of institutional learning as regulated by highly specific structures is well-attested in classroom-interaction research; for a state-of-the-art account see Redder (1983), for an analysis of reading in class see Van Peer (forthcoming b). Besides analyzing these structural qualities, it is also possible to concentrate on the development of more adequate teaching techniques, so that teachers may be equipped with these. However, before we turn to such alternative teaching methods, it will be useful to look rather more closely at some other characteristics of textual structure. It is on the basis of these characteristics that the alternative techniques will be proposed.

11.5 FUNDAMENTAL CHARACTERISTICS OF TEXT STRUCTURE

One crucial feature of texts is their 'open-ness', i.e. the fact that they do not formally contain all elements that are needed for their comprehension. Two aspects may be distinguished causing this open-ness, the first of which is illustrated in the following short text-fragment:

(1) . . . I had to leave. The engine did not start . . .

Most people will interpret this fragment somewhat along the following lines: the I-person telling the story had to go home, but he could not get the engine of his car started. The interesting thing, however, is that no such information is actually contained in the text. First of all, *engine* does not necessarily refer to a car;

one might also imagine it to be the engine of a motorbike, a boat, a plane, or a helicopter. Secondly, it is not said explicitly that the I-person tried to start the engine himself. Perhaps someone else was in charge. Thirdly it is not mentioned where and why the I-person has to go. Fourthly, the particular actions to be carried out in order to get an engine started are left out. For instance, if the text refers to a car, it would mean a series of coordinated actions such as: going to the car, getting hold of the door handle, pushing the knob, pulling the door towards yourself, seating yourself in the car, inserting the ignition key, checking the gears, turning the key in the right direction, etc. Of course such an enumeration of activities would make the text highly trivial (and perhaps unreadable). The point is, however, that even a short text as banal as the above relies for its comprehension on a considerable amount of educated guesswork on the part of the reader. Psycho-linguistic approaches to text comprehension use the term *inference* for this kind of mental activity required to make sense of texts. In such cases, the text is incomplete with reference to the *reality* it purports to depict. In order to bridge this incompleteness, the reader has to rely on world knowledge, as stored in his memory. But this is only one aspect of the open-ness of texts. Consider, for instance, the following example:

(2) Dave had a ski-accident. John had more luck.

Readers will in general derive from such a fragment that John did *not* have a ski-accident. In some way or other, the second sentence is hooked onto the first one, and a link is established in the reader's mind between *more luck* and '(the bad luck of having) *a ski-accident*'. In other words, texts do not only display an openness with respect to reality. It is also the case that relationships *within* the text are incomplete and the reader has to conjecture what kind of internal links are necessary. In general, then, readers tend to interpret text-internal relations when this is demanded in order to make sense of the text. The mental activity needed in order to achieve text-comprehension in this respect may be labelled *integration*: the reader has to integrate separate textual elements into a general meaning.

The activities of *integrating* and *inferencing* may be directly linked to reading processes that have (in recent psychological literature) been called *bottom-up* and *top-down* respectively. Bottom-up processes take the text as the point of departure, starting from elementary 'building blocks' of the text, and try to integrate their meanings systematically. Top-down processes start from the reader, and display his efforts to infer from the text typical states, events, actions, etc. as are known to him in reality. Theoretical models of text processing have sometimes been based on either of these strategies: see Jager Adams and Collins (1979) for the top-down approach, and Kintsch and Van Dijk (1978) for the bottom-up process. For a model taking into account both strategies, see Rumelhart (1977).

It should be added here that these psychological notions have their counterpart in the linguistic structure of the text. To the notion of *integration* corresponds the concept of *cohesion*, i.e. the fact that texts 'hang together': specific linguistic devices, such as anaphoric expressions, conjunctions, enumeration, time adverbials, etc. may link up different parts of a text. *Inference*, on the other hand, is the result of a strategy based on the assumption that the meaning structure of a text shows *coherence*: it refers to a (real or imagined) world that is coherent. This coherence may be brought about by verbal repetition, coreference, determinate and deictic expressions, personal pronouns, proper names, and the like. The problem outlined here is that both (text-internal)

Fig. 11.4   Openness in text

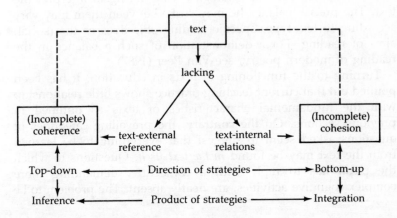

cohesion and (text-external) coherence are necessarily incomplete. Hardly any text explicitly mentions all text-internal relations, and no text provides a full picture of events described. Hence the use of text calls for complex mental activities on the part of the reader, so that cohesion and coherence may be constructed as adequately as possible in the course of text-processing.

By way of a summary, the two characteristic forms of open-ness displayed by texts are cast into Figure 11.4.

11.6 IMPLICATIONS FOR TEACHING TEXTS

This has important consequences for the social functions texts fulfil, and for the ways individuals may make use of them. Although, as has been seen above, texts occupy a crucial place in the transmission of traditional knowledge and values, their structure displays a fundamental open-ness. This means that one of the most important achievements of textual communication, i.e. to bridge gaps in time and space, thereby transcending the immediacy and the transience of face-to-face interaction, has its hazards too: the loss of unproblematic referencing and of fluent joining together of utterances. Hence a reader/listener confronted with a text will necessarily have to make *inferences* where the text leaves out detailed references to the empirical world. Simul-taneously, he will have to *integrate* text-internal relationships that are not spelt out explicitly. For most instances, it will be imper-ative for him to use *both* strategies while trying to interpret the text. The precise balance he may strike between them may vary according to text-type, specific reading objectives or the (social) aims of reading. For a demonstration of such a balance in the reading of modern poetry, see Van Peer (1987).

Turning to the functioning of texts in education, it has been pointed out that current teaching practice shows little relationship with the fundamental characteristics of texts as outlined in previous sections. On the contrary, the prevailing categories of questions asked seem to suggest that everything to be learned from the text may be found *in the text itself*. Questions to which the pupil has to reply with a conjecture, demanding more complex cognitive activities, are nearly absent. The problem to be addressed should therefore be in what way teachers may make pupils:

(a) *aware* of the characteristics of open-ness in terms of coherence and cohesion;
(b) *skilled* in the mental activities required to cope with these characteristics, i.e. inferencing and integrating.

In what follows, four methods will be suggested for simultaneously heightening this awareness and skill. Examples from literary texts will be provided, but the procedures suggested may easily be adapted to the teaching of non-literary texts.

11.6.1 Two methods for teaching integration

In order to confront pupils with the internal openness of texts, I shall propose a method taken from a quite different field of linguistic analysis, i.e. the cloze-test, used as a measure of comprehension or of general language proficiency. As such it is known well enough in applied linguistics; see, for instance Oller (1979: 340–80). Space forbids a discussion of the particular techniques involved, and of the problems and pitfalls that hamper its use. By thus abandoning its qualities as a diagnostic instrument I want to alienate it from its original context and to introduce it into a didactic one. Practical applications in the classroom have shown to me that pupils generally react enthusiastically to this transplantation. This is corroborated also by the Bullock report (1976: 93).

The rationale for using the technique lies in the fact that cloze-versions provide the possibility of confronting pupils with texts that are *open* in the material sense of the word, and having them reconstruct, on the basis of (the remaining) cohesion, the original text, or a version corresponding as closely as possible to its meaning. The mental activity of filling in the deleted items in such a cloze-*text* mirrors the general skill of integrating implicit relations in the text. No measurement is thereby aimed at, but the (regular) training of integration skills.

Two ways of preparing cloze-versions suggest themselves. First of all, words from a text may be deleted randomly, e.g. every third, fourth or fifth word: the resulting version may present a pupil with various difficulties pertaining to the integration of preceding and following text-material. In other words, he comes to realize that the slot may only be filled by words which are *consistent* with the linguistic context of the slot, i.e. words which show *cohesion* with the rest of the text. As an illustration of this technique, Faulstich (1976) presented one of Stephen Crane's poems to a group of students in the following cloze-version, in which every third word had been deleted:

I stood _____1_____ a high _____2_____ ,
And saw, _____3_____ , many devils
_____4_____ , leaping,
And _____5_____ in sin.
_____6_____ looked up, _____7_____ ,
And said:" _____8_____ ! _____ !"

Stephen Crane

The reader may try for himself the kind of possibilities that suggest themselves, before comparing them with the results obtained by Faulstich in this particular experiment. Table 11.1 summarizes the response of some readers (numbers refer to the slots in the poem):

Table 11.1 Reader response

Item No.	Original Word	Version Reader 1	Version Reader 2	Version Reader 3
1	upon	on	on	on
2	place	mountain	hill	mountain
3	below	below	terrified	below
4	running	dancing	singing	dancing
5	carousing	living	indulging	wallowing
6	one	I	I	they
7	grinning	sadly	to heaven	laughing
8	Comrade. Brother	Go away	Help me	Join us

Various observations may be made concerning the text-integrations provided by the readers, both with respect to their (near) correct guesses, as in items 1–4, and to differences in lexical associations or rhythmic structure, as in items 5 and 7. Perhaps the most striking feature is that only one reader (3) has captured the essential meaning of the Crane poem: the devils seeing the I-person as one of them. Pupils (1) and (2) have chosen for a more standard moral line, i.e. the I-person looking for salvation from evil. This difference between pupils is already apparent in item number 5, where pupils (1) and (2) have chosen the more neutral verbs *living* and *indulging*, while pupil (3) selected the pejorative *wallowing*, thereby coming closer than the others to the (similarly pejorative) original *carousing*. But the crucial difference sets in with item number 6, where a selection has to be made with reference to the subject of the verb _____ *looked up*. As an agent for this action, two pupils have selected *I*, while both pupil (3) and Crane chose (one of) the devils. An analysis of these differences may be readily provided in the light of what has been said about text-cohesion. Let us consider for a moment the spatial relationships as they are depicted in the text. The *I* is standing *high* and the *devils* are *below*. Schematically this is shown in Figure 11.5.

Fig. 11.5

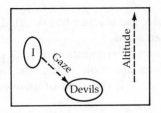

Therefore when item number 6 is followed by 'looked up', it seems, on the basis of the principle of cohesion, to be more in line with the rest of the poem to suppose that it must be one of the devils looking *up*, since they are already *below*. It is quite possible, of course, for the I-person to look up, as is indicated by the fact that the versions provided in this way by readers (1) and (2) are fully acceptable texts. But by doing so, they select a possibility that shows less cohesion with previous elements of the text. Moreover, there is another cohesive tie to be found at this point in the poem. The verbs used to refer to the I-person are *statives* (*stood, saw*), while the devils are portrayed by way of *active* verbs (*running, leaping*). This may be yet another reason for deciding that *devils* must be the agent of the active verb to come (*looked up*). (Note that readers (1) and (2) have achieved syntactic parallelism between *I stood* and *I looked up*. This itself provides cohesion too, but the other cases of cohesion then vanish. Note also that this kind of parallelism presents a simpler kind of narrative and tends to lead to a static description, while Crane's original drew a more dynamic, interactive picture.)

More observations of the kind could be made if more reader-reactions were thrown into the picture. The important issue, however, is that this procedure allows both pupil and teacher to study in detail the various possibilities in which open-ness of texts may be interpreted. Defenders of the 'questions-approach' might counter that it is equally possible to 'ask' pupils why *carousing* is a well-suited word in the context of this poem. Several arguments may be offered against such a stance, based on the earlier insights:

(i) the question remains vague and its terms not well-defined (i.e. what is meant by 'well-suited'?);

(ii) pupils may not have other words available for comparison;

(iii) it is not clear to pupils why such a question should be asked at all;

(iv) nor is it clear why the teacher has decided to question the use of this particular word;

(v) the question offers no suggestion of how possible answers are to be found (does one look in the text, in the dictionary, in one's memory, or is it the kind of answer one has to 'dream up'?);

(vi) the question is aimed at the word in isolation, thereby missing the central fact that words in texts are strongly interwoven.

I should therefore wish to defend the following position: the cognitive activity pupils get involved in when comparing their own (and their peers') solutions to the cloze-text must be of a higher complexity than when they are answering the question; the latter may be accomplished through memory-searching, while the former will at least require analytical operations, most probably also critical and/or evaluative thinking. (The same can, in general, be said against most efforts to capture the effects as illustrated in the cloze-versions by making use of questions. When providing further alternatives to questioning later in this article, I shall not repeat the arguments given here.) As a conclusion I should like to propose that questions are often not particularly well-suited to teach textual structure of any degree of (realistic) complexity. In any case it is a hard task to develop questions that are geared towards such issues, while other teaching techniques, such as the use of cloze-versions, readily present themselves as more convenient alternatives.

Nothing has been said so far about the *randomness* of the deletions in the poem. It is clear that such a procedure has its own limitations. Perhaps the most important ones are that:

(a)   the teacher has *no control* over the items deleted;
(b)   the pupil does not build up specific sub-skills, but with each new cloze-text is confronted with *general* skills of integration.

To remedy this, I suggest that the teacher arranges for variation in the two kinds of cloze-texts, i.e. *randomly constructed* or *controlled*. The latter provides interesting possibilities for directing the pupils' attention to more specific aspects of cohesion. One such illustration may be seen in the following cloze-version of a poem by e.e. cummings:

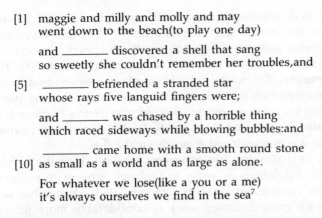

[1]   maggie and milly and molly and may
      went down to the beach(to play one day)

      and _____ discovered a shell that sang
      so sweetly she couldn't remember her troubles,and

[5]   _____ befriended a stranded star
      whose rays five languid fingers were;

      and _____ was chased by a horrible thing
      which raced sideways while blowing bubbles:and

      _____ came home with a smooth round stone
[10] as small as a world and as large as alone.

      For whatever we lose(like a you or a me)
      it's always ourselves we find in the sea[7]

The solution is easy, if trivial enough, but crucial. As many teachers will recognize, most (poor) readers in their classes, when presented with the original poem, would read on line by line, while in fact from verse 1 a quick glance over the poem would reveal its composition: each successive stanza opens with one of the names of the four persons introduced in the first line, and in that order; for a further discussion of this poem, see Short (1986). By using such a doctored version of the poem, the teacher may make pupils *aware* of such cohesive devices as lists or enumerations which serve as signposts for the rest of the text. (This principle is perhaps even more important in non-literary texts, when it comes to teaching paragraph structure in argumentative or demonstrative texts.) Apart from gearing pupils' attention to such organizing principles, one may prepare cloze-texts aimed at the detection of specific linguistic elements responsible for cohesion, e.g. verb tense, anaphora, conjunctions, linking adverbials, definite articles, lexical repetition (or substitution), ellipsis, parallelism, etc. Consider, for instance, the opening passage from Henry James's *Daisy Miller*:

> [1]   At the little town of Vevey, in Switzerland, there is a particularly comfortable hotel, there are, indeed, many[1] _____ ; for the entertainment of tourists is the business of the place, which, as many[2] _____ will remember, is seated upon the edge of
> [5]   a remarkable blue lake a[3] _____ that it behoves every[4] ____ to visit. The shore of the[5] _____ presents an unbroken array of[6] _____ of this order,. . .

Cohesion is constituted here by *lexical repetition* in (1), (3), (4) and (5), where the words *hotel, lake* and *tourist* are exact repetitions from previous sentences. In addition, the fragment also exhibits what is known as *elegant variation* (see Leech and Short 1981: 107) in item number (2), where *travellers* replaces *tourists*, and in (5), where *establishments* is used in variation to *hotels. Training* pupils in guessing lexical items or lexical fields may greatly increase both their reading speed and their ability to detect cohesive relationships that are not spelt out formally in the text.

Finally, it is also possible to *augment* gradually both the number and kinds of deletions, in order to confront pupils with progressively more complex integration activities. (Note again that such planning for more complex work is considerably more difficult when using questions only.) Consider, for instance, the following doctored version of Hemingway's opening to *For Whom the Bell Tolls*:

> [1]   He lay flat on the brown, pine-needled floor of the ___1___,
> ___2___ chin on ___3___ folded ___4___ , and ___5___
> overhead ___6___ wind ___7___ in ___8___ tops of
> ___9___ pine ___10___. The mountain side sloped gently
> where ___11___ lay; ___12___ below ___13___ was ___14___
> and ___15___ could see ___16___ dark of the oiled road
> winding through ___17___ pass.

In this passage more than 30 per cent of the total number of words have been deleted and different kinds of cohesive ties have been tampered with. Even so, trained readers will not have great difficulties in reconstructing the original passage.[8]

We have dwelt on several advantages of the cloze-text. But the method has its limitations too. Two such limits may be pointed out:

(1)   the teacher has little control over the 'fillers' provided by pupils; if these are highly idiosyncratic, specific teaching problems present themselves;
(2)   the pupil may, certainly in the beginning, encounter difficulties conjuring up suitable filler-words.

To remedy these shortcomings, a variation of the cloze technique may be employed by actually providing pupils with alternative words to fill in the empty slots. Since this resembles the multiple-choice testing technique, the method may be called the *multiple-choice text*. Again, as with cloze-texts, it is necessary to keep in mind that the technique is not being employed as a *testing*, but as a *teaching* instrument. To illustrate the method, here are some possible examples of particular verse-lines, where the choice from alternatives may highlight important issues of style-as-choice for the pupil:

(i)   Tyger! Tyger! _____ bright   (W. Blake, 'The Tyger')
       a. looking
       b. burning
       c. being
       d. coloured
       e. brown

(ii)   This bread I _____ was once the oat   (D. Thomas, 'This
       a. eat   Bread I Break')
       b. swallow
       c. break
       d. got
       e. see

(iii) The palm at the end of the _____   (W. Stevens, 'Of Mere
                                 a. beach Being')
                                 b. desert
                                 c. street
                                 d. mind
                                 e. horizon

Beyond the last _____
                a. station
                b. thought
                c. wood
                d. mountain
                e. sea

In each of the three cases, the reader has to consider both content
and form. So, for instance, in (1) and (2) considerations of metre
and alliteration may accompany those of thoughts and images
conveyed. Example (3) illustrates how concrete and abstract
words may be contrasted in the list of alternatives, and how
different choices may impinge on one another as for instance
between *beach* and *sea*, or between *mind* and *thought*.

A multiple-choice version may also be used to illustrate the
crucial point made by the text, as can be observed in the following
poem of Emily Dickinson.

When Etna basks and purrs
Naples is more afraid
Than when she shows her Garnet Tooth;
Security is _____ .
                a. silent
                b. safe
                c. loud
                d. dangerous
                e. dark

The mental effort demanded of a reader in projecting his choice
on to the complete meaning of the text will more easily lead to
insight into Emily Dickinson's crucial message. Again the reader
is confronted with the problem of the open-ness of texts, one
which continually haunts any reading activity. The *more . . . than
. . .* structure seriously constrains the selection to be made from
the alternatives offered, thereby establishing a firm premise on
which a reader may base his *integrating* activity. At the same time

one may notice that the mental activity of guessing the original wording (in both cloze and in multiple-choice texts) directs the attention of the reader towards the central qualities of the text-as-speech-act. They bring to light the fact that the writer intends to transcend time/space barriers by communicating some form of valued knowledge or experience.

11.6.2 Two methods for teaching inference

Both the cloze-text and the multiple-choice text illustrated possibilities of training students to overcome the fundamental openness of textual structure. At the basis of these techniques lies the assumption that in presenting pupils with *explicit* 'holes' in texts, they are confronted with essentially the same problem as when they have to fill in *implicit* 'holes', i.e. unmentioned cohesive relationships. The methods are attractive, both motivationally and from a developmental point of view, because of the complexity of the cognitive activities involved, i.e. because they constitute a kind of *problem-solving*. Finding the most appropriate 'fillers' or 'alternatives' on the basis of subtle (and unmentioned) cohesive ties is a technique that may only be acquired through training; compare also Holyoak (1982), who presents interesting possibilities for learning literary interpretations as a kind of problem-solving.

Let us now turn to the problem of how students can be made aware of and be trained to cope with the openness of texts with reference to the *reality* they describe. A first technique to be considered consists of directing pupil attention towards the *hierarchical* nature of actions, states, or events. Consider, for instance, an example similar to the one given in section 11.5.

(3) He had to leave. He went to his car and drove off.

The different actions involved may be categorized according to the degree of generality they refer to. In other words, descriptions of actions or events may be highly *detailed*, or may be stated in very *general* terms, or some mode in between. The example given may thus, for instance, be illustrated as in Figure 11.6. Of course this representation remains highly incomplete; each of the actions

Fig. 11.6

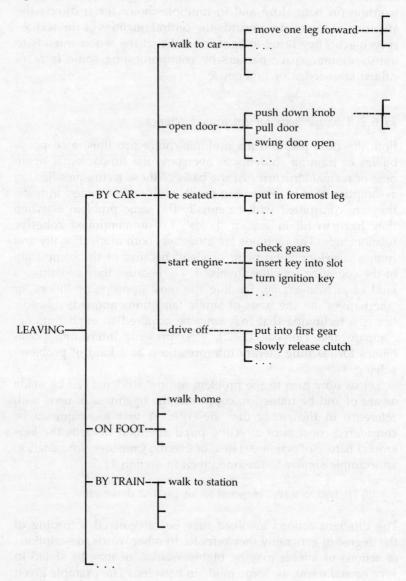

at the right-hand side of the diagram may itself be described in terms of sub-actions, and this process may go on until one reaches the physico-chemical level, both within and outside the organism. It is this possibility of distinguishing between different *levels of generality* in description that lies at the basis of the openness that texts have with respect to reality. Hence a text-fragment such as the example given above may leave a million (sub-)actions unspecified, and still be understood rather well, because readers will *infer* what kind of things are left unmentioned. It follows that adequate reading presupposes the ability to distinguish between such levels of generality, in order to infer the global meaning of a text. Learning to do this may be achieved through various methods, such as summarizing texts, paraphrasing, distinguishing between main and side issues, etc. It is also possible to use a somewhat more rigorous technique by having pupils *rank order text elements* according to their general importance. Consider, for instance, the following anonymous Chinese poem:[9]

[1] Green rushes with red shoots,
Long leaves bending to the wind –
You and I in the same boat
Plucking rushes at the Five Lakes.

[5] We started at dawn from the orchid-island:
We rested under elms till noon.
You and I plucking rushes
Had not plucked a handful when night came!

To a trained reader even a quick glance will reveal that the main point is to be found in the final line. To make pupils aware of such differences in importance, and to train their skills in perceiving these, one may ask them to rank order the lines according to their importance, e.g. by giving a number one to the line they judge as most important, a number two to the following one in the importance hierarchy, and so on. From such an exercise pupils may come to grips with the fact that not everything needs to be mentioned in the text, and that this is possible only because some things in the text have a more general character than others. This in itself is not a completely new idea; teachers have always stressed the fact that pupils should learn to read 'between the lines'. The problem, however, is to develop adequate teaching methods that may help pupils to discover what there is to be found 'between' those lines. Rank ordering them is one potential step in that direction. Again the procedure may be used to build up reading speed together with interpretative skills, as may be seen in the following extract from T. S. Eliot's *Four Quartets*:[10]

[1] In my beginning is my end. In succession
     Houses rise and fall, crumble, are extended,
     Are removed, destroyed, restored, or in their place
     Is an open field, or a factory, or a by-pass.
[5] Old stone to new building, old timber to new fires,
     Old fires to ashes, and ashes to the earth
     Which is already flesh, fur and faeces,
     Bone of man and beast, cornstalk and leaf.
     Houses live and die: there is a time for building
[10] And a time for living and for generation
     And a time for the wind to break the loosened pane
     And to shake the wainscot where the field-mouse trots
     And to shake the tattered arras woven with a silent motto.

It is clear that lines 1–2 and 9–10 contain the central idea advanced by the text; everything else is illustration of this idea. Hence a rank ordering carried out by pupils would reveal whether they have grasped this compositional property of the text. Because of the difficulties of interpretation pupils often encounter in reading (modern) poetry, a comparison with each others' rankings may lead to a fruitful discussion along inter- pretative lines. My own experience with such a method is that, certainly in the beginning stages of its use, classes show both high correlations *and* significant differences in their ranking orders. Exactly these coincidences and these differences provide a highly interesting starting-point for discussion under the teacher's guidance. In general, the discussions generated in this way in my classes proved to be of a much more penetrating nature than I experienced when I used to ask pupils about the 'main point' of the text. Presumably it was their own involvement with the ranking procedure, and the clear discrepancies with their peers' rankings that set off motivational processes accounting for the liveliness and thoroughness with which they approached the texts. A second observation I have made when applying the rank ordering method as a teaching aid was that pupils gradually, over a period of months, showed higher agreements in their rankings, both within the class-group, and with reference to what I myself considered to be some rough objective measure of the importance of lines or sentences. This may perhaps be taken as an indication that pupils became more proficient in distinguishing main and side issues in texts by applying this teaching technique. It does not imply, however, that there exists a fail-safe system for allocating rank orders to text-parts. This remains essentially a heuristic procedure, in which, however, the teacher's richer and longer experience may be used to help pupils overcome some limitations of their own interpretative strategies. Naturally, as with all teaching methods, this demands for flexibility in its application, not for rigidly clinging to the details of its procedure.

The ranking procedure is a method that may be employed in order to teach pupils to distinguish between central and subsidiary information in texts. Such a distinction often forms the basis of inference, for instance that in the Chinese poem the lovers' plucking of the rushes is only a pretext for their meeting, or, that in the Eliot poem the rise and fall of houses may come about in a large variety of ways.

Another, and perhaps more straightforward way to teach inferencing, may consist in explicitly encouraging pupils to *do* so. However, such a direct approach may easily lead to frustration, resulting from pupils' inability to provide suitable inferences. This in itself shows that pupils are at least aware of the fact that not everything goes as an interpretation. In order to take them beyond this awareness and to help them construct meaningful interpretations, I have often found it effective to *provide them with explicit interpretations* of (parts of) texts. Here is an example:

> We are the hollow men
> We are the stuffed men
> Leaning together
> Headpiece filled with straw. Alas!
>
> T. S. Eliot, 'The Hollow Men'

This poem is about:
1. Madame Tussaud's
2. scarecrows in a field
3. the condition of modern man
4. dummies in an empty shop-window

For pupils, the difficulty of a passage like this often consists of the fact that certain lexical items, e.g. *hollow, stuffed,* or *straw* are not to be taken literally. In the example given here, four alternative inferences are provided for pupils, three of which are based on literal interpretations of these items, and hence are at odds with Eliot's general intentions. Only one of the inferences, i.e. item (3), is based on a figurative interpretation of the ambiguous lexical items. By contrasting this *one* figurative interpretation with three literal ones, and by keeping the wording of (3) in rather general terms, pupils may get hold of the kind of mechanism at work in drawing inferences from the Eliot text in a rather direct way. By using this method, it likewise becomes possible gradually to increase the difficulties involved in the selection process, for instance in a case like the present one, by offering *several* competing figurative interpretations.

Again, building up such a progression in the complexity of mental activity involved in inferencing is less easily achieved through asking questions about the author's 'intent', or the poem's 'central meaning'. Space forbids an extensive treatment here of all the possibilities provided by the technique; perhaps another example may illustrate the kind of complex thinking (even on a micro-textual level) involved in the decision-making process:

> The country-handed grave boxed into love.
>
> Dylan Thomas, 'A Grief Ago'

This verse-line means:
1. a rural picture of a farmer growing flowers and corn;
2. the grave in the likeness of a boxer with fists as big as countries;
3. the shock of death moving us to sympathy with all things.

In this example a critic's[11] interpretation of a particular verse-line by Dylan Thomas (item 1) is set against the poet's own interpretation (item 2), followed by yet another interpretation (item 3). The advantage of this method lies in the fact that it allows pupils the choice among alternative inferences that they might not have conjured up themselves. Making a choice between the alternatives involves decision-making on the basis of complex thinking processes. As such, it widens the scope of their own interpretative horizon. As a result of frequently being confronted with different interpretations related in a complex way to the original text, one may expect pupils to produce inferences of a more complex kind themselves.

11.7 CONCLUSION

Four alternatives to the traditional method for the teaching of texts have been outlined in the previous section. It was thereby assumed that cloze and multiple-choice versions of texts may be geared more to the teaching of *integration* processes, while the use of rank ordering and the procedure of eliciting choices between different interpretations would stimulate the development of *inferencing* strategies. However, a word of caution may be relevant here. The openness of texts, as described in section 11.5 is almost certainly of a more complex nature than the simple cohesion/coherence dichotomy suggests. To take only one example: what to do with text-fragments of the following kind:

(4) She is very beautiful. But she is quite a brilliant student.

Here the cohesion between the two sentences is spelt out explicitly by means of the contrastive conjunction *but*. However, the precise assumptions of this *cohesive* relation are difficult to interpret without recourse to *coherence* relations in reality, i.e. sexist presuppositions that women must be *either* beautiful *or* clever. Consequently, one must conclude that the openness of texts with reference to either internal relations or external coherence is not a matter of a simple dichotomy. Rather it is the case that the two structures interact in a complex way. This has been noted by Leech and Short (1981: 249–54) when they speak of 'inferred cohesion'. The term is quite accurate, as may be seen in the light of the previous example. In such cases, integrating textual elements cannot be successfully accomplished without simultaneous inferencing on the basis of one's knowledge of the world. The reverse occurs too, as will be clear if one substitutes other conjunctions, e.g. *so, hence* or *furthermore* for the *but*. What happens in such a case is that the text-external reference becomes quite different for each of the cohesive words inserted. In other words, cohesive ties not only relate different text-parts, they also relate textual elements to states, events or actions in reality. Consequently, *cohesion* and *coherence* (and hence the psychological processes of *integration* and of *inference*) are not isolated principles, but constitute textual structures and procedures that interact in a complex way.

In the light of this caveat one might reconsider the teaching techniques that have been suggested previously. One case may perhaps suffice to illustrate the point. It was argued in section 11.6.1 that in the cloze version of the Stephen Crane poem cohesion led one to suppose that the person looking up had to be one of the devils. But such a supposition is also built on the picture of the spatial relations between the participants described in the poem, which is a relationship with reference to a reality created by the writer, hence a relationship of *coherence*.

As a consequence, the teaching methods suggested here should not be taken as useful with respect to *either* cohesion *or* coherence. In many cases it will be imperative for the teacher to be on the look-out for possible interrelationships of the two principles of openness. Further research will be necessary to establish the precise way in which these two characteristics of texts interact with each other, with individual reader characteristics, or with general reading expectations. It will also be necessary to elaborate the pragmatic definition of text and its links with the linguistic characteristics of texts. At present, however, the methods suggested here may already be tested for their efficiency. Measuring and comparing reading scores of classes trained with these methods, and with other, more traditional ones, such as questioning, may provide a sound basis for developing yet better ways of teaching texts. Considering the immense use of texts in all kinds of socialization, the development of these teaching methods has become a highly desirable educational instrument, and a highly relevant social aim. In the same way as actors have to invent new and inspiring ways to highlight meanings and functions of texts, teachers should have at their disposal a wide variety of methods to train pupils in the construction of such meanings and functions. Presumably it is not an easy task to develop these, but the difficulty should be taken as a challenge, not as an excuse.

NOTES

1. From the weekly horoscope in *Woman's Realm*, 3 April 1982.
2. Notice that some forms of communication, e.g. writing letters or calling someone over the telephone, violate this principle. Space forbids an extensive discussion of these phenomena here.
3. For further discussion of such pragmatic issues, see Austin 1962; Searle 1969; Leech 1983; Levinson 1983.
4. *The Koran*. Harmondsworth, Pelican, 1974, p. 24.
5. It will be evident that category (a) demands a much simpler mental activity on the part of the pupil than is the case for categories (d) and (f). In general, therefore, the order of the categories roughly corresponds to the taxonomy of educational objectives, as advanced by Bloom (1956).
6. Clearly recalling word meanings, as in (a), is of very little pragmatic interest. Category (c) does already reflect some basic characteristics of texts. Obviously the final categories are of primary interest if one considers texts as knowledge or value-delivering speech acts.
7. maggie and milly and molly and may
    went down to the beach(to play one day)

    and maggie discovered a shell that sang
    so sweetly she couldn't remember her troubles,and

    milly befriended a stranded star
    whose rays five languid fingers were;

    and molly was chased by a horrible thing
    which raced sideways while blowing bubbles:and

    may came home with a smooth round stone
    as small as a world and as large as alone.

    For whatever we lose(like a you or a me)
    's always ourselves we find in the sea

8. 1: forest; 2: his; 3: his; 4: arms; 5: high; 6: the; 7: blew; 8: the; 9: the; 10: trees; 11: he; 12: but; 13: it; 14: steep; 15: he; 16: the; 17: the.
9. J. Stallworthy (ed.), *The Penguin Book of Love Poetry*. Harmondsworth, 1973, p. 102.
10. T. S. Eliot, *Four Quartets*, London, Faber & Faber, p. 23.
11. For a discussion of these interpretations of the Thomas line, see Leech (1969: 60).

Bibliography

[The place of publication of books is London unless otherwise stated]

Adamson, S. M. (1985) 'Diglossie littéraire et apprentissage des langues', *Triangle*, 4, 55–66.
_____ (forthcoming) *The Active Voice: the representation of subjectivity in literature.* Macmillan.
Alderson, J. C. and Alvarez, G. (mimeo 1977) 'The development of strategies for the assignment of semantic information to unknown lexemes in text'. *Research and Development Unit Report No 10*, Centro de Enseñanza de Lenguas Extranjeras, Universidad Nacional Autónoma de Mexico.
_____ and Hughes, A. (1981) *Issues in Language Testing.* The British Council.
_____ and Urquhart, A. H. (eds) (1984) *Reading in a Foreign Language.* Longman.
Alexiou, M. (1982) 'Diglossia in Greece' in Haas (1982), 156–92.
Allen, J. P. B. and Corder, S. P. (eds) (1973) *The Edinburgh Course in Applied Linguistics.* Oxford: Oxford University Press.
Allott, K. (ed.) (1950) *The Penguin Book of Contemporary Verse.* Harmondsworth: Penguin.
Amante, D. J. (1980) 'Ironic language: a structuralist approach', *Language and Style*, 13, 15–26.
Ardener, E. (ed.) (1971) *Social Anthropology and Language.* Tavistock Publications.
Armstrong, N. (1983) 'A language of one's own: communication modelling systems in Mrs Dalloway', *Language and Style*, 16, 343–60.
Attridge, D. (1982) *The Rhythms of English Poetry.* Longman.
Austin, J. L. (1962) *How to do Things with Words.* Oxford: Clarendon Press.
Babb, H. S. (ed.) (1972) *Essays in Stylistic Analysis.* New York: Harcourt, Brace Jovanovitch Inc.
Bally, C. (1912) 'Le style indirect libre en français moderne', *Germanisch-Romanische Monatsschrift*, 4, 549–56, 597–606.
Banfield, A. (1973) 'Narrative style and the grammar of direct and indirect speech', *Foundations of Language*, 10, 1–39.
_____ (1981) 'Reflective and non-reflective consciousness in the language of fiction', *Poetics Today*, 2, 61–76.
_____ (1982) *Unspeakable Sentences.* Routledge & Kegan Paul.

Barber, C. (1976) *Early Modern English*. Andre Deutsch.

Barrell, J. (1983) *English Literature in History*. Hutchinson.

Barry, P. (1983) 'Discourse analysis revisited: a reply to H. Sopher and Tony Deyes', *English Language Teaching Journal*, **37**, 44–7.

Bates, H. E. (1974) 'The Tiger Moth', in *'The Song of the Wren' and Other Stories*, Harmondsworth: Penguin.

Baugh, A. C. (1959; 2nd edn) *A History of the English Language*. Routledge & Kegan Paul.

Belsey, C. (1980) *Critical Practice*. Methuen.

Benveniste, E. (1966) 'Les relations de temps dans le verbe français', in Benveniste (1966) *Problèmes de Linguistique Générale*. Paris: Gallimard, 237–50.

Bickerton, D (1968) 'Modes of interior monologue', *Modern Language Quarterly*, **28**, 229–39.

Birch, D. (ed.) (1985) 'Style and structure in criticism: papers in literary and linguistic stylistics', *Indian Journal of Applied Linguistics*, **10**, 1–2.

Bloom, B. S. (1956) *Taxonomy of Educational Objectives*. Longman.

Bloom, H. *et al.* (1979) *Deconstruction and Criticism*. Routledge & Kegan Paul.

Boardman, R. and McRae, J. (1984) *Reading Between the Lines*. Cambridge: Cambridge University Press.

Bolinger, D. (1977) *Meaning and Form*. Longman.

Booth, W. (1961) *The Rhetoric of Fiction*. Chicago: Chicago University Press.

Bradley, H. (1904; rev. edn 1968) *The Making of English*. Macmillan.

Bransford, J. D., Stein, B. S. and Shelton, T. S. (1984) 'Learning from the perspective of the comprehender', in Alderson, J. C. and Urquhart, A. H. (1984).

Breen, M. and Candlin, C. N. (1981) 'The essentials of a communicative curriculum in language teaching', *Applied Linguistics*, **2**,' 89–112.

Brown, G. and Yule, G. (1983) *Discourse Analysis*. Cambridge: Cambridge University Press.

Brumfit, C. J. (1980) *Problems and Principles in English Teaching*. Oxford: Pergamon Press.

—— (1981) 'Reading skills and the study of literature in a foreign language,' *System*, **9**, 243–8.

—— (ed.) (1983) *Teaching Literature Overseas: language-based approaches*. Oxford: Pergamon Press.

—— and Carter, R. A. (eds) (1986) *Literature and Language Teaching*. Oxford: Oxford University Press.

Bullock, A. (1975) *A Language for Life*. HMSO.

Burton, D. (1975) 'Concrete poetry – "The general art of the word"', *Nottingham Linguistic Circular*, **4**, 17–31.

—— (1980) *Dialogue and Discourse*. Routledge & Kegan Paul.

—— (1982) 'Through a glass darkly: through dark glasses', in Carter, R. A. (ed.) (1982), 196–217.

Byers, P. (1983) 'The auditory reality of the verse line', *Style*, **17**, 27–36.

Candlin, C. N. (1981) *The Communicative Teaching of English: principles and an exercise typology*. Longman.

―――― and Edelhoff, C. (1982) *Challenges – Teacher's Guide*. Longman.

Carpenter, R. H. (1982) 'The symbolic substance of style in presidential discourse', *Style*, **16**, 38–49.

Carter, R. A. (ed.) (1982) *Language and Literature*. Allen & Unwin.

―――― (1985) 'Stylistics', in Kaplan, R. B. (ed.) (1985).

―――― (1986a) 'Linguistic models, language and literariness: study strategies in the teaching of literature to foreign students', in Brumfit, C. J. and Carter, R. A. (eds) (1986), 110–32.

―――― (1986b) 'A question of interpretation: an overview of recent developments in stylistics', in D'Haen, T. (ed.) (1986), 7–26.

―――― and Burton, D. (eds) (1982) *Literary Text and Language Study*. Arnold.

―――― and Long, M. (1987) *The Web of Words: language-based approaches to literature: students' and teachers' book*. Cambridge: Cambridge University Press.

―――― and Nash, W. (1983) 'Language and literariness', *Prose Studies*, **6**, 124–41.

―――― and Simpson, P. (1982) 'The sociolinguistic analysis of narrative', *Belfast Working Papers in Language and Linguistics*, **6**, 123–52.

Carton, A. S. (1971) 'Inferencing: a process in using and learning a second language', in Pimsleur, P. and Quinn, T. (1971), 45–58.

Chatman, S. (ed.) (1973) *Approaches to Poetics*. New York: Columbia University Press.

―――― and Levin, S. R. (eds) (1967) *Essays on the Language of Literature*. Boston: Houghton-Mifflin.

Ching, M. K. L. *et al.* (eds) (1980) *Linguistic Perspectives on Literature*. Routledge & Kegan Paul.

Clark, H. H. (1977) 'Inferences in comprehension', in Laberg, D. and Samuels, S. J. (eds) (1977).

Cluysenaar, A. (1976) *Introduction to Literary Stylistics*. Batsford.

―――― (1982) 'Formal meanings in three modern poems', *The Dutch Quarterly Review*, **4**, 302–20.

Cole, P. and Morgan, J. L. (eds) (1975) *Syntax and Semantics III: speech acts*. New York: Academic Press.

Corder, S. P. and Allen, J. P. B. (eds) (1974) *The Edinburgh Course in Applied Linguistics, III*. Oxford: Oxford University Press.

Coward, R. and Ellis, J. (1977) *Language and Materialism*. Routledge & Kegan Paul.

Crane, R. S. (1970) *The Languages of Criticism and the Structure of Poetry*. Toronto: Toronto University Press.

Crombie, W. (1983) 'Raymond Chandler: burlesque, parody, paradox', *Language and Style*, **16**, 151–68.

Crystal, D. and Davy, D. (1969) *Investigating English Style*. Longman.

Culler, J. (1975) *Structuralist Poetics*. Routledge & Kegan Paul.

―――― (1976) *Saussure*. Fontana.

―――― (1981) *The Pursuit of Signs*. Routledge & Kegan Paul.

Cummings, M. and Simmons, R. (1983) *The Language of Literature*. Oxford: Pergamon Press.

Davis, F. B. (1968) 'Research in comprehension in reading', *Reading Research Quarterly*, **3**, 499–545.

De Beaugrande, R. and Dressler, W. (1981) *Introduction to Text Linguistics*. Longman.

De Man, P. (1979) 'Shelley disfigured' in Bloom, H. *et al*. (1979).

Denison, N. (1971) 'Some observations on language variety and plurilingualism', in Ardener, E. (ed.) (1971) 157–83.

Deyes, A. (1982) 'Discourse analysis and literary interpretation', *English Language Teaching Journal*, **36**, 119–24.

D'haen, T. (ed.) (1986) *Linguistics and the Study of Literature*. Amsterdam: Rodopi.

Dillon, G. (1978) *Language Processing and the Reading of Literature*. Bloomington: Indiana University Press.

—— (1981) *Constructing Texts*. Bloomington: Indiana University Press.

Dornic, S. (ed.) (1977) *Attention and Performance*. Hillsdale: Erlbaum.

Eagleton, T. (1983) *Literary Theory: an introduction*. Oxford: Basil Blackwell.

Ehlich, K. (1981) *Text, Oral and Written Tradition*. Mimeo: Tilburg University.

—— (1984) 'Zum textbegriff', in Rothkegel, A. and Sandig, B. (1984) 9–25.

Empson, W. (1961) *Seven Types of Ambiguity*. Harmondsworth: Penguin.

Enkvist, N. E., Spencer, J. and Gregory, M. J. (1964) *Linguistics and Style*. Oxford: Oxford University Press.

Ervin-Tripp, S. (1973) *Language Acquisition and Communicative Choice*. Palo Alto, California: Stanford University Press.

Fasold, R. (1984) *The Sociolinguistics of Society*. Oxford: Blackwell.

Faulstich, W. (1976) 'Die relevanz der cloze-procedure als methode wissenschaftlicher text-untersuchung', in *Lili. Zeitschrift für Literaturwissenschaft und Linguistik*, **6**, 81–95.

Ferguson, C. A. (1959) 'Diglossia', *Word*, **15**, 325–40, reprinted in Giglioli, P. P. (ed.) (1972), 233–51.

Ferrar, M. (1984) 'Linguistics and literary text', *The Use of English*, **35**, 33–40.

Firth, J. R. (1957) *Papers in Linguistics 1934–1951*. Oxford: Oxford University Press.

Fish, S. E. (1970) 'Literature in the reader; affective stylistics', *New Literary History*, **2**, 123–62.

—— (1973a) 'What is stylistics and why are they saying such terrible things about it?', in Chatman, S. (ed.) (1973), 109–52.

—— (1973b) 'How ordinary is ordinary language?', *New Literary History*, **5**, 41–54.

—— (1980) *Is There a Text in This Class?* Cambridge, Mass.: Harvard University Press.

Fishman, J. A. (1967) 'Bilingualism with and without diglossia; diglossia with and without bilingualism', *J. Soc. Issues*, **23**, 29–38.

Fowler, R. (ed.) (1966) *Essays on Style and Language*. Routledge & Kegan Paul.

—— (ed.) (1971a) *The Languages of Literature*. Routledge and Kegan Paul.

—— (1971b) 'Introduction', in Fowler, R. (1971a), 1–31.

—— (ed.) (1973) *A Dictionary of Modern Critical Terms*. Routledge & Kegan Paul.

—— (ed.) (1975) *Style and Structure in Literature: essays in the new stylistics*. Oxford: Basil Blackwell.

—— (1981) *Literature as Social Discourse*. Batsford.

—— (1982) 'How to see through language: perspective in fiction', *Poetics*, **11**, 213–35.

—— (1986) *Linguistic Criticism*. Oxford: Oxford University Press.

Fransson, A. (1984) 'Cramming or understanding', in Alderson, J. C. and Urquhart, A. H. (1984), 86–121.

Freeborn, D. (1982) 'Varieties of English', *Times Educational Supplement*, 26 November.

Freedle, R. O. (ed.) (1979) *New Directions in Discourse Processing*. Norwood, N. J.: Ablex Publishers.

Freeman, D. C. (ed.) (1970) *Linguistics and Literary Style*. New York: Holt, Rinehart & Winston.

Gardner, W. H. (rev. 2nd edn, 1969) *Gerard Manley Hopkins (1844–1889): a study of poetic idiosyncrasy in relation to poetic tradition*. Oxford: Oxford University Press.

—— (ed.) (1953) *Gerard Manley Hopkins: Poems and Prose*. Harmondsworth: Penguin.

Garvin, P. L. (ed. and trans.) (1964) *A Prague School Reader on Esthetics, Literary Structure, and Style*. Washington D.C.: Georgetown University Press.

Giglioli, P. P. (ed.) (1972) *Language and Social Context*. Harmondsworth: Penguin.

Gimson, A. C. (2nd edn, 1970) *An Introduction to the Pronunciation of English*. Arnold.

Gläser, R. (1975) 'Emotive features in scientific and technical English', in Ringbom, H. (ed.) (1975), 190–201.

Goody, J. (1977) *The Domestication of the Savage Mind*. Cambridge: Cambridge University Press.

Gower, R. (1984) 'Review of B. Lee, *Poetry and the System*', *English Language Teaching Journal*, **38**, 63–6.

Gowers, E. (1948) *Plain Words*. HMSO.

Greenhough, J. B. and Kittredge, G. L. (1901) *Words and their Ways in English Speech*. New York: Macmillan.

Gregory, M. (1965) 'Old Bailey speech in *A Tale of Two Cities*', *Review of English Literature*, **6**, 42–55.

—— and Carroll, S. (1978) *Language and Situation*. Routledge & Kegan Paul.

Grice, H. P. (1975) 'Logic and conversation', in Cole, P. and Morgan, J. L. (eds) (1975), 41–58.

Haas, W. (ed.) (1982) *Standard Languages Spoken and Written*. Manchester: Manchester University Press.

Halliday, M. A. K. (1967) 'The linguistic study of literary texts', in Chatman, S. and Levin, S. R. (eds) (1967), 217–23.

_____ and Hasan, R. (1976) *Cohesion in English*. Longman.

Hamburger, K. (1973) *The Logic of Literature*. Bloomington: Indiana University Press.

Harri-Augstein, E. S. and Thomas, L. F. (1984) 'Conversational investigations of reading; the self-organized learner and the text', in Alderson, J. C. and Urquhart, A. H. (1984), 250–80.

Hartmann, P. (1968) 'Zum begriff des sprachlichen zeichens', *Zeitschrift für Phonetik, Kommunikationsforschung und Phonetik*, **21**, 205–22.

Hartmann, R. R. K. (1981) 'Style values: linguistic approaches and lexicographic practice', *Applied Linguistics*, **11**, 263–73.

Hayashi, T. (1978) *The Theory of English Lexicography 1530–1791*. Amsterdam: John Benjamins.

Herman, V. (ed.) (1983) *Prose Studies*, **6**.

Hernadi, P. (1971) 'Verbal worlds between action and vision: a theory of the modes of poetic discourse', *College English*, **33**, 18–31.

Holst, J. (1980) 'Linguistics and the teaching of poetry to advanced learners of EFL', in Pincas, A. (1980), 2–25.

Holyoak, K. J. (1982) 'An analogical framework for literary interpretation', *Poetics*, **11**, 105–26.

Hosenfeld, C. (1977) A preliminary investigation of the reading strategies of successful and non-successful second language learners', *System*, **V**, 110–23.

_____ (1984) 'Case studies of ninth grade readers', in Alderson, J. C. and Urquhart, A. H. (1984), 231–49.

Hudson, R. A. (1980) *Sociolinguistics*. Cambridge: Cambridge University Press.

Hutchinson, T. (1985) *Project English*. Longman.

_____ and Waters, A. (1984) *Interface*. Longman.

_____ and Waters, A. (1987) *English for Specific Purposes*. Cambridge: Cambridge University Press.

Iser, W. (1978) *The Act of Reading: a theory of aesthetic response*. Routledge & Kegan Paul.

Jager Adams, M. and Collins, A. (1979) 'A schema-theoretic view of reading', in Freedle, R. O. (ed.) (1979), 1–22.

Jakobson, R. (1960) 'Closing statement: linguistics and poetics', in Sebeok, T. A. (1960), 350–77.

Jespersen, O. (9th edn, 1958) *Growth and Structure of the English Language*. Oxford: Blackwell.

Johnson, B. (1981) 'Rhetoric and deconstruction', in Young, R. (1981), 225–43.

Johnson, S. (1755; 1825) *A Dictionary of the English Language*.

Jones, C. (1968) 'Varieties of speech presentation in Conrad's *The Secret Agent*', *Lingua*, **20**, 162–76.

Jones, R. F. (1953) *The Triumph of the English Language*. Palo Alto, California: Stanford University Press.

Joos, M. (1961) *The Five Clocks*. Bloomington: Indiana University Press.

Kachru, B. B. (1983) 'The bilingual's creativity: discoursal and stylistic strategies in contact literatures in English', *Studies in Linguistic Sciences*, **13**, 37–55.

―――― and Stahlke, F. W. (eds) (1972) *Current Trends in Stylistics*. Edmonton, Alberta: Linguistic Research Inc.

Kaplan, R. B. (ed.) (1985) *Annual Review of Applied Linguistics 5*. New York: Cambridge University Press.

Kintgen, E. R. (1977) 'Reader response and stylistics', *Style*, **11**, 1–18.

―――― (1983) *The Perception of Poetry*. Bloomington: Indiana University Press.

Kintsch, W. and Van Dijk, T. A. (1978) 'Toward a model of text comprehension and production', *Psychological Review*, **85**, 363–94.

Klein, W. (1985) *Second Language Acquisition*. Cambridge: Cambridge University Press.

Knight, R. (1982) 'Literature and the language of linguists', *The Use of English*, **33**, 58–67.

Laberg, D. and Samuels, S. J. (eds) (1977) *Basic Processes in Reading: perception and comprehension*. Hillsdale, N. J.: Erlbaum.

Labov, W. (1970) 'The study of language in its social context', repr. in Giglioli, P. P. (ed.) (1972), 283–307.

―――― (1972) 'The transformation of experience in narrative syntax', in *Language in the Inner City*. Oxford: Blackwell, 354–96.

Lakoff, R. and Johnson, M. (1980) *Metaphors We Live By*. Chicago: Chicago University Press.

Larkin, P. (1955) *The Less Deceived*. The Marvell Press.

―――― (1974) *High Windows*. Faber.

Leavis, F. R. (1952) *The Common Pursuit*. Chatto & Windus.

Leech, G. N. (1965) '"This Bread I Break": language and interpretation', *Review of English Literature*, **6**, 66–75; repr. in Freeman, D. C. (ed.) (1970), 119–28.

―――― (1966a) *Language in Advertising*. Longman.

―――― (1966b) 'Linguistics and the figures of rhetoric', in Fowler, R. (ed.) (1966), 135–56.

―――― (1969) *A Linguistic Guide to English Poetry*. Longman.

―――― (1977) 'Literary criticism and linguistic description', *The Dutch Quarterly Review*, **7**, 2–22.

―――― (1983) *Principles of Pragmatics*. Longman.

―――― and Candlin, C. N. (1986) *Computers in English Language Teaching and Research*. Longman.

―――― and Short, M. H. (1981) *Style in Fiction: a linguistic introduction to English fictional prose*. Longman.

Levin, S. R. (1965) 'Internal and external deviation in poetry', *Word*, **21**, 225–37.

Levinson, S. (1983) *Pragmatics*. Cambridge: Cambridge University Press.

Lewis, C. S. (1969) *Selected Literary Essays*. Cambridge: Cambridge University Press.

Lindemann, B. (1983) 'Text as process: an integrated view of a science of texts', *Journal of Literary Semantics*, **12**, 5–37.

Littlewood, W. (1976) 'Literary and informational texts in language teaching,' *Praxis*, **1**, 19–26.

Long, M. (1985) 'A feeling for language: the multiple values of teaching literature', in Brumfit and Carter (eds) (1986), 42–59.

MacCabe, C. (1981) 'Language, linguistics and the study of literature', *Oxford Literary Review*, **4**, 68–82.

McHale, B. (1978) 'Free indirect discourse: a survey of recent accounts', *PTL*, **2**, 249–87.

_____ (1983) 'Unspeakable sentences, unnatural acts: linguistics and poetics revisited', *Poetics Today*, **4**, 17–45.

McHoul, A. (1978) 'Ethnomethodology and literature: preliminaries to a sociology of reading', *Poetics*, **7**, 113–20.

Magalhaes, I. (1976) *Free Indirect Speech*. Lancaster: MA dissertation.

Mailloux, S. (1982) *Interpretive Conventions*. Ithaca & London: Cornell University Press.

Maley, A. and Grellet, F. (1981) *Mind Matters*. Cambridge: Cambridge University Press.

Mirambel, A. (1964) 'Les aspects psychologiques du purisme dans la Grèce moderne', *Journal de Psychologie Normale et Pathologique*, **4**, 405–36.

Morgan, J. and Rinvolucri, M. (1983) *Once Upon a Time*. Cambridge: Cambridge University Press.

Mukařovský, J. (1964) 'Standard language and poetic language', in Garvin, P. L. (1964), 17–30; repr. in Freeman, D. C. (ed.) (1970), 40–56.

Mummert, I. (1985) '"... Und dann habe ich gemerkt, dass ich gern dichte und lese": untersuchungen zum kommunikativen literaturunterricht mit fremdsprachigen texten', *Triangle*, **4**, 113–23.

Muyskens, J. A. (1983) 'Teaching second-language literatures: past, present and future', *Modern Languages Journal*, **67**, 413–22.

Nash, W. (1980) *Designs in Prose*. Longman.

O'Donnell, W. R. and Todd, L. (1980) *Variety in Contemporary English*. George Allen & Unwin.

Oller, J. W. (1979) *Language Tests at School: a pragmatic approach*. Longman.

Olsen, D. R., Torrance, N. and Hildyard, A. (1985) *Literacy, Language and Learning*. Cambridge: Cambridge University Press.

O'Neal, M. J. (1983) 'Point of view and narrative technique in the fiction of Edith Wharton', *Style*, **17**, 270–89.

Orwell, G. (1946) 'Politics and the English language', in *Collected Essays* (1961). Heinemann, 337–51.

Page, N. (1973) *Speech in the English Novel*. Longman.

Petöfi, J. and Rieser, H. (1973) *Studies in Text Grammars*. Dordrecht: Reidel.

Pickett, D. (ed.) (1982) *Literature in Foreign Language Teaching*. The British Council.

Pimsleur, P. and Quinn, T. (1971) *The Psychology of Second Language Learning*. Cambridge: Cambridge University Press.

Pincas, A. (ed.) (1980) *English Literature for EFL: working documents no. 2*. University of London Institute of Education.

Plath, S. (1965) *Ariel*. Faber & Faber.

Porter, P. (1978) 'Peter Porter writes . . .', *The Poetry Book Society Bulletin*, **96**.

Power, H. W. (1981) 'Literature for language students: the question of value and valuable questions', *Forum*, **19**, 8–10.

Pratt, M. L. (1977) *Toward a Speech Act Theory of Literary Discourse*. Bloomington: Indiana University Press.

Preminger, E. (ed.) (1974) *Princeton Encyclopaedia of Poetry and Poetics*. Macmillan.

Pride, J. B. and Holmes, J. (eds) (1972) *Sociolinguistics*. Harmondsworth: Penguin.

Pulman, S. G. (1982) 'Are metaphors creative?', *Journal of Literary Semantics*, **11**, 78–89.

Quirk, R. *et al.* (1972) *A Grammar of Contemporary English*. Longman.

Redder, A. (1983) 'Kommunikation in der schule: zum forschungsstand seit mitte der siebziger jahre', *OBST*, **24**, 118–44.

Reeves, C. E. (1983) 'Literary competence and the linguistic model', *Journal of Literary Semantics*, **12**, 30–72.

Riffaterre, M. (1972) 'Describing poetic structures: two approaches to Baudelaire's "Les Chats"', in Babb, H. S. (1972), 362–92.

—— (1973) 'Interpretation and descriptive poetry: a reading of Wordsworth's "Yew Trees"', *New Literary History*, **4**, 229–56.

Ringbom, H. *et al.* (eds) (1975) *Style and Text: studies presented to Nils Erik Enkvist*. Stockholm: Språkforlaget Skriptor AB and Åbo Akademi.

Rodger, A. (1982) '"O where are you going?": a suggested experiment in classroom stylistics', in Carter, R. (1982), 123–61.

Rothkegel, A. and Sandig, B. (1984) *Text – Textsorten – Semantik*. Hamburg: Buske Verlag.

Rumelhart, D. E. (1977) 'Toward an interactive model of reading', in Dornic, S. (ed.) (1977), 573–603.

Rutter, T. *et al.* (1985) *British Council Activity Review No. 4: English Language and Literature*. The British Council.

Salisbury, R. F. (1972) 'Notes on bilingualism and linguistic change in New Guinea', in Pride, J. B. and Holmes, J. (eds) (1972), 52–64.

Sankoff, G. (1971) 'Language use in multilingual societies,' in Pride J. B. and Holmes, J. (eds) (1972), 33–51.

Schmidt, S. J. (1973) *Texttheorie*. Munich: Fink.

Schumann, J. H. (1975) 'Implications of pidginization and creolization for the study of adult second language acquisition', in Schumann and Stenson, N. (1975) *New Frontiers in Second Language Learning*. Rowley, Mass.: Newbury House.

Searle, J. R. (1969) *Speech Acts*. Cambridge: Cambridge University Press.

Sebeok, T. A. (ed.) (1960) *Style in Language*. Cambridge, Mass.: MIT Press.

Short, M. H. (1973) 'Some thoughts on foregrounding and interpretation', *Language and Style*, **2**, 97–108.

_____ (1981) 'Discourse analysis and the analysis of drama', *Applied Linguistics*, **2**, 180–202.

_____ (1982) '"Prelude I" to a literary linguistic stylistics', in Carter, R. (ed.) (1982), 55–62.

_____ (1986) 'Literature and language teaching and the nature of language', in D'haen, T. (ed.) (1986), 152–86.

_____ and Candlin, C. N. (1986 and this volume) 'Teaching study skills for English literature', in Brumfit, C. J. and Carter, R. A. (eds) (1986), 89–109.

Sibley, F. (1965) 'Aesthetic and nonaesthetic', *Philosophical Review*, **74**, 135–59.

Sinclair, J. McH. (1966) 'Taking a poem to pieces', in Fowler, R. (ed.) (1966), 68–81.

_____ (1972) 'Lines about "Lines"', in Kachru, B. B. and Stahlke, F. W. (1972), 251–61.

_____ (1982) 'The integration of language and literature in the English curriculum', in Carter, R. and Burton, D. (eds) (1982), 9–27.

_____ and Coulthard, R. M. (1975) *Towards an Analysis of Discourse*. Oxford: Oxford University Press.

Sopher, H. (1981) 'Discourse analysis as an aid to literary interpretation', *English Language Teaching Journal*, **35**, 328–33.

Sorenson, K. (1957) 'Latin influence in English syntax', *Travaux du Cercle Linguistique de Copenhague*, **11**, 131–55.

Starnes, D. T. and Noyes, G. E. (1946) *The English Dictionary from Cawdrey to Johnson 1604–1755*. Chapel Hill, N.C.: University of North Carolina Press.

Steiner, W. (1981) '*Res Poetica*: the problematics of the concrete program', *New Literary History*, **12**, 529–45.

Stubbs, M. (1982) 'Stir until the plot thickens', in Carter, R. A. and Burton, D. (eds) (1982) 57–85.

Tannen, D. (ed.) (1982) *Spoken and Written Language*. New Jersey: Ablex.

Taylor, T. and Toolan, M. J. (1984) 'Recent trends in stylistics', *Journal of Literary Semantics*, **13**, 57–79.

Thurley, G. (1983) *Counter-modernism in Current Critical Theory*. Macmillan.

Toolan, M. J. (1983) 'The functioning of progressive verbal forms in the narrative of *Go Down Moses*', *Language and Style*, **16**, 211–30.

Traugott, E. C. and Pratt, M. L. (1980) *Linguistics for Students of Literature*. New York: Harcourt Brace Jovanovich Inc..

Trengove, G. (1983) 'Language as a literary medium', in Brumfit, C. J. (ed.) (1983), 103–19.

Trudgill, P. (1974a) *Sociolinguistics*. Harmondsworth: Penguin.

_____ (1974b) *The Social Differentiation of English in Norwich*. Cambridge: Cambridge University Press.

Van Dijk, T. A. (1972) *Some Aspects of Text-Grammars*. The Hague: Mouton.

Van Peer, W. (1983) 'Poetic style and reader response: an exercise in empirical semics', *Journal of Literary Semantics*, **12**, 3–18.

—— (1986a) 'Pulp and purpose: stylistic analysis as an aid to a theory of texts', in D'haen (ed.) (1986a), 268–86.

—— (1986b) *Stylistics and Psychology: investigations of foregrounding*. Croom Helm.

—— (1987) 'Top-down and bottom-up: interpretative strategies in reading e. e. cummings', *New Literary History*, **18**, 597–609.

—— (forthcoming a) 'The concept of cohesion: its empirical status in a definition and typology of texts', in Conte, M. E., Petöfi, J. S. and Sözer, E. (1986) *Text and Discourse Connectedness*. Amsterdam: Benjamins.

—— (forthcoming b) 'Oral reading practice: an institutional constraint on the development of functional literacy', in Zuanelli-Sonino, E. (ed.) (forthcoming) *Literacy in School and Society: international trends and issues*. New York: Plenum

Wadman, K. L. (1983) '"Private ejaculations": politeness strategies in George Herbert's poems directed to God', *Language and Style*, **16**, 87–105.

Walker, R. (1983) *Language for Literature*. Glasgow: Collins.

Weber, J. (1981) 'Inferences and ideological point of view in Joyce's *Eveline*', *UEA Papers in Linguistics*, **16**, 1–21.

—— (1982) 'Frame construction and frame accommodation in a Gricean analysis of narrative', *Journal of Literary Semantics*, **11**, 90–5.

Weinrich, H. (1976) *Sprache in Texten*. Stuttgart: Klett.

Werth, P. (1976) 'Roman Jakobson's verbal analysis of poetry', *Journal of Linguistics*, **12**, 21–73.

Widdowson, H. G. (1974) 'Stylistics', in Corder, S. P. and Allen, J. P. B. (eds) (1974), 202–31.

—— (1975) *Stylistics and the Teaching of Literature*. Longman.

—— (1979a) *Explorations in Applied Linguistics*. Oxford: Oxford University Press.

—— (1979b) 'The process and purpose of reading', and 'Interpretative procedures and the importance of poetry', in Widdowson, H. G (1979a).

—— (1980) 'Stylistic analysis and literary interpretation' in Ching, M. K. L. *et al.* (eds) (1980), 235–41.

—— (1983) 'Talking shop: literature and ELT', *English Language Teaching Journal*, **37**, 30–5.

Young, R. (1981) *Untying the Text: a post-structuralist reader*. Routledge & Kegan Paul.

Index